The Dyslexia Handbook 2008/9

Edited by **Dr Chris Singleton**

Managing Editors **Jennifer Owen Adams and Rachel Lawson**

Published by
The British Dyslexia Association
Unit 8 Bracknell Beeches, Old Bracknell Lane, Bracknell, RG12 7BW

Helpline: 0845 251 9002
Administration: 0845 251 9003
Website: www.bdadyslexia.org.uk

Front Cover designer **Jon Adams**

9 781872 653020

£10.00 (inc. P&P)

The British Dyslexia Association

President
Baroness Warnock of Weeke

Chair
Margaret Malpas

Vice Presidents
Lord Addington
Diana Baring
Professor Angela Fawcett
Lady Jane Lloyd
Professor Tim Miles OBE PhD FBPsS
Sir Nick Monck KCB
Professor Kevin Morley
Professor Peter Pumfrey CPsychol FBPsS
The Lord Renwick
Professor Margaret Snowling
Sir Jackie Stewart OBE
Anne Watts CBE

The British Dyslexia Association aim to ensure that there is a way forward for every dyslexic person, so that he or she receives appropriate teaching, help and support, and is given an equal opportunity to achieve his or her potential in order to lead a fulfilled and happy life.

The Dyslexia Handbook 2008/9

A compendium of articles and resources for dyslexic people, their families and teachers.

The Dyslexia Handbook is substantially updated and revised each edition.

Edited by **Dr Chris Singleton**

Managing Editors **Jennifer Owen Adams and Rachel Lawson**

Published by
The British Dyslexia Association

Editorial Note

The views expressed in this book are those of the individual contributors, and do not necessarily represent the policy of the British Dyslexia Association.

The BDA does not endorse the advertisements included in this publication.

Whilst every effort has been made to ensure the accuracy of information given in this handbook, the BDA cannot accept responsibility for the consequences of any errors or omissions in that information.

In certain articles the masculine pronoun is used purely for the sake of convenience.

British Dyslexia Association
    The Dyslexia Handbook 2008/9
    1.   Great Britain. Education
    I.   Title II. Dr Chris Singleton
    ISBN 978-1-872653-02-0

Published in Great Britain 2008 Copyright © British Dyslexia Association 2008.

All rights reserved. No part of this publication may be reproduced or transmitted in any form or by any means, electronically or mechanically, including photocopying, recording or any information storage or retrieval system worldwide, without prior permission in writing from the publisher.

Printed by Blackmore, Shaftesbury, Dorset
www.blackmore.co.uk

Advertising sales by Space Marketing
Tel: 01892 677740
Fax: 01892 677743
Email: brians@spacemarketing.co.uk

British Dyslexia Association

Unit 8 Bracknell Beeches, Old Bracknell Lane, Bracknell, RG12 7BW
Helpline: 0845 251 9002
Administration: 0845 251 9003
Fax: 0845 251 9005

Website: www.bdadyslexia.org.uk

BDA is a company limited by guarantee, registered in England no. 1830587.

Registered Charity No. 289243.

Contents

Introduction

Judi Stewart

Information about dyslexia is useful for the dyslexic individual as well as those with whom they come into contact. This can be a direct and very close relationship such as that between a parent and child or a professional relationship such as an employer and employee. There is also the need for knowledge and expertise from teachers and those who set and implement policies and laws. The British Dyslexia Association (BDA) Handbook is a compendium of facts, ideas and views that is useful to anyone who has an interest in dyslexia. It is published annually so that the reader is kept up-to-date with the latest views and activities.

One of the more notable features of the previous year has been the growing interest in the positive aspects of dyslexia. Dr Julie Logan, Professor of Entrepreneurship at Cass Business School, has undertaken two studies looking at the relationship between dyslexia and entrepreneurship. The initial research found that there was a significantly higher incidence of dyslexia in people who own and manage their own companies than those who work as a manager for a company. The dyslexic entrepreneurs showed higher degrees of creativity and oral skills than their non-dyslexic counterparts. In a second very recent study, undertaken in the UK and US, it was found that dyslexic entrepreneurs were better at managing staff and this is possibly based on the need for dyslexic people to develop coping strategies such as delegation.

Setting aside the good news, the same study found both the US and UK school systems fail to help students who are dyslexic to achieve academically, but those in the US said they actually enjoyed their school years compared with those in the UK who spoke about their negative experience. Dr Logan advocates "lessons that encourage both left and right brain learning and that encourage soft skill development" are essential to support learning.

The key organisations representing people who are dyslexic would agree with Dr Logan. All the major dyslexia organisations advocate the use of multi sensory teaching and the use of synthetic phonics as the best way to support children who are dyslexic. Four of theses organisations, including the BDA, launched a project in February 2007 called Xtraordinary People "No to Failure". The project has been part funded by the Department for Children, Schools and Families (DCSF). The aim is to demonstrate that a teacher in every school trained to Approved Teacher Status (dyslexia), alongside basic foundation training for all teachers, will provide a sustainable way to enable dyslexic children to become independent. The DCSF is also supporting an Inclusion Development Programme which will provide dyslexia awareness materials of the very highest standard to all schools via National Strategies.

The need for a specialist dyslexia teacher is widely held as the right answer to support dyslexic children, as the BDA found when it debated 'when' and 'how' children should be screened in school. Baroness Warnock, the President of the BDA, led a Working Group on this issue and after much debate from members, academics and teachers, the BDA members voted to endorse the concept of a specialist teacher. Dyslexia is such an individual condition that any mandatory ruling would create further difficulties rather than provide solutions. It is the specialist teacher who can support the class teacher to provide the right screening and programme of support.

In December 2007 the Secretary of State for Children announced a £3,000,000 package of support for dyslexic children. The Government is faced with recent studies showing British school children falling behind those of other countries (Pisa Study) and Key Stage 2 test results showing that nearly three in ten 11-year olds failed to meet expected standards for their age in English, maths and science by the time they left for secondary school. The package from the DCSF included £150,000, over two years, to help support the work of the BDA Helpline. The Helpline receives approximately 16,000 calls a year from right across the country and relies on a very experienced group of volunteers who give freely of their expertise and time.

The year ahead promises to be a very active one for issues concerning dyslexia. The BDA, along with the other dyslexia organisations, will be working to make sure that every child, young person and adult who has dyslexia gets the opportunity to develop the skills they need to be independent, and to focus on the many talents that are so often associated with dyslexia.

Judi Stewart is Chief Executive of the British Dyslexia Association.

Assessment · Education · Training

Dyslexia Action is a national charity and the UK's leading provider of services and support for people with dyslexia and literacy difficulties.

We specialise in assessment, teaching and training. We develop and distribute teaching materials and undertake research.

Our services are available through our 26 centres and 160 teaching locations - many in schools - around the UK. Over half a million people benefit from our work each year.

We offer a one-stop shop of services including:
- Free surgeries and advice
- Assessments by chartered psychologists
- Specialist literacy, study skills and maths tuition
- First-class teacher training to develop careers helping dyslexic people
- Online shopping for our own and other specialist resources

Contact Dyslexia Action
T 01784 222300 **F** 01784 222333 **E** info@dyslexiaaction.org.uk
www.dyslexiaaction.org.uk

Dyslexia Action is the working name of the Dyslexia Institute. Reg. Charity No. 268502

Definition of dyslexia

Dyslexia is a specific learning difficulty that mainly affects the development of literacy and language related skills. It is likely to be present at birth and to be life-long in its effects. It is characterised by difficulties with phonological processing, rapid naming, working memory, processing speed, and the automatic development of skills that may not match up to an individual's other cognitive abilities. It tends to be resistant to conventional teaching methods, but its effects can be mitigated by appropriately specific intervention, including the application of information technology and supportive counselling.

Editor's Note

This definition of dyslexia was approved by the Management Board of the British Dyslexia Association on 17 October 2007 and replaces previous definitions published by the Association. The BDA definition of dyslexia is consistent with current scientific knowledge and professional experience. However, a cautionary note on definitions in general, and definitions of dyslexia in particular, is in order because most people view definitions differently from the way scientists see them, and this can lead to misunderstanding.

How definite is a definition?

To an ordinary person, a definition – as the name implies – is usually something *definite* (i.e. 'certain') and *definitive* (i.e. 'final'). We typically use a dictionary to look up a definition of a word in order to resolve disagreement about what it means. A definition of a word describes the meaning of that word and we commonly regard the dictionary definition as certain and final (despite the fact that the meanings of words can and do change over time). By contrast, scientific definitions are neither certain nor final, and never can be. A scientific definition is just a convenient way of describing, as briefly as possible, the key features of something according to current scientific knowledge. In essence, science is a search for understanding. It can never be said that a scientific theory or scientific definition is *true*, nor that it is certain or final, because there is always the possibility that new discoveries will require us to revise our understanding of something. What we *can* say, however, is whether a scientific theory or definition is *consistent* with current knowledge. If it is, then it helps us to understand the subject better. If it isn't consistent with current knowledge then obviously it won't improve our understanding – instead, it will probably just confuse us.

A good scientific theory or scientific definition should also enable us to make *predictions*. For example, on the basis of the BDA definition of dyslexia, we would predict that people with dyslexia would probably have difficulties with phonological processing, rapid naming, working memory, processing speed, and the automatic development of skills. Furthermore, it would be predicted that specialist teaching and assistive technology would be likely to help people with dyslexia.

The British Psychological Society definition of dyslexia

Some readers will be familiar with other definitions of dyslexia. One of the most widely used in the UK at present is the so-called 'BPS definition':

Dyslexia is evident when accurate and fluent reading and/ or spelling develops very incompletely or with great difficulty. This focuses on literacy learning at the 'word level' and implies that the problem is severe and persistent despite appropriate learning opportunities. It provides a basis for a staged process of assessment through teaching.

Although the name of this definition implies that the British Psychological Society has approved it, this is not strictly the case; the definition was actually put together by a working group convened in 1999 by the Division of Educational and Child Psychology of the British Psychological Society.

The BPS definition has been criticised on several grounds. Many critics feel that it casts the net too wide. Some children who do not have dyslexia can nevertheless experience serious difficulties with learning to read and spell, but the definition does not make any distinction between dyslexics and non-dyslexics in this respect. The definition also suggests that dyslexia can only be identified if it is severe and persistent, which in turn implies waiting to see whether the problem will resolve itself over time and if it doesn't, then it is dyslexia! Clearly, this is contradictory to the important principle of early identification of all special educational needs, including dyslexia, which is explicit in all SEN legislation. Some people have interpreted the BPS definition to mean that dyslexia cannot be remediated (which is not the case), or that dyslexia is always so severe that it will inevitably have been identified when the person is at school (which is also not the case).

A significant proportion of individuals with dyslexia are not formally diagnosed until they reach further or higher education. This is partly because the procedures for identifying dyslexia in further or higher education are, on the whole, better developed than they are in schools, and partly because dyslexia can vary in severity. Some children with milder forms of dyslexia manage to survive through their school years without formal recognition of, or support for, their difficulties. But in further or higher education, where much tougher demands are made on learning skills, they typically find they are unable to cope, and fail to achieve as expected. At this point dyslexia is often identified, although it would have been much better had it been spotted when the person was in primary school.

Despite its rather obvious deficiencies, the BPS definition has gained wide currency, largely because many educational psychologists have endorsed it. Educational psychologists are usually the professionals that have greatest influence over dyslexia policy in local education authorities. In recent years, increasing numbers of LEAs have created or adopted a policy on dyslexia that includes provision for teachers to identify children with dyslexia, so that they can be given appropriate support without having to wait to see an educational psychologist. This approach is particularly welcome because educational psychologists are currently in short supply. By adopting the BPS definition as the lynchpin of the LEA's policy, the problem of complicated diagnostic criteria for dyslexia, which can lead to endless and often fruitless debates, is immediately overcome. This is undoubtedly a step in the right direction, but will only work if LEAs can channel sufficient funds into good-quality training for teachers so that they can reliably spot pupils with dyslexia as early as possible, and have the know-how to provide effective intervention.

Should the definition also stress positive aspects of dyslexia?

A definition should ideally be brief (otherwise it becomes an essay!) and therefore some aspects inevitably have to be omitted. In writing a definition, different experts may choose to emphasise different features of dyslexia. It was for this reason that the BDA's Management Board decided that it would be sensible to adjudicate upon what definition of dyslexia should be adopted by the Association. However, previous editions of the BDA Dyslexia Handbook have included somewhat different definitions of dyslexia. One definition that found favour amongst many individuals with dyslexia was produced by Lindsay Peer (a former Education Director of the BDA), which was published in the BDA Dyslexia Handbook for 2004–05. It was a much longer definition and as well as incorporating all the features explicit in the current BDA definition (albeit in more detail), also stressed the 'positive' aspects of dyslexia. For example, Peer's definition portrayed dyslexia as 'a combination of abilities and difficulties that affect the learning process' and that 'some learners have very well developed creative skills and interpersonal skills, others have strong oral skills.' Although she admitted 'some have no outstanding talents', she also claimed 'all have strengths'.

The problem with Peer's definition is not that it is wrong – indeed, many of those working in the field of dyslexia would readily agree with it – but that it has not yet been well supported by empirical evidence. This is partly because research to date has focused largely on the disadvantages of having dyslexia, rather than on the possible advantages. Fortunately the balance of research is now beginning to be redressed and we are seeing more scientific interest in the 'positive' aspects of dyslexia. In due course the outcome of these lines of research may well cause the BDA to revise its definition once more. This is just as it should be, because a proper definition should be consistent with current knowledge.

Conclusions

Like any scientific definition, the BDA definition of dyslexia should not be regarded as definite or definitive, but rather as a shorthand way of indicating the major features of dyslexia for which we currently have good scientific evidence. In this respect it is arguably a more appropriate definition than the BPS definition, although the BPS definition might be seen to have some practical advantages in education. At the present time the evidence on positive aspects of dyslexia is too incomplete for us to be able to include this confidently in a definition of the condition, but as research science and professional practice both develop, the definition will almost certainly change.

Chris Singleton

Dyslexia: an overview

Chris Singleton

Dyslexia is an inherited neurological condition that affects the acquisition and development of literacy skills and is found in about 5–10% of the population. Dyslexia is one of a number of developmental disorders that often go by the general label 'specific learning difficulty' ('SpLD' for short). The use of the word 'specific' implies that the effects of the learning difficulty are not general but specific to certain skills, such as reading and writing. Developmental coordination disorder (sometimes called dyspraxia) and specific arithmetic disorder (sometimes called dyscalculia) are other types of specific learning difficulty. Dyslexia has long-term impact on many aspects of life and learning. It does not only affect reading, writing and spelling, but often extends to the acquisition of foreign languages, mathematical skills and musical notation. Dyslexia is independent of intelligence and social class. It can affect children right across the intelligence spectrum and those from disadvantaged backgrounds as well as those from privileged backgrounds.

In school and further education throughout the UK dyslexia is regarded as a special educational need (except in Scotland, where dyslexia is classed as an 'additional learning need'). Dyslexic pupils are entitled to special provision to help them learn to read and write, to enable them to access the curriculum, and are usually allowed additional time in written examinations. In higher education across the UK dyslexia is classed as a disability and consequently dyslexic students are eligible for special allowances to enable them to purchase computer technology and other support for their studies. In employment law in the UK dyslexia is also regarded as a disability. Workers with dyslexia have particular rights provided under disability discrimination legislation.

Positive aspects of dyslexia

Although dyslexia is widely regarded as a special educational need or disability that merits extra or particular provision, it should not necessarily be thought of as undesirable. Adults who have dyslexia do not automatically regard themselves as being disabled – if anything, they are more likely to say that they are 'differently abled'. There are large numbers of highly successful dyslexics in all walks of life. In certain professions dyslexics are unusually common, suggesting that many dyslexics possess extraordinary talents. These professions are typically ones in which visual thinking skills and creative abilities are more highly valued than are traditional literacy skills or the acquisition and application of academic knowledge. Hence dyslexics may frequently be found amongst artists, musicians, sculptors, designers, architects, engineers, technologists and entrepreneurs. This may be described as a 'positive' aspect of dyslexia.

Despite the obvious talents and success of a great many dyslexic individuals, we should not assume that all dyslexics naturally possess outstanding visual or creative abilities. It could certainly be the case that the dyslexic brain is predisposed to visual and creative thinking – we do not have the scientific evidence to rule this out at the present time. But it could equally be the case that dyslexic people gravitate towards careers where visual and creative skills are most important because they find it hard to succeed in other pursuits. Certainly, many adult dyslexics say that the difficulties that their dyslexia created for them at school made them even more determined to succeed in life. To resolve these issues more research on the 'positive' aspects of dyslexia is required.

Can dyslexia be cured?

Ostentatious claims for 'cures' for dyslexia appear in the media from time-to-time. Parents are often desperate to help their dyslexic children and may be vulnerable to the promises made by companies peddling dubious treatments. The truth, however, is that because dyslexia is a neurological condition it is life-long and cannot be 'cured'. The scientific evidence shows that the cognitive difficulties that underpin dyslexia (such as problems with the sounds of language – 'phonology' – and with verbal memory) persist into adulthood, even in people whose literacy difficulties have been largely overcome and who progress to the highest levels of education.

The fact that dyslexia cannot be cured does not mean it cannot be treated. There is ample evidence that early intervention using well-structured multisensory approaches concentrating on the intensive, systematic teaching of phonic skills (i.e. letter-sound relationships) is usually successful with dyslexic children. Dyslexic children who are taught in this manner and given appropriate opportunities to practise and consolidate the necessary skills, will usually acquire a reasonable standard of basic literacy. Some literacy weaknesses may remain – generally in spelling, carrying out lengthier pieces of writing, and in speed of reading and assimilating large amounts of text – but typically the person will develop strategies for dealing with these challenges. Dyslexic people now increasingly rely on using computer technology (including word processing, spell checking, mind mapping, and programs that convert text to speech) to overcome many of their difficulties.

Theories of dyslexia

In recent years there has been major progress in our scientific understanding of the nature and causation of dyslexia. Evidence from studies using brain scanning shows that brain activity in dyslexic people when carrying out literacy tasks is different from that seen in non-dyslexic people. Brain scanning also shows that there are observable changes in brain activity of dyslexics who have received remediation. Although there are several theories about the nature of dyslexia – indicating that there is still plenty of research to be done in this field – one theory predominates and has the greatest weight of scientific evidence to support it. This theory is generally known as the phonological deficit theory, which maintains that dyslexia is caused primarily by deficiencies in the brain systems that are responsible for processing and storing information relating to the sounds of language (phonology).

Having observed for over half a century that dyslexia tends to run in families, researchers have long suspected that it is genetically inherited. More recently, genetic studies using large samples of twins have shown that the factors involved in reading as well as reading difficulties all have a significant inherited component. Of course, we do not inherit genes for reading because reading is not a skill we have evolved. Rather, we inherit genes that determine the cognitive skills which enable us to learn to read. Many genes on several chromosomes seem to be involved and the environment is concerned as well. For this reason, dyslexia differs in severity from person to person, and close relatives of people with dyslexia often display mild difficulties of a dyslexic nature although they may not be classed as having outright dyslexia.

The impact of dyslexia also varies according to the orthography (written language) that the person is acquiring. Languages with regular orthography (in which each letter corresponds to only one sound, and each sound is represented by only one letter) are easier for learning to read and write. Consequently the effects of dyslexia in languages that have highly regular orthographies (such as Norwegian, Finnish, Italian and Spanish) are not as severe as they are in less regular languages such as English and French.

Educational difficulties of the dyslexic child

Children with dyslexia whose difficulties have not been properly recognised or addressed show characteristic problems in reading. They are not as fluent as average readers at recognising words in the text. There will be a high proportion of words they have difficulty in decoding. They will stumble over these words and often resort to guessing. If they do try to 'sound out' words they will often make mistakes so that they end up with the wrong word or just nonsense. So much time and mental effort will be taken up in trying to decode 'problem' words that they will be unlikely to retain much of the meaning of what they are reading.

Similar difficulties can be seen in the writing of dyslexic children who have not received appropriate help or support. They will struggle over the spelling of a high proportion of words needed to convey their meaning, and often resort to substituting a different, simpler word because they are unable to spell the word they wanted to use. The time and mental effort devoted to the process of finding words to use and deciding how to spell them disrupts the fluency of their writing. They are liable to lose track of what they are trying to say, and may fail to notice that essential words have been omitted. The result will almost certainly fail to convey their intended meaning and in quality will fall far short of what would be expected of them from their oral skills and general intelligence.

The fact that reading ability has a significant genetic component does not mean that the environment makes little difference: quite the contrary, in fact. There is ample evidence that environmental factors such as home background and quality of education make a huge difference to literacy development. Nor does the fact that dyslexia is an inherited condition mean that that it cannot be treated. Multisensory phonics-based techniques for teaching children with dyslexia have been widely used for over 50 years. Extensive, well-controlled research studies have shown that these techniques, provided they are delivered early enough and with sufficient intensity, are usually effective in raising the literacy skills of dyslexic children to within the normal range. There is also good evidence that the use of information technology can help dyslexic students practise essential skills in word recognition and spelling, as well as providing support for reading and writing so that they can achieve their educational goals.

Identifying the dyslexic child

In the past, identification of children who have dyslexia has been largely based on waiting for them to fail and then deciding what to do about it. But because many dyslexic children have cognitive strengths that enable them to compensate for their dyslexic difficulties to some extent, the true nature of their problems can easily remain unnoticed for several years. Many children with dyslexia have good visual memory and can remember many words purely on visual appearance. The teacher may be misled into thinking that the child's reading development is progressing well. The child's inability to decode unfamiliar words may not be appreciated as a problem until relatively late in primary school. In some cases it is only when the pupil is overwhelmed by the avalanche of new words in unfamiliar areas of the secondary school curriculum that dyslexia finally comes to light.

There are many ways in which dyslexia can be identified. Because dyslexia is an inherited condition, when a family member is known to have dyslexia parents should be on the lookout for dyslexic signs in their children. Most dyslexic children display problems with learning at the pre-school stage, especially in acquiring pronunciation and discriminating speech sounds. Dyslexic children tend to have poor phonological awareness (i.e. appreciation of the sound structure of language), which is often evident in the child's inability to produce or recognise rhymes. Typically they show little interest in books, reading or writing. However, the significance of these 'early warning signs' should not be over-estimated. Although the factors mentioned here are all connected with dyslexia, they are not always reliable indicators because many children who experience these problems do not subsequently go on to develop dyslexia. Early warning signs should *alert parents to the possibility* that their child has dyslexia but they do not definitely mean that the child has dyslexia.

The *Special Educational Needs Code of Practice* (called 'Supporting Children's Learning Code of Practice' in Scotland) places emphasis on the importance of early identification of all special educational needs, including dyslexia. The Code encourages the use of appropriate screening and assessment tests. There are legal requirements for schools to follow this Code of Practice. A number of screening tests for dyslexia are now available to schools and are quite widely used, although not all schools use them routinely yet. Usually these screening systems consist of a number of short tests of key indicators of dyslexia, such as phonological awareness, short-term working memory and phonic skills. They take about 15–30 minutes and may be administered by a teacher or delivered via computer. These tests can be given from age 4, although probably age 5–6 is a more appropriate age because many 4-year-olds are still quite immature, which can affect the reliability of such tests.

It is usually expected that the results of tests will be shared with the child's parents, especially if the outcome is positive. On the whole, these screening tests are very helpful but that does not mean they are infallible. In fact, the very nature of screening means that all screening tests inevitably have a degree of error. Occasionally the test will classify a child as having dyslexia when in fact the child *does not* have dyslexia (this is called a 'false positive') or the test will classify a child as not having dyslexia when in fact the child *does* have dyslexia (this is called a 'false negative'). The producers of screening tests try to ensure that levels of false positives and false negatives are as low as possible. However, they are rarely lower than 5–10% for each type of misclassification, which means that if one hundred children were selected at random and screened, we would expect that between ten and twenty of them will be wrongly classified. In practice, however, the way that children are selected for screening is not random because few schools screen all their pupils. Instead, teachers tend to screen pupils who are experiencing problems with reading and writing. In such circumstances, the screening test should be more accurate. On the other hand, unless all children are screened it is likely that many of the dyslexics will be missed because they will not necessarily appear to have significant difficulties with reading and writing at this early stage.

The roles of teachers and educational psychologists

The most important factor in identifying dyslexic children is not the test used nor when it is given, nor to which pupils, but the skills of the teacher to recognise the signs of dyslexia and to interpret the results of tests appropriately. Although there is increasing awareness of dyslexia in schools, at the present time very few schools have teachers with an adequate knowledge of dyslexia. Traditionally, teachers have relied on educational psychologists to identify pupils with dyslexia. Educational psychologists are trained to assess children for dyslexia and other learning difficulties and have at their disposal a wide range of psychometric tests to which teachers do not have access. Some local education authorities do not allow teachers to describe children as 'dyslexic' unless an educational psychologist has assessed them. Unfortunately, there are not enough educational psychologists available to provide dyslexia assessments for all children who will need them. Many children wait several years for an assessment by an educational psychologist, by which time their dyslexic difficulties will probably have got worse and their motivation and self-image will be very low. Educational psychologists also have many other demands on their time, such as assessing and advising on the education of children with a wide range of difficulties.

Although educational psychologists undoubtedly have important roles to play in the education of children with dyslexia, it is clear that any system of dyslexia identification that relies solely on educational psychologists is never going to be adequate. Furthermore, such a system fails to meet the requirements of the Code of Practice regarding early identification of special educational needs. In recent years many local education authorities have recognised this problem and have implemented new policies on dyslexia that place the responsibility for identifying dyslexia with teachers. Of course, for this approach to work there has to be appropriate training for teachers but there are several signs of progress on this issue.

Over the past year a large-scale government-funded project called 'No To Failure' has been evaluating the use of screening to identify children at risk of dyslexia/SpLD and providing intensive specialist tuition for them (see www.notofailure.com). This project involves the cooperation of four national organisations concerned with the education and needs of people with dyslexia: the British Dyslexia Association, Dyslexia Action, PATOSS (Professional Association of Teachers of Students with Specific Learning Difficulties), and Xtraordinary People. The ultimate goal of the 'No To Failure' project is to demonstrate the benefits of every school having one specialist teacher with the skills required to identify and support pupils with dyslexia. In May 2008, Ed Balls, Secretary of State for Children, announced that Sir Jim Rose has been asked to look at dyslexia provision in schools in England, taking into account evidence from 'No To Failure' project. Rose has been asked make recommendations on identifying and teaching children with dyslexia and is expected to report early in 2009. In Scotland, the inspectorate for education (HMIe) has asked all local authorities to supply information regarding their policies and provision for children with dyslexia, and a report on this is expected towards the end of 2008.

Conclusions

The major challenge at the present time is not how to teach or support children and adults with dyslexia. The most effective methods for doing this have been established for some considerable time. The most significant challenges currently are, firstly, to ensure that all children with dyslexia are identified at an early age, and secondly, to ensure that sufficient numbers of teachers have the training they need to enable them to give appropriate teaching and support for dyslexic pupils. These two objectives are closely linked. In order to identify dyslexic children we first need teachers who know enough about dyslexia to recognise a dyslexic child or who can use the necessary assessment and screening tools effectively. And there is little point in identifying children who have dyslexia unless we also have teachers with the professional skills and time to address their learning needs effectively.

Suggested reading

'Dyslexia: A Practitioner's Handbook' by Gavin Reid. Wiley, 3rd edition, 2003.

'Dyslexia: A Complete Guide for Parents' by Gavin Reid. Wiley, 2004.

'Dyslexia' by Margaret Snowling. Blackwell, 2nd edition, 2000. *[This book reviews much of the research evidence on dyslexia.]*

Dr Chris Singleton is Senior Lecturer in Educational Psychology at the University of Hull, Research Director of Lucid Research Ltd, and Associate Editor of the Journal of Research in Reading.

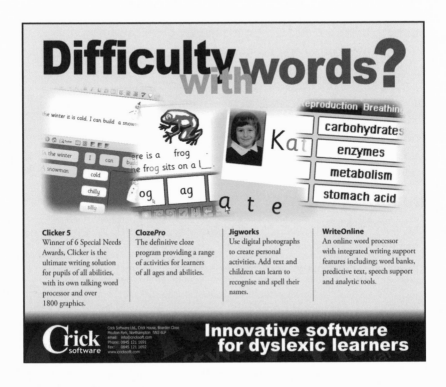

National initiatives

No To Failure

Chris Singleton and Rosie Wood

The *No To Failure* project is a major national study that aims to demonstrate the importance of screening for dyslexia and to show how dyslexia, if ignored, can lead to educational failure. The project is also evaluating the impact of specialist teaching on the literacy skills and educational development of pupils found to be at risk of dyslexia. The project is funded by the Department for Children, Schools and Families (DCSF) and involves the participation of four organisations concerned with the education of children with dyslexia: Xtraordinary People (XP), the British Dyslexia Association (BDA), Dyslexia Action, and PATOSS (Professional Association of Teachers of Students with Specific Learning Difficulties).

Intervention for children with dyslexia

The most widely supported research view on dyslexia is that it is a constitutional, specific language-based disorder characterised by difficulties in single-word decoding, which are attributable to weaknesses in the ability to process the phonological features of words (Vellutino et al, 2004). Specialist teaching for dyslexic children is characterised by use of intensive multisensory methods that are highly-structured, cumulative, and phonologically rich, to establish firm phoneme-grapheme links as well as giving children a variety of strategies for processing text, spelling and writing (Rack, 2004).

Surprisingly, very few studies of the impact of specialist teaching on the learning of children with severe reading difficulties or dyslexia have been carried out in the UK, although there have been many studies of different intervention schemes for children who are behind in reading. However, fewer than half of the 48 studies reviewed by Brooks (2007) have included control or comparison groups, making evaluation difficult. Torgeson (2005) has carried out a series of well-controlled studies in the USA using intensive, phonologically-based, individually delivered intervention for pupils with dyslexia. The children in these studies made significant improvements in word reading, phonic skills and reading comprehension and generally maintained these improvements over time. The nearest comparable controlled study in the UK was the Cumbria Reading Intervention project in which a highly structured reading scheme, combined with systematic activities to promote phonological awareness, was found to be effective with 7-year-old children who had reading difficulties (Hatcher, Hulme and Ellis, 1994). Hatcher (2003) reported on a further study with10-year-old dyslexic children, for whom the reading-plus-phonology technique yielded an impressive 2.89 months improvement per month in reading and 2.07 months improvement per month in spelling.

Design of the No To Failure project

Twenty primary and secondary schools from three different local authorities are participating in the *No To Failure* project. All the pupils in Years 3 and 7 in these schools were screened using tests of reading, writing, spelling; the total number of children screened was 1,341. Pupils scoring at or below standard score 85 on these literacy measures were then given tests of cognitive skills such as phonological awareness and verbal memory, which underpin literacy development and dyslexia. These data were then used to identify 'at risk' pupils, defined as those having a dyslexia/SpLD profile, i.e. significant impairments in reading and/or spelling together with either a clear pattern of cognitive deficits in phonology and/or verbal memory, or showing other indicators of SpLD, such as persistent problems of coordination, attention or visual-perceptual skills that are reflected in classroom activities such as writing, mathematics, following instructions, learning and recall. This approach is not being put forward as the only, or necessarily the best, way to identify pupils at risk of dyslexia/SpLD; in this project, however, the critical factor is the professional training of specialist teachers, enabling them to select and apply the most suitable tests based on evidence, and in interpreting and acting appropriately on the test results.

Pupils judged to be at-risk of dyslexia/SpLD on the basis of these results (N = 243) were then allocated to one of two groups: the intervention group, which is currently receiving 20 hours of tuition from trained dyslexia specialist teachers, and the control group, which is receiving normal schooling. After the initial screening, the at-risk children were given pre-tests to assess their literacy skills in more detail. The assessments used in the screening and pre-testing are being re-administered after 10 weeks (post-test 1) and 20 weeks (post-test 2). These data will be used to evaluate the effectiveness of the intervention, the results of which will be published at the end of the study. After post-test 2 the control group will become a delayed intervention group, which will then receive specialist tuition, and a further assessment (post-test 3) will evaluate the subsequent progress made by children in this group.

Results of the screening phase of the project

Overall, 21% of the pupils were classified as being at risk, this proportion being very consistent across the three local authorities. A higher proportion of the Year 3 group (26%) was found to be at risk compared with a lower proportion (18%) of the Year 7 group (see Figure 1). 25% of the overall sample did not reach target levels in SATs (i.e. at Key Stage 1, level 2C or below in reading and writing; at Key Stage 2, level 3 or below in English overall score). Overall, about 55% of those children who did not achieve target levels in SATs fell into the at-risk group.

Dyslexia has been shown to be associated with an identifiable set of cognitive difficulties, of which the principal ones are in phonological processing, working memory, and phonological decoding (Vellutino et al, 2004). Data from the screening enabled an analysis of the number and type of these deficits in the at-risk group. Overall, 58% of at-risk children were found to have a working memory (WM) deficit, 39% to have poor phonological decoding (PD) skills, and 28% to have phonological processing (PP) deficits (see Figure 2).

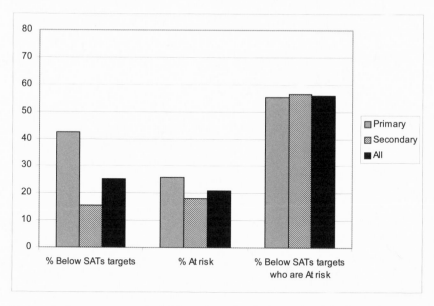

Figure 1. Percentages of children found to be at risk of dyslexia/SpLD.

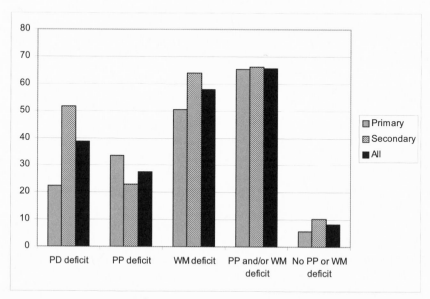

Figure 2. Percentages of at-risk children with various cognitive deficits.

Using these data, it is possible to divide the at-risk group into the following three subgroups based on the degree and type of cognitive impairment.

Subgroup 1. High risk of dyslexia/SpLD (phonological type)

Poor reading and/or spelling skills (standard score 85 or below) with TWO OR MORE areas of cognitive deficit (i.e. phonic decoding, and or phonological processing, and or working memory). It is likely that most of the pupils in this category would have 'classic' phonological dyslexia to a severe or fairly severe degree. About 39% of the at-risk group and 8% of the total sample fell into this category.

Subgroup 2. Moderate risk of dyslexia/SpLD (phonological type)

Poor reading and/or spelling skills (standard score 85 or below) with ONE area of cognitive deficit (i.e. phonic decoding or phonological processing or working memory). It is likely that most of the pupils in this category would have less severe dyslexia of the 'classic' phonological type. About 35% of the at-risk group and 7.5% of the total sample fell into this category.

Subgroup 3. Moderate risk of dyslexia/SpLD (non-phonological type)

Poor reading and/or spelling skills (standard score 85 or below) without deficits in either phonic decoding, phonological processing or working memory, but with other indicators of dyslexia/SpLD, such as persistent difficulties with handwriting or mathematics, coordination problems, or attentional difficulties. It is likely that most of the pupils in this category would have either atypical types of dyslexia not characterised by phonological difficulties, or other forms of SpLD. About 26% of the at-risk group and 5.5% of the total sample fell into this category.

Discussion

The finding that the 21% at-risk level was very similar across the three local authorities despite socio-economic differences confirms not only that consistent criteria have been applied, but also that these criteria relate to the identification of learning difficulties that are largely independent of socio-economic factors. Although the 21% figure is higher than many estimates of the prevalence of dyslexia it is not inconsistent with recent international estimates, which place the overall prevalence of impairments of a dyslexic nature at about 15-20% of the general population (International Dyslexia Association, 2007). It should also be stressed that the screening carried out in this project was fairly broad and intended to identify a wide variety of children at risk of SpLD, rather than to 'diagnose' dyslexia *per se*.

Over half of the pupils who did not reach target levels for SATs fell into the at-risk group and 80% of the pupils at risk of dyslexia/SpLD did not reach expected levels for SATs. These findings suggest that unidentified dyslexia/SpLD or other learning difficulties are a major cause of educational failure that could be remedied but which at present do not appear to be being addressed in ways that enable children to fulfil their potential. The proportion of pupils found to be at risk of dyslexia/SpLD was relatively higher for Year 3 and somewhat lower for Year 7, the results indicating that during the course of four school years of ordinary schooling from Year 3 to Year 7 less than a third of at-risk children are lifted out of risk, leaving the majority in educational jeopardy

It is notable that subgroup 1 accounts for a relatively greater percentage of the at-risk group in Year 7 than it does in Year 3, and correspondingly, subgroup 2 accounts for a relatively greater percentage of the at-risk group in Year 3 than it does in Year 7. This reflects the likelihood that the older the pupils, the more likely it will be that those who are at educational risk will have more severe problems. The reason for this effect is because a relatively greater proportion of pupils with less severe problems will have been taken out of risk as a result of educational input. This, in turn, underlines the importance of identifying children with dyslexia/SpLD as early as possible because, unless given appropriate specialist intervention, they are likely to continue to experience major difficulties throughout secondary education.

References

Brooks, G. (2007) *What works for pupils with literacy difficulties? The effectiveness of intervention schemes.* (3rd Edition) Department for Children, Schools and Families.

Hatcher, P. (2003) A conventional and successful approach to helping dyslexic children acquire literacy. *Dyslexia, 9,* 140-145.

Hatcher, P., Hulme, C. & Ellis, A.W. (1994) Ameliorating early reading failure by integrating the teaching of reading and phonological skills: the phonological linkage hypothesis. *Child Development, 65,* 51-57.

International Dyslexia Association (2007) Dyslexia basics. *IDA Fact Sheet 62.* http://www.interdys.org/FactSheets.htm

Rack, J. (2004) The theory and practice of specialist literacy teaching. In G.Reid & A. Fawcett (Eds.) *Dyslexia in Context: Research, Policy and Practice.* London: Whurr, pp. 120-131.

Torgeson, J. (2005) Recent discoveries on remedial interventions for children with dyslexia. In M.J.Snowling and C.Hulme (Eds.) *The Science of Reading: A Handbook.* Oxford: Blackwell, pp. 521-537.

Vellutino, F. R., Fletcher, J. M., Snowling, M. J. & Scanlon, D. M. (2004) Specific reading disability (dyslexia): what have we learned in the past four decades? *Journal of Child Psychology & Psychiatry, 45,* 2–40.

Postscript

A version of this article was published in *Literacy Today.*
The Interim Report of the *No To Failure* project, which contains all the results of the screening phase of the study, can be downloaded from www.notofailure.com
The Final Report of the project is scheduled for publication early in 2009.

Dr Chris Singleton is Senior Lecturer in Educational Psychology at the University of Hull, and Independent Evaluator to the No To Failure project.

Rosie Wood is Specialist SpLD Adviser to the No To Failure project. She was formerly Director of the Helen Arkell Dyslexia Centre.

'Could do better': improving literacy in schools

Kerry Bennett

With one in five eleven-year-olds leaving primary school without a basic level of literacy what can we do to improve standards in reading and writing across the UK? This chapter looks at underlying reasons for this worrying statistic and outlines what can be done to rectify the situation. The perspective is that of Dyslexia Action, the UK's leading provider of services for people with dyslexia and other literacy difficulties.

Current provision

What is causing so many children to struggle to learn to read and write? And what can be done to address this problem earlier in a child's life, when support is easier and less expensive to provide, and results more quickly in improved literacy, self esteem and school success? In 2006 the government approved the recommendations of the Rose Review of the teaching of reading and its emphasis on the importance of using synthetic phonics to teach reading. This method underpins the teaching methods used by Dyslexia Action and we welcome its introduction to the curriculum in due course. We believe this will go some way to improving standards of reading.

Dyslexia Action remains concerned, however, that a formal articulated special educational needs policy and national standards for service provision for this area are crucial – and still waiting to be introduced – in order to help the many children currently 'falling though the cracks' and who will still struggle. Many children would

not be adding to the poor reading statistics if they were properly identified and supported from an early age at school.
Up to 10% of the UK populations are affected by dyslexia. That's two to three children in every primary school classroom. If dyslexia is not recognised early and a pattern of reading failure has set in, children become frustrated and depressed and are often labelled as either 'lazy', 'stupid', or both. Many children lose confidence in their abilities and frequently become school failures.

The figures from the Department for Children, Schools and Families (DCSF) show that in excess of 9,000 children are permanently excluded from school and over 60% of these are identified as children with special needs. At least 80% of these children will have dyslexia or other specific learning difficulties (SpLD). The National Foundation of Educational Research (NFER) has noted that the cost of provision for a child who is excluded is £9,900 per annum.

Effects of poor literacy beyond school

Undiagnosed dyslexic children also contribute to the large numbers of poor readers who do not have the required skills to get a job after leaving school. The government has estimated that adults with poor literacy and numeracy skills could earn up to £50,000 less over their lifetime and are more likely to have health problems. In addition the government's own statistics estimate that poor skills cost the country's economy in excess of £10 billion every year.

A lack of skills for education and employment, combined with a loss of self-esteem, results in individuals with undiagnosed dyslexia being over represented in all areas of poverty and disadvantage. This not only has a direct affect on the individual but also upon the economy as a whole. There is strong evidence that individuals with undiagnosed dyslexia/SpLD and other hidden disabilities are 'over represented' in the prison and probation populations. In 2004, Dyslexia Action conducted a national research project to find out the incidence of hidden disabilities in the prison population. The study revealed that 20% of prisoners had dyslexia and related learning problems. This is exactly double the number of dyslexic individuals that would be expected in prison given the population norm of 10%. Significant numbers of these offenders might have been steered away from crime and its costly outcomes by early intervention. Based on prison costs if these individuals had been identified early and provided with adequate support, this could make a saving of more than £300 million per annum. Drawing on similar statistics from the Probation Service, early intervention might have saved around £80 million per annum. The same arguments can be applied to the long-term unemployed.

SEN pupils in mainstream schools

The Education and Skills Select Committee's report on SEN in July 2006 concluded that a bigger investment in teacher training and support for SEN was vital, stating that without adequate intervention many children are left unable to fully engage within classroom activities or access the curriculum. Dyslexia Action's Chief Executive, Shirley Cramer, gave evidence to the Select Committee, stating that the current 'wait and fail' model is failing children and their parents.

Most children with dyslexia/SpLD, with, and without, statements of SEN, are educated in mainstream schools. But the levels of support they receive vary throughout the country, as the result of a number of factors:

1. There are no standard policies related to dyslexia provision across local authorities and this has resulted in a postcode lottery in terms of provision.

2. Delegated funding for SEN to individual schools has, in many cases, had a detrimental effect on the provision of specialist services and the quantity and quality of provision for children with dyslexia/SpLD. As this funding is not ring fenced for SEN pupils, schools may have used the money for other purposes. (See Ofsted report *Inclusion: the impact of LEA support and outreach services*, July 2005.)

3. As dyslexia is a hidden disability, information from parents across the country indicates that theirs are often the children

least likely to receive adequate support, as their problems are not obvious to those without knowledge of the issue. In consequence many children are failing who should be thriving in the mainstream environment.

4. Teaching and support staff do not have the information or expertise to know what the appropriate evidence-based services are for students with dyslexia/SpLD. There is a need for improved awareness and training about dyslexia in schools.

5. Delegated funding has diminished the capacity of Local Authorities to monitor the progress of pupils with SEN. Dyslexia Action has found that it has also reduced the numbers of staff with specialist dyslexia expertise who previously offered advice, guidance and support to mainstream staff.

Improving skills and expertise of staff

One of the single most important barriers to achievement for children with dyslexia is the lack of expertise on the issue in the education system. Dyslexia Action's experience is that head teachers who have a good understanding of dyslexia have better support in place. Dyslexia Action's model of good practice encourages a 'whole school' approach to understanding dyslexia, so that head teachers and governors are aware of the needs of all pupils, and that parents also get opportunities to increase awareness and support.

Currently, Initial Teacher Training (ITT) does not cover special needs in any depth and new teachers are mostly unaware of evidence-based practices to support dyslexic learners. There is a need to ensure that all teachers are aware of the warning signs and at risk factors so that they can refer children to appropriate support at the right level. Classroom teachers have a role in delivering the curriculum in ways that support those with dyslexia and many of these strategies are helpful for all pupils. Dyslexia Action strongly recommends increasing the knowledge and training given to new teachers.

Children with moderate/severe dyslexia need access to a teacher who has specialist training in dyslexia and literacy. At the present time there is a shortage of qualified staff to support dyslexic learners. Classrooms are not resourced to support the numbers of children with difficulties. In April 2004 a National Union of Teachers Survey of Special Needs Coordinators (SENCOs) revealed that there were long waiting lists for support and that any support available was focused on advice rather than direct help to the children in need.

There has been little statutory funding available to train specialist dyslexia teachers and many teachers who have chosen to obtain their certificate or diploma have had to pay for their own training. If we want children to be included, funding must be made available to support the training of specialist teachers and to train professionals at every level in the system.

Early intervention can prevent children with dyslexia/SpLD from requiring more intensive and costly support throughout their lives. There is evidence that many educational settings are providing appropriate support for children with dyslexia. Guidelines and policy have offered opportunities for good practice to be developed. However, as already outlined, there are still major gaps in effective provision for children with dyslexia. These deficiencies have been highlighted in a series of reports by the Audit Commission and Ofsted.

Dyslexia Action believes that a comprehensive and strategic approach to supporting children with dyslexia is critical. If inclusion is to become a reality for all children with dyslexia/SpLD the right support and resources need to be widely available in all schools, together with a comprehensive training programme to ensure the most effective delivery.

Partnership for Literacy

The *Partnership for Literacy* programme encompasses the principles of Dyslexia Action's approach to this problem. This is a unique initiative, using the specialist knowledge of Dyslexia Action teachers to develop a cost-effective sustainable model of provision for primary age children who are struggling with literacy. It incorporates whole school awareness, family learning and apprentice-style training in each partner school. It gives school staff the expertise both to identify which children are at risk and to develop strategies to support their needs. Reinforcement of the learning provided at school is made possible at home by offering awareness training and teaching resources to parents.

The stages of the project for each primary school are as follows:

- Awareness training for all staff
- Screening of all pupils within Years 2, 3, 4 and 5, to identify those at risk of literacy failure
- Screening training to enable staff to continue this process in the future
- A teaching programme, over two terms, for a selected group of pupils, using Dyslexia Action resources
- Two terms of apprentice style training for staff responsible for supporting SEN pupils (usually the Special Needs Coordinator and 2-4 Teaching Assistants)
- Resource training on the use of Dyslexia Action's computer program *Units of Sound* and on the *Active Literacy Kit*, for key members of staff and others from the LEA and neighbouring schools
- Parents' awareness training
- Study skills sessions for Year 6 pupils
- Consultancy following the apprentice training to support school staff

The project was launched in January 2006, initially working with four schools in the first year and then completing work with a further four schools at the end of the summer term 2007. These schools are in the London, Hull, Coventry and Nottingham areas. The project is funded by independent donations. The current costs of this project are approximately £27,000 per partnered school. This is a cost-effective model as the school is provided with the knowledge and expertise to continue to deliver a programme of identification and support for generations of children to come.

Partnership for Literacy is being evaluated and monitored by the Centre for Evaluation and Management (CEM Centre) at Durham University. Initial results for the first four schools show that the bottom 20% of children gained an average of seven standard score points over a six month period, with 102 children from the four schools moving from 'below average' into the 'average' category.

The schools involved welcomed the additional support, as Steve Farr, Head Teacher of Whitegate Primary School, commented: "This joint literacy project has opened our eyes to another group of children with 'disguised needs'. Careful assessment, training and use of the resources provided have enabled our staff to move some way towards addressing the needs of the identified children. All our staff, but especially those working with the project, have appreciated the input by Dyslexia Action and the progress made by the children. We intend to continue the work in future years."

Karen O'Keefe, Head Teacher of Oak Cottage, added: "The Partnership for Literacy project has been an exciting and informative initiative. Both our staff and children have benefited from the expertise of the Dyslexia Action teachers and we look forward to celebrating the children's progress and achievements."

From September 2007, further independent donations will enable Dyslexia Action to work with nine more schools. These will be in the London, Coventry, Sutton Coldfield, Tonbridge, Bath, Lincoln, Newcastle, Sheffield and Wilmslow areas. With further funding it is hoped that this intervention programme will be more extensively rolled out across the UK.

Government initiatives to improve teacher expertise

The Inclusion Development Programme (IDP) is a four-year cross-phase continuing professional development (CPD) programme for teachers in all schools, accessed on CD ROM and also via the internet. The programme is aimed at practitioners, teachers and leadership teams in mainstream education. In the first of four years the IDP will focus on dyslexia and speech, language and communications. CPD on supporting autism, behavioural needs, etc., will be addressed in later years. A series of regional events and workshops to promote the CPD, increase awareness and understand and encourage take up, will take place during 2007–08. The Government is also investing in the *No To Failure* project through which local authorities and schools are working with the national dyslexia organisations to train teachers to become specialists in this area and to eliminate failure in reading and writing.

Costs – the bottom line!

Shirley Cramer has spoken in public many times about the costs to the UK economy of failing to deal with poor literacy: "The cost to the taxpayer to train one teacher in every primary school to support children with hidden disabilities, such as dyslexia, would be £36 million. Projects such as the Partnership for Literacy currently cost approximately £27,000 per partner school. This is a fraction of the cost to the treasury of the long-term problems for adults with dyslexia later in life, not to mention the wasted potential, tax revenues and missed contributions to society. Providing the right help early in a child's life can help prevent major difficulties later. We should be investing in these children now which will reap rewards for the individual, the public purse and contribute to the competitiveness of the UK."

For more information please visit www.dyslexiaaction.org.uk or call 01784 222300.

Kerry Bennett is Public Relations Manager for Dyslexia Action.

Recent national initiatives on dyslexia in Scotland

Pamela Deponio

The Scottish Executive has funded various initiatives to facilitate the support of pupils with dyslexia over the last few years. The Education (Additional Support for Learning) (Scotland) Act 2004 placed new duties on education authorities to identify, assess and support pupils with additional needs, including dyslexia [1]. This chapter looks at some recent developments in Scotland.

'The Additional Support for Learning Act introduces a new framework for supporting children and young people in their school education, and their families. This framework is based on the idea of additional support needs. This new term will apply to children and young people who, for whatever reason, require additional support, long or short term, in order to help them make the most of their school education.'

Supporting children's learning: code of practice (2005), Scottish Executive.

Dyslexia at Transition

Dyslexia at Transition is an interactive DVD-ROM, which is the result of a Scottish Executive grant awarded to Dyslexia Scotland in 2004. Directed by Pamela Deponio, University of Edinburgh, the project was carried out by a team of education professionals, which involved the Universities of Aberdeen and Strathclyde along with five local education authorities.

The project undertook a longitudinal research study of pupils with dyslexia, and their parents, over the transition year from primary to secondary education to establish their hopes, concerns and experiences. Key issues arising from the research were selected to form the basis of Continuing Professional Development activities (known as i-Papers) for primary and secondary teachers.

The DVD-ROM comprises six separate sections and is designed for use by teachers, pupils and parents. Materials are arranged in the following formats:

What is dyslexia? (for teachers)
This is a voiced PowerPoint, which offers an introduction to dyslexia in terms of the nature of the difficulties experienced by learners, how they may be identified and how responses to support individual needs can be made. This section is particularly beneficial to teachers who identify dyslexia awareness as an area of professional development need.

i-Papers (for teachers)
These interactive papers encourage teachers to examine the key issues that arose from the study. Each paper invites teachers to select an issue of interest, listen to the views of pupils, parents and teachers and reflect on their own practice by discussing and noting any possible changes they may want to implement. The i-Papers are arranged under the following themes:

- the affective domain

- the curriculum

- modern languages

- the process of transition

- transfer of information

- use of technology

Pupils' transition experiences (for pupils)
Interviews with some of the pupils are presented at the three key points over the year, namely the end of the final year of primary education, the first term of the first year of secondary education, and the very end of the first year. This section is designed for pupils so that they may listen to the experiences of others who have already made the move.

Pupil booklet (for pupils)
This booklet is designed to prepare pupils with dyslexia for the move to secondary school. Schools may individualise the booklet by adding the name of the receiving secondary and other specific information. It can then be downloaded and printed in colour. Pupils may either work through the booklet at home with a parent/carer or in school with a support assistant. Copies may be downloaded at www.dyslexiatransition.org

Parents' transition experiences (for parents)
Designed for parents of pupils who are about to make the move to secondary school, this section allows parents to share in the hopes and concerns of others as they support their children through the transition process. Although designed for parents, this section gives teachers valuable insights into parents' expectations and experiences over the transition year.

Sir Jackie Stewart lecture (for teachers and parents)
Sir Jackie Stewart is president of Dyslexia Scotland. As a contribution to this project Sir Jackie delivered a lecture to a group of students from the PGDE programme at Moray House. The lecture, which addresses the impact of dyslexia from the point of view of an individual with dyslexia, was recorded in December 2006 and can be heard at www.dyslexiatransition.org

The DVD-Rom has been distributed to all primary and secondary schools in Scotland to encourage learning communities to consider pupils with dyslexia at the time of transfer and to support secondary subject teachers in their understanding of the impact of dyslexia in the early years of secondary education.

SQA Digital Exam Papers

The Communication Aids for Language and Learning (CALL) Centre, which is based at the University of Edinburgh, has recently collaborated with the Scottish Qualifications Authority (SQA) to pilot the use of digital exam papers for candidates with additional support needs. The papers were first used in 2006 and offer pupils with dyslexia a more independent way of taking exams, eliminating the need for readers and scribes. The papers, sent to schools on a CD, are opened on candidates' computers. They are 'speech enabled' so that pupils can click on the text and have the questions read out by the computer. The addition of response sections allows pupils to type answers on screen. Background and/or text can be colour adapted to accommodate visual disturbance.

Feedback from pupils and staff who have used the papers has been extremely positive and it is anticipated that the SQA will make digital papers widely available to any pupil with dyslexia in Scotland from 2008 onwards. This initiative is led by Paul Nisbet, Joint Co-ordinator of the Centre. Further information about the digital papers and the CALL Centre is available at http://callcentre.education.ed.ac.uk/digitalexams

Books for All

Pupils with dyslexia who cannot read standard textbooks, reading books, worksheets, assessments and exam papers in school are obviously disadvantaged. Some pupils are supported by other students or staff reading to them. This means, however, that pupils are dependent on someone else. A more appropriate approach for some is to convert the printed book or worksheets into an alternative, accessible format, e.g. to 'adapted print' using a more readable font, or audio or digital format that can be opened and read on a computer.

Pupils can then access the books in their own time and place. Pupils can use text-to-speech software and ICT to access and write their answers independently.

In 2006 the CALL Centre was commissioned by the Scottish Executive to conduct a study into the need for learning materials in formats for pupils with all print disabilities, including dyslexia. The *Books for All* project found that there is a need to produce and disseminate materials in accessible formats to support all pupils with literacy needs. At present, many pupils cannot find books in formats that are accessible to them. Most publishers do not sell adapted print, audio or digital versions.

Alternative formats of print (e.g. braille, large print, audio books, etc) have long been used by pupils with visual impairment and copyright law currently allows books to be converted for pupils with a visual impairment. In contrast, copyright law prevents such adaptation for pupils with dyslexia. Schools can adapt printed materials for pupils with dyslexia but permission must first be obtained from the publisher. Furthermore, there is huge duplication of effort since pupils, parents and staff all over the country make the same accessible versions of the same books because the law prevents the books from being shared.

The *Books for All* report proposes setting up a 'The Scottish Accessible Learning Resources Network' with a view to:

- offering advice and support to education authority staff to help create libraries of accessible books;

- serving as a link between publishers, education authorities and the Copyright Licensing Agency (CLA) to arrange licences;

- sourcing electronic versions of texts from which a range of accessible formats can be produced;

- supporting the cataloguing and sharing of the resources.

The report was delivered to the Scottish Executive in April 2007 and a Stakeholder's Group has been set up to take the recommendations

forward. More information is available from www.booksforall.org.
uk

WordTalk

Some pupils with dyslexia who have difficulty reading find they can access text more easily or more quickly when it is read out by the computer. There are many computer programs that can do this, but most are relatively expensive. The Scottish Executive has therefore funded the CALL Centre and Rod Macaulay, a teacher based in TASSCC (Technological Assessment and Support Service for Children and the Curriculum) in Aberdeen to develop and distribute *WordTalk* free of charge to Scottish education. *WordTalk* is a very simple toolbar that can read out any Microsoft Word document on a PC. It has proved very popular in the UK and also internationally and Rod was awarded a prestigious Microsoft Innovative Teacher Award in March 2007 for his work. *WordTalk* can be downloaded free of charge from www.wordtalk.org.uk

Inclusive Practice Project

Research reports suggest that many teachers are not fully prepared to meet the needs of all pupils. Indeed, many mainstream teachers still do not regard the support of pupils with additional needs as within their remit. Traditionally, initial teacher education has addressed the issue of additional or 'special' needs through the use of specialist lecturers offering 'one off' lectures on particular aspects of additional needs or offering 'opt-in' courses. Following a meeting between Sir Jackie Stewart, the University of Aberdeen and the Scottish Executive, an initiative at the University of Aberdeen known as the *Inclusive Practice Project* has been set up. This project aims to reform initial teacher education by addressing the issue of additional support needs within the core curriculum. Professor Martin Rouse is leading this project, which to date has reviewed the Postgraduate Diploma in Education. The project will also work with fully registered teachers in local authorities on collaborative action research projects in the area of additional support.

Showcasing dyslexia in Scottish education

The national initiatives described above, and many of the education authority initiatives described elsewhere in this Handbook by Marie Lockhart, the National Coordinator Dyslexia Scotland, came together in May 2007 at an event jointly hosted by the University of Edinburgh and the Scottish Executive, entitled *Showcasing Dyslexia in Scottish Education*. This event was attended by representatives from many authorities in Scotland and was chaired by Professor Martin Rouse, University of Aberdeen. Mike Gibson, Head of Additional Support for Learning at the Scottish Executive set the policy context for pupils with additional support needs in general and dyslexia in particular. He stated that, despite progress in Scotland with regards to the identification and support of pupils with dyslexia, there was no room for complacency and that the HMIe (Her Majesty's Inspectorate of Education in Scotland) would undertake a review of policy and provision in Scotland from 2007–08. The results of this review will inform future policy and practice.

Reference

[1] www.clacks.gov.uk/site/documents/policies/supportingchildrenslearningcodeofpractice

Pamela Deponio is Academic Coordinator of the Programmes in Additional Support for Learning at Moray House School of Education, University of Edinburgh, and a member of the Scottish Parliament's Cross-Party Group on Dyslexia.

The National Coordinator Dyslexia Scotland Project

Marie Lockhart

Funded by the Scottish Executive Education Department, the National Coordinator Dyslexia Scotland Project began in April 2006. As part of the National Coordinator's remit was to investigate models of good practice, visits were made to 25 of the 32 Scottish local authorities, representing inner city, urban and rural areas. Initial meetings were held with identified key personnel and, because the main focus was on provision for children with dyslexia in primary schools, two of the major areas of discussion centred round early identification and effective interventions currently in place. Follow-up visits were made to local authorities and schools identified as good practice models, some of which are outlined in the following examples.

Outreach support

Peripatetic outreach work is undertaken by network support teams in some local authorities whilst, in others, teachers in specialist bases provide advice and support for individual pupils and their teachers at a local level. Besides having a teaching commitment in the literacy base within a mainstream primary school, the staff who provide outreach support to schools in one local authority fulfil a number of roles. This includes working alongside class teachers, modelling good practice, providing resources as well as being involved in assessments. With a focus on inclusion and the aim of empowering mainstream colleagues, their remit also includes delivery of whole-school and authority-wide in-service training. "Drop-in" sessions are held on a regular basis in the base, which is an example of a 'dyslexia-friendly' classroom environment. Teachers from this and other schools can visit the base to access resources as well as advice.

The remit of the dyslexia support teachers in another area, whose main role is to provide peripatetic support, is to develop ICT and thinking skills. During the summer term, a transition programme is also provided for groups of primary 7 pupils who have been referred with literacy difficulties. This involves teaching the children strategies to be used across all areas of the curriculum in secondary school. The design and delivery of continuing professional development training on dyslexia to mainstream teachers and support for learning staff is an integral part of their role.

Members of a specialist ICT support team, in a large inner-city local authority, have produced a film. This shows some of the ways in which ICT is being used in schools to help pupils who have literacy difficulties to cope independently with the reading and writing requirements of the curriculum. The film highlights the benefits for pupils of a variety of software, most of which is already in schools. It aims to encourage more staff to make use of these ICT resources in their own schools and classrooms. It also emphasizes that children's access to the resources relies on whole school commitment - from head teachers, class teachers, support for learning teachers, ICT coordinators and support staff.

In one of the largest local authorities, mainstream support for learning teachers, who have gained additional qualifications in dyslexia, is provided by members of a specialist ICT team, working on a part-time basis in their ICT role. Led by a coordinator, they also deliver staff training as well as providing direct support and appropriate resources for children with dyslexia.

Although these and several other authorities provide exemplary outreach services in response to referrals, the following example of one local authority's provision is a model which ensures that support for children with dyslexia is available to every primary school.

A team of three specialist teachers is centrally managed by the Additional Support for Learning (ASL) Coordinator. Each of these teachers is deployed to specific schools, which enables regular visits to be made and positive working relationships to be established with mainstream and support for learning staff. Close links are also maintained with the educational psychology service.

These teachers carry out a variety of roles and provide a range of services, which include:

- Working collaboratively with class teachers, advising on appropriate interventions, resources and programmes. A 'tool-kit', which includes classroom resources and a checklist, is provided for every class teacher.

- Mentoring newly-appointed support for learning teachers.

- Carrying out assessments of individual children, supporting colleagues in interpretation of findings and confirmation of identification of children 'at risk of dyslexia'.

- Keeping abreast of developments and introducing innovative approaches.

- Attendance at meetings in their allocated schools at the beginning of each session to discuss the needs of identified children.

- Liaison with parents, particularly at the primary 7 transition stage, and attending case conferences, if necessary.

They also provide various levels and types of training, e.g. for newly qualified teachers, input into post-graduate certificate courses as well as responding to requests from individual schools. Their remit also includes support for children with dyspraxia and Asperger's syndrome.

Early identification and intervention

One local authority has introduced several initiatives to improve provision and practice as part of its 'Dyslexia Strategy', with a particular focus on early identification and intervention. During the session 2005/2006, a pilot project on *Lucid CoPS (Cognitive Profiling System)* and *LASS (Lucid Assessment System for Schools)*, which are computer-based assessment systems designed for children in the 4 – 8 and 8 – 11 years age ranges, respectively, was established. Designed to run for 15 months (5 school terms), this involved 20 support for learning teachers and covered approximately 30 primary schools. These programs are used to assess children's difficulties when transitioning from Stage 1 to Stage 2 of the Additional Support for Learning staged intervention process. (Stage 1 involves the Class Teacher using differentiated approaches, additional resources, etc., and Stage 2 is based on whole-school approaches, including referral to and intervention by the support for learning teacher.) The teachers involved in the project received rigorous training, which included interpretation of results and intervention strategies.

In recognition of the importance of early identification and intervention, some local authorities are focusing on phonological awareness and/or oral language and communication skills at the pre-school stage. For a number of years, the synthetic phonics approach to literacy development has been implemented in primary schools in several regions, which is also having a positive impact on children's early literacy skills development. Some authorities have developed intervention programmes which are reported as being successful in alleviating individual children's literacy difficulties in the early stages of their school career, ensuring that progress is sustained and preventing problems associated with erosion of self-esteem.

Several years ago, in one of the local authorities, a 12 – 16 week early years intervention programme, *Intensive Support for Reading* (ISR), was devised and piloted by an educational psychologist and support for learning teacher. Based on Edinburgh Council's updated version of Marie Clay's *Reading Recovery* programme, identified children receive one-to-one support. Due to its success, this is firmly embedded in practice in schools throughout the region.

Several teachers have been trained to deliver the programme and a coordinator has recently been appointed.

In another local authority a pilot of a multi-sensory approach to spelling has already raised the attainment of many pupils, including those with dyslexia. Founded on well-researched and recommended teaching and learning strategies for pupils with dyslexia, the programme includes metacognition and paired learning. An important success factor has been the insight gained into the importance of learning style and the use of this to maximise all pupils' learning. The programme has been used successfully with children from Primary 3 to Primary 7.

As well as local authority initiatives, examples of good practice were also found in the course of follow-up visits to schools. Individual teachers have developed innovative programmes to support children with dyslexia, irrespective of whether local authorities have these arrangements in place.

One example of an excellent inclusive initiative is the *Literacy Workshop for Early Years*. Based on synthetic phonics, this programme has evolved over several years from the work of a learning support teacher. It has now become a comprehensive package, which can be delivered by a team of teachers and support assistants, in whole class or small group settings throughout the primary school. Although the programme is targeted at children at risk of reading failure, it is proving beneficial for all children with a range of abilities in the Primary 1 mainstream class. Above all, the *Literacy Workshop* is to be enjoyed, its main aim being to ensure that no child becomes 'locked out' of the world of books. It is hoped that this will be rolled out to other schools within the authority.

Dyslexia Friendly Schools Award

Although examples of good practice have been identified in several authorities, East Renfrewshire Council has become the flagship of the Dyslexia Friendly Schools Award in Scotland and could provide the blueprint for others that may decide to follow their lead. At the outset of the initiative, designated members of staff were appointed as Dyslexia Advisors (DAs) in every primary and secondary school.

Initial training sessions were targeted at DAs; however, subsequent rounds have been attended by support for learning teachers and, more recently, mainstream staff who wish to expand their knowledge. Because dyslexia-friendly schools are based on a whole-school approach and commitment, *all* staff in *all* schools have received basic awareness training. Subsequently, development needs have been identified through consultation with DAs as well as through issues being raised by the Dyslexia Friendly Schools Field Officer/Project Manager on her assessment of schools. Parents' groups have been set up and local authority representatives also attend meetings. This ensures that open lines of communication are maintained. Evaluation of the initiative, as a whole, has identified specific areas that require adaptations or improvements to be made. On-going monitoring ensures that standards are maintained after a school has gained this award and tracking children's progress is an essential element of this process.

Plans for future development

Whilst there are some similarities in dyslexia provision and training there are also considerable variations, both within and between authorities. Changes cannot be achieved overnight but there are positive indicators that several local authorities already have systems in place which could form the basis of plans to ensure that support for children with dyslexia is available to every primary school. Throughout the course of the National Co-ordinator Project, local authority personnel who are keen to move practice forward have requested advice and support to develop more dyslexia friendly provision and practice. Measures are also being taken to review current training programmes. However, overall, these developments are still very much 'work-in-progress'.

Having identified some examples of best practice models, Dyslexia Scotland is in a position to be pro-active and solution-focused. Future plans for a short continuation of the National Co-ordinator

Project include disseminating good practice and investigating how to develop the dyslexia friendly schools initiative. This will involve consideration of the major issues of teachers' professional development and the need for early identification and intervention.

As well as improving provision for children with dyslexia and autism, initial teacher education and Continuing Professional Development for teachers are high on the Scottish political agenda. HMIe are currently carrying out a review of dyslexia, and their findings, due to be published towards the end of 2008, will inform future developments in training and provision. It is hoped that the work of Dyslexia Scotland, together with the commitment and will of politicians and personnel at all levels of the education system, a highly-trained workforce and the requisite funding, will ensure that children with dyslexia will be enabled to thrive and achieve their full potential.

Marie Lockhart is the National Coordinator, Dyslexia Scotland, and a member of the Scottish Parliament's Cross-Party Group on Dyslexia.

Good practice in schools

Identifying and supporting pupils with dyslexia: the Loretto Experience

Stuart Lucas

Loretto School is a small co-educational independent school just outside Edinburgh that offers parents the options of day schooling, flexi-boarding or boarding. There are approximately 340 pupils on the school roll at present. Through having a small school outlook we have the opportunity of individualising a pupil's timetable to meet their individual needs. We have three full-time teachers (two of whom are undertaking diplomas in dyslexia) and one part-time teacher. By the end of the 2007–08 academic year all our support teachers will have a specialist qualification in dyslexia. Currently, one teacher specialises in reading skills, one in pastoral support, one in numeracy support, and one in literacy skills.

Our aim is to provide the best support that best fits the needs of our pupils, the caveat being that we understand that at times there are inevitable constraints such as the timetable, subject choice, and the motivation of the pupils. Sometimes it is a fine balancing act, but with the use of initial and follow-up screening procedures and the allocation of support, we can guide our pupils towards success at GCSE and on to AS and A2 and, for the vast majority, college or university.

Types of support available

In the 2nd and 3rd forms support learning is offered to those pupils with dyslexia. This comprises small group teaching with a maximum of four groups of five students for four lessons per week. The support learning option is chosen instead of a second modern language. The Director of Studies, advised by the Head of Support for Learning, deals with subject choice. In addition, subject teachers can request, via their Head of Department, in-class support for pupils, which will be dependent on need, staffing and timetabling. If pupils have 'Additional Support Needs' which cannot be met within the above support measures, then these can be discussed with both the Head of Support for Learning and the Director of Studies. The aim is to offer a broad curriculum and support the needs of pupils with dyslexia either through direct literacy support or by developing specific study skills, such as ways of analysing texts (e.g. poetry, short stories and film) combined with re-enforcement of essay writing skills. We aim to support all subject areas but this is not always possible at GCSE level and hence additional workshops are offered by some academic departments, including one in maths and physics. In addition, some teachers offer individualised support where a greater need has been identified, though this is at the discretion of the individual teacher.

If required, pupils can continue with support during their GCSE course in the 4th & 5th forms; they opt to take eight GCSEs instead of the usual nine. As always, however, needs are considered on an individual basis. Pupils once more join a small group (maximum of five students) and work on their current coursework, although assistance with literacy and numeracy skills is also available. In addition, study skills and exam revision skills can be incorporated into any support programme. For the academic year 2007–08 we are introducing a specific reading group with a minimum of two pupils and a maximum of four per group. We also aim to offer a specific numeracy group in the academic year 2008–09.

Support is also catered for in 6th form, though to a lesser degree. At this stage many pupils who have previously had support are

Northease Manor School

Changing lives, building confidence, creating independent citizens

A small Independent School for pupils aged 10 to 17 with Specific Learning Difficulties including Dyslexia and Dyspraxia

"Northease Manor is an excellent school"

"Outstanding value for money"
"Curriculum is outstanding"

"Progress that pupils made is outstanding"
Source: Ofsted - July 2007

"Boarding and Care are outstanding"
Source: Ofsted - November 2007

✓ For Girls and Boys aged 10 to 17

✓ Weekly Boarding or Day placements

✓ On-site Speech and Language Therapy and Occupational Therapy

✓ Individual learning programmes in small classes where everyone is valued

✓ Access for all to GCSE examinations with highly successful results record

To find out more, or to arrange an appointment to visit us, please contact the Secretary:
Northease Manor School, Rodmell, Lewes, East Sussex, BN7 3EY
Tel: 01273 472915 Fax: 01273 472202 E-mail:
office@northease.co.uk
Or visit our website: www.northease.co.uk

Registered Charity no. 307005

ready to become more independent, although the established links with support staff make it easier for students to request support if required. Pupils who enter Loretto at 6th form level are usually catered for through providing exam access arrangements, such as extra time. For some of our new pupils it can come as a 'shock' or a 'release' when they are picked up by our screening procedures and identified as having dyslexia. It is at this stage that they may find life slightly easier because they have the opportunity to receive support as well as having exam access arrangements.

In a few specific cases one-to-one tuition is given, though this is agreed before acceptance and is usually for those pupils with a Statement of Needs or a Coordinated Support Plan (in Scotland). A few parents request one-to-one tuition for their children, especially in the lead-up to exams, and if this can be timetabled it is provided although parents have to meet the extra costs. At times, support is only allocated once screening procedures have been carried out and after consultation with the individual pupil, their parents, their tutor (whom they meet with daily and receive effort grades and academic grades once per month), and their subject teachers.

For those pupils who have been identified with dyslexia or who have been referred for support to be screened or to be monitored then their names are appended to our 'Pupil List' and this is then available to all teachers via the school's intranet. This is updated on needs basis but certainly every month.

Screening

All new 2nd, 3rd and 4th form pupils are screened for dyslexia using the **LASS Secondary** computerised assessment system. In addition, through looking at the test results from 'Cave' (visual memory), 'Reading' and 'Spelling', in association with our own vision screening checklist, a decision can be taken whether or not to recommend orthoptic assessment (treatment for pupils with reading difficulties). Furthermore, the test results from 'Nonwords' and 'Segments' (tests of phonological skills), in particular, but also 'Mobile' (forward auditory sequential memory) and 'Spelling', may indicate whether or not pupils may benefit from improved auditory processing through Johansen Sound Therapy.

We have also just started to screen all 6th form pupils for dyslexia using **LADS** – Lucid's computerised Adult Dyslexia Screening Test. LADS incorporates three tests that have been designed to measure phonological processing and working memory skills, which are typically weak in dyslexic adults and young people (post 16) despite educational intervention.

We also use the **NFER Single Word Spelling Test** to screen all new 2nd and 3rd form pupils. We find that this test is a good additional indicator to help us identify pupils with dyslexia. The **Dyslexia Screening Test (DST)** and the **Dyslexia Adult Screening Test (DAST)** can also used to determine whether or not a referral to an Educational Psychologist is required.

If a more detailed assessment of a pupil is required we may use **SNAP** (Special Needs Assessment Profile). If a teacher suspects that a pupil has a learning difficulty that has not been identified, or if they wish a more detailed report with accompanying advice sheets, then the pupil can be assessed using SNAP. This is done through the pupil's teachers completing a questionnaire (parents may also be asked to complete a small questionnaire) and if need be a selection of small tests, known as probes, may be used. The results are shown in a bar graph and may show the co-occurrence of specific learning difficulties.

Assessments by outside agencies

We use several outside agencies to provide specialised assessment and intervention, although all costs relating to these have to be agreed with parents prior to assessment and/or treatment.

When a pupil is screened by the Support for Learning Department and found to be at risk of dyslexia then the parents are informed and a request is made to have the pupil assessed by an educational psychologist. From this assessment the school will be informed as to whether or not the pupil has dyslexia and recommendations will be made regarding appropriate teaching strategies and support. This will also help to determine – in consultation with subject teachers and tutors – what examination access arrangements would be appropriate. We have the services of an independent educational psychologist who visits the school twice per term and another one who visits as required.

Orthoptic assessment and treatment is also available through the Support for Learning Department. A state-registered orthoptist holds a monthly eye clinic during term-time for those pupils who have visual difficulties, be they dyslexic or not. Information on orthoptic vision screening and a request form for orthoptic assessment are available to parents from the Head of Department.

In addition, the services of a speech and language therapist, using Johansen Sound Therapy is available through the Support for Learning Department. We find that a few pupils have problems with the processing of language; their ability to organise, store and retrieve information is weak and this weakness directly affects reading, spelling and learning as well as concentration and the development of spoken language. Hence we aim to address these difficulties in a few of our pupils per year. One of the outcomes we have found is greater concentration when in class and hence an improved processing of language.

Pupil profiles and technology

Once pupils have been assessed by an educational psychologist then a Pupil Profile is compiled, which states that they have dyslexia, lists their strengths and weaknesses, and specifies the school's responsibilities (the amount of support given and exam access arrangements), teachers' responsibilities, teaching recommendations, and pupil responsibilities (use of support time and relevant software, e.g. Inspiration). Other information can be added as required

For those pupils who have a Statement of Needs or a Coordinated Support Plan then a Pupil Plan (Individual Education Plan) is drawn-up and re-visited at the end of term. At the present time this measure applies only to a few pupils at Loretto.

During 2007–08 we will be introducing the software **Kurzweil** to assist pupils with reading difficulties. The school has bought a 25-user site licence, which we will be able to 'lend' to pupils on a needs basis: a bit like a library system. We are also considering investing in a site licence for *TextHelp Gold* in order to assist our pupils in becoming more independent in their learning. Both of these programs will complement our existing software programs, for which we have school site licences, including *Inspiration*, *Mindmanager 2006*, and *Visual Thesaurus*.

Conclusions

In getting the Support for Learning Department off the ground seven years ago and in keeping the department staffed at the appropriate level and with necessary funding, we have found that the support and encouragement of two key senior staff has been central. These are our excellent line manager (Director of Studies) and the Headmaster, who supports our ideas and gives the department enough freedom to continue to expand its vision. On the other hand, it must always be noted that the Financial Operations Officer and Governors keep a close eye on staffing costs and our annual budget. Thanks must also go to Dr Gavin Reid who assisted our department with many enquiries in the early days and with assessments and follow-up recommendations over the years. Above all, the continued success of the department, and ultimately that of our pupils, relies on good teamwork and the daily imparting of knowledge from class teacher to pupil.

Resources

www.gavinreid.co.uk
DST/DAST: www.pearson-uk.com
www.inspiration.com
www.johansensoundtherapy.com
www.kurzweiledu.com
LASS/LADS: www.lucid-research.com
Mindmanager 2006: www.Mindjet.com
www.nfer-nelson.co.uk
www.snapassessment.com
www.texthelp.com

Stuart Lucas is Head of Support for Learning, Loretto School, Musselburgh, Scotland, and a member of the Scottish Parliament's Cross-Party Group on Dyslexia.

Tackling the spelling problems of dyslexics

Jonathan Ferrier

Spelling is all about hearing the sounds in words and transcribing these sounds on to paper, using the correct symbols (letters) in the correct order. Here is an example taken from a piece of writing by Michael, a 13-year-old boy who has dyslexia:

on niy Fist bay at sheool I came home wive too blak iser.

[On my first day at school I came home with two black eyes.]

Understanding the problems

A brief inspection of Michael's writing shows a number of points for which help is required, but also reveals some basics that he has mastered. At least he writes from left to right, and his letters, although not cursive (joined up), are all firmly on the lines and are recognisable.

Looking more closely at what he has written:

1. *'on'* is correct but he has not started with a capital letter. Does he know the difference between capital letters and lowercase letters, and does he know when to use them?

2. Where does *'niy'* come from? It is certainly very unusual, but it suggests that Michael cannot hear the difference between 'm' and 'n' since he correctly uses a letter 'm' in came and home.

3. *'Fist'* starts with an inappropriate capital, so he may not know how to write a lowercase 'f'. (Indeed many dyslexics who are less severe than Michael, seem to have difficulty in writing an 'f' and often sit it on the line rather than making it an ascender and a descender). Obviously *'Fist'* is phonetically incorrect and shows that he does not know how to make an 'er' sound in English (er/ir/ur). On the other hand he has heard and written correctly the 'st' sounds.

4. *'bay'* - the most blatant piece of b/d confusion that I have ever seen. More commonly you will see capital Bs and Ds scattered through the text because the child/student can remember the difference between B and D, but not which sound goes with 'b' or 'd'.

5. *'at'* looks as if it started out as *'an'* but was then changed to *'at'*, in which case Michael is at least trying to get the correct sounds on to the paper.

6. *'shcool'*. The correct spelling of school is such an extraordinary piece of irregular spelling that it always amazes me how many dyslexics actually manage to spell it correctly, but then they do see it written very frequently. Michael's spelling may be how he says the word, in which case it is a piece of phonetic spelling (phonetically correct but not the actual spelling used in English). However, I suspect that he has in fact done what many dyslexics do, which is to remember the letters in the word, but not in their correct order.

7. *'wive'* – 'wiv' would be phonetically correct for Michael's Oxfordshire accent, where in this age group 'th' is frequently pronounced 'v', so this misspelling may not mean that he does not know how to write a 'th' sound. However, the word should definitely not end in 'e', and he has obviously not understood about 'silent E'.

8. *'too'* is a homophone (same sound, different meaning) for 'two'. The different 'too's need explaining to Michael (to, too, two) and it may be helpful to pronounce 'too' and 'two' with a longer 'oo' than

in 'to' to help him grasp this. Arguably, however, Michael has more pressing problems than getting involved in too/two at present!

9. '*blak*' is the first proper phonetic spelling. It demonstrates the need to sort out the different 'k' sounds and particularly the common '-ck' ending with single syllable words.

10. '*iser*'. Another phonetic spelling for 'eyes', but where did the final 'r' come from? We need to ask him.

Overall most of Michael's phonemes (sounds) are in the correct order, which is a good start. However, he has a very poor grasp of how to write the sounds he is hearing, and does not understand the 'silent E' rule.

Tackling the problems

When there is uncertainty about what appears to be a problem, you can and should ask the child/student. For instance, in Michael's case, you might ask:

'How do you write the sound 'th' (or 'f')?'

'Can you hear the difference between 'm/n', or 'th/f'? How do you write those sounds?'

'Tell me each of the sounds in 'school' in order (s.k.oo.l).'

Once a student's problems have been identified, a plan can be drawn up of what to teach and when.

Teaching phonetics

Virtually all dyslexics are unable to learn by 'look and say' methods. Consequently:

■ They have to have a phonetic approach.

- They have to learn to hear the sounds in each word in the correct order.

- They have to understand and learn most of the 144 ways of spelling the 44 phonemes (sounds) in the English language.

These are what all the methods of teaching synthetic phonics do, in one way or another.

I think it is pointless and the cause of much misery to try to get dyslexics to spell every word correctly. However, it is quite possible for them to learn a phonetically correct spelling for everything they write so they can produce spellings that are easily recognisable. In Michael's case, I would praise him for spelling *'blak'* with a phonetically correct spelling, while pointing out the various ways of writing the 'k' sound and the fact that the actual spelling is 'black'.

Whichever method of teaching phonetics you use (and I would strongly recommend using one of the synthetic phonics methods), dyslexics need a clear, simple, progression, starting with phonetically regular CVC words. Irregular spellings should be avoided as much as possible in the early stages, at least until all the letter sounds have been firmly established.

In English, life is made much more difficult because we have a 26 lowercase letters and 26 capital letters (i.e. 52 written symbols) as well as 26 letter sounds and 26 letter names (i.e. 52 sounds): a total of 104 symbols which easily get confused.

It amazes me how many dyslexic teenagers are still unsure of the sounds of letters such as w, v, x, and y, in spite of seven or more years of schooling. Even more children are confused by the difference between the letter names and the letter sounds. Start by using letter sounds and only introduce letter names when the sounds are known, making sure the child knows the difference between the two.

A particularly helpful exercise for dyslexics at all stages is phoneme manipulation, which can be practised by making and changing nonsense words that can only be pronounced phonetically.

1. Take a selection of about 10 letters (including at least two vowels), each letter being on a separate card (scrabble letters will serve this purpose well), and lay them out in a row.

2. Ask the child to make a simple word, e.g. *Pull the letters forward to make 'sog'.*

3. Then ask him/her to change it by one letter, e.g. *Now make 'spog'.*

4. Continue making new words, changing one letter at a time, keeping to three- or four-letter words at first. It is best to have a list of words from the letters you are going to use, so that you cover the particular range of sounds that you wish to work on in each lesson.

As you increase to more complex five-letter words, e.g. *Change 'tasp' to 'trasp'*, you will see and hear the child start to separate the sounds in the word into individual phonemes, and then compare those phonemes with the letters on the table.

When this happens **you have won**!! You have started to establish:

- That letters are pictures of sounds
- That the sounds have to be written in order
- That the order is shown on paper from left to right
- That you have to hear the sounds in order to write them in order

N.B. In this exercise you can use digraphs (two letters, one sound, e.g. ch, sh, th) putting the two letters on to one card. You can also reinforce 'silent E', e.g. *Change 'spot' to 'spote'*.

b/d and p/g confusion

Many dyslexics, particularly those with visual problems, continue to have confusion about b/d and p/g two pairs of letters. The confusion is not about the different sounds or about the capital letters, it is simply that they cannot remember which way round the lowercase letter should be written to go with the sound they want. Unfortunately every time they get it wrong, they reinforce the fact that they don't know.

The answer lies in the word 'bed'. The 'bed' has a headboard and a foot to it (the uprights at each end of the word) and if it helps children to remember it, you can draw a stick man lying on the bed. A similar strategy can be used with 'peg', where the pegs hang down from the line but the letters again face inwards. Young dyslexic children may wish to put three or four people to 'bed' every night at their own bedtime, e.g. by writing *me in bed, bob in bed, dad in bed,* perhaps accompanied by a drawing. Older students may just wish to write *'bed'* or *'peg'* at the top of everything they write, so they can refer to it when needed.

'Silent E' and some other important rules

'Silent E' (sometimes called 'Magic E') is one of the few rules in English that has to be taught (and the most important one). Firstly the pupils must know the vowels (A,E,I,O,U), and in this case it is helpful to use their names, but then to back this up by asking for their sounds. The actual rule is *'silent E makes the vowel say its name'* (or *'the silent E changes the preceding vowel to say its name'* for the older student who wishes to be more precise). You then have to establish the sounds with and without the final E. I get the student to write the five vowel sounds across the page and write under each vowel the appropriate 'b-t' word (i.e., bat, bet, bit, bot, but), saying each word as it is written. I then get them to put an arrow down to make the same word with 'silent E' added (i.e. bate, bete, bite, bote, bute), again saying each word as it is written. It does not matter that some of these words will be nonsense words or incorrect spellings for words that are spelt differently (e.g. bote/boat); you should explain that although this is not the accepted way 'boat' is spelt, the word (bote) can only be pronounced in that way in the English language.

This exercise should be then be repeated as often as necessary, using different consonants (but not C or G, because the 'silent E' also changes the sound of the C and G) until it has been thoroughly understood and learnt. I back it up by playing pellmanism with pairs of rhyming words and getting the student to read each word with and without the final e.

The only other rule that I teach specifically to all students is soft C and G. In this case, C changes its sound from 'k' (as in *cat*) to 's' (as in *cent, ice, icy*) when it is followed by 'e', 'i' or 'y'. The same applies to G which changes from 'g' (as in *gun*) to 'j' (as in gent/gin). However, with the letter G there are a number of major exceptions (e.g. get, gig, giggle).

Final phonetics

If you teach students to hear all the sounds in a word, you do not need to teach them **blends** (st, pl, dr, gl, etc). In fact if you teach them blends, you will get some dyslexics who will misread the first letter as a blend when it is not (e.g. reading 'bread' for 'bead').

One of the greatest problems in written English is the many different ways of writing the same sound, particularly the **long vowel sounds**. Thus the long ō can be written 'oa' (as in boat), 'ow' (as in snow), 'o-e' (as in note), 'oe' (as in toe), 'o' (as in go/so), 'ough' (as in though). This has to be addressed and personally I like using the phonetics methods that tackle it head on (such as *PhonoGraphix* and *Sound Reading*). In these, you ask students to underline every example of particular sound in a piece of text and then list all the different groups on a separate sheet of paper. (You can create these texts for yourself, e.g. 'Joe rowed the boat so slowly that he had to ask for a tow with a rope from his old foe').

Resources

Some popular synthetic phonics teaching methods (principal designer's name in brackets)

Jolly Phonics (Sue Lloyd) – Jolly Books
Phono-Graphix (Diane McGuiness) – ReadAmerica
ReadWrite (Ruth Miskin) – Oxford University Press
Sound Reading System (Fiona Nevola) - Oxford

Some useful teaching aids

ACE Spelling Dictionary – LDA.
Exercise Your Spelling [Photo-copiable work sheets] – Elizabeth Wood; Hodder & Stoughton.
Lexia Reading System [Computer based spelling and reading practice] – Lexia UK.
Wordshark [Computer based spelling program with 36 games] – White Space Ltd.
Word Tracking [Teaches scanning and common word recognition] – Ann Arbor.

Jonathan Ferrier is a dyslexia tutor based in Oxfordshire.

Dyslexia and mathematics

Anne Henderson

Mathematics – the very word can make some students shake with fear!

For the dyslexic coping with maths can be very difficult. If a student continually gets the answer wrong then very quickly there will be a loss of confidence and a lowering of self-esteem. Once this starts to happen the student becomes unhappy in school, starts to fail in other subjects and, indeed, in all areas of life. Often for dyslexics, lack of self esteem means that everyday life starts to disintegrate so they find themselves on a downward spiral where failing becomes the norm. It is essential to recognise that every dyslexic is an individual with individual needs.

When faced with a maths question a dyslexic student has to read and understand complex maths words. Then there is the problem of trying to remember the correct method that will result in a successful solution. Usually on top of this, because it is maths speed is essential, you have to complete questions quickly. If you struggle with basic maths skills – such as simple subtraction – then anxiety takes over. Sweaty hands that can't hold a pencil, messy pages and disorganised thinking will guarantee a wrong answer.

A dyslexic learner will value teachers who understand his difficulties in maths and give praise for any amount of learning that has taken place. A teacher who focuses on strengths and creates positive learning experiences, will encourage that student to try even harder to overcome barriers to learning in mathematics. Early intervention is vital if we are going to help these students to achieve in maths.

Spotting students who struggle with maths

Does the student:

- Lack confidence when doing maths?
- Read and write numbers incorrectly or reverse them?
- e.g. S for 2 or 21 for 12?
- Confuse telephone numbers?
- Muddle digits and symbols?
- e.g. 6 + 3 read as 9 x 3
- Struggle with mental maths?
- Have poor estimation skills?
- Struggle to read and understand written maths problems?
- Struggle to remember the sequence he needs to problem solve?

Understand and support

A teacher who understands the problem, works with individual learning styles, uses appropriate apparatus to assist and provides strategies that support throughout all teaching, will benefit all dyslexic students.

Reading

Dyslexics often struggle with reading a maths book so need to become familiar with the maths words that are being used. A list of these words should be put on walls in the classroom. The words should be written in colour on blank cards, these could be stored in a 'special maths' box. A teacher must use these words, repeating them frequently and discussing their meaning with pictures. So not only do children see the spelling of the written words, but also hear the words being said. If a child reads slowly, allow him to sit with a good reader who will be able to help.

Understanding text

Understanding the words in context is most helpful. A teacher or parent should read the maths word problems with the child and discuss the meaning of the question. This gives the children who are struggling the opportunity to ask questions to clarify their difficulties. We should regard maths as a foreign language so we must translate from maths to English and English to maths. Some examples are shown in Table 1.

Six plus seven	6 + 7
Find the total of six plus seven	6 + 7
9 – 5=?	Nine take away 5
9 – 5+?	What is 5 less than 9?
I have six apples and eat two. How many do I have left?	6 – 2=?
8 + 2 =?	I have eight pens then find two more. How many pens have I got now?

Table 1. Examples of translation of mathematical expressions

Presentation

Different maths books present questions in very differing ways. Students need to experience these differences and have the opportunity to practise various strategies to help them problem solve.

Memory

Dyslexic students often forget verbal instructions, questions written on the board and lose personal belongings. Give the instructions several times and write them down for those students who really struggle. Teaching information in small chunks, using multi-sensory methods, and allowing enough time to complete work will enhance maths lessons for all students. When dealing with maths symbols put the symbol in the corner of the card with the word the student associates with it. The corner picture is a visualisation prompt for memory. Examples then can be written on the card.

If strategies are taught to help memory recall, then all children in the group, not just the dyslexics, will benefit. A piece of practical apparatus called **Audiblox** [www.audiblox2000.com] can help children develop their own strategies to improve memory. Children with learning disabilities in maths should be given peace and quiet to exercise their memory skills.

Help memory by encouraging students to:

- Trace digits in sand and say it aloud
- Trace the same digit, say it aloud, close eyes and picture it mentally
- Draw the digit in the air using a straight arm and big sweeping movements
- Draw the digit with noses, elbows and feet in the air. Say the digit but now picture it mentally with eyes open
- Trace the same digit on the skin
- To recall the digit – encourage the student to re-trace it on his skin
- Working in twos – one student traces the number on the other student's back and this student then has to say the number or write it on his whiteboard and ask: 'Is this the number?'
- Some students like to make their own personal links with numbers, e.g. 1 is a walking stick, 2 is a duck, 8 is a snowman, etc.

Direction

It is very helpful to discuss regularly and remind students about the meanings and positions of spatial relationships such as left and right, up and down, before and after, backwards and forwards. If necessary put stickers on their hands to denote left and right. Find a rhyme that will help the student to remember these directions. Children need to know where to begin a written calculation so possibly using a green spot (traffic light for 'go') will enable them to start in the right place.

Estimation

Estimation is an important mathematical skill that everyone uses throughout their lives. Children should always be encouraged to continue to give estimates to maths questions. Once they have developed this skill it will enable them to check whether or not their calculation is about the right size. If they know that an answer is roughly correct then this helps with using a calculator correctly.

Following a sequence of instructions

Maths is all about following a series of instructions from the start to the end so that an answer may be reached. These students may like the help of a sequence sheet that will help them remember what to do next. An example is shown in Figure 1.

Question………		
Read and re-read question. Highlight important words, underline important numbers.		
The question is asking me to find out……………		
Symbols I will use	Key words	I estimate the answer will be
+ − X ÷		More than Less than
My working out is		
Check answer against estimate		
Check answer against question		
My final answer is		

Figure 1. An example of a sequence sheet

Recognising patterns

Once students begin to see the patterns in the number system they are able to understand what maths is all about. Counting enables children to give names to the digits (1 – 'one', 2 – 'two', etc.). Later, understanding the patterns in the place value system (23, 24.., 33, 34.., etc.) allows children to count to huge numbers as they recognise the patterns in the system. The *Numicon* teaching approach uses multi sensory number shapes and rods that allow children to see the patterns in numbers [www.numicon.com]. In fact the *Numicon* apparatus is the most efficient that I have ever used to teach basic number concepts.

Perseveration

Some students do not notice that the calculation has changed from addition to subtraction so carry on doing addition. Encourage students to use different coloured highlighter pens to identify different maths symbols. In this way they will begin to notice when the colour changes the symbol also has changed. Some older students may do a series of different calculations but although the workings may be different for each calculation the answers will always be the same. Use a piece of cardboard to cover work already done so that the student can lift the card to check what has gone before but will not copy the answer. Discussing this problem can often prevent it from happening.

Work with learning styles

A teacher should always be aware that we all have individual learning styles. Working with these styles enables the student to maximise learning time.

A *visual learner* learns through seeing. He will enjoy reading books, watching a demonstration, seeing a video, using a map and following written instructions.

An *auditory learner* learns through hearing. He will learn best when told information, listening to instructions, hearing stories, talking to himself when learning and telling other what he knows.

A *kinaesthetic learner* learns through moving, doing and touching. He likes using apparatus, making models, using a computer, moving around the room as he works.

Teachers can often spot a learning style by spending time with a student and closely observing how he learns best. Make a chart showing how the student learns best using pictures and colours. A valuable piece of apparatus called the *Portable Classroom* is useful for a peripatetic teacher wishing to use multi-sensory approaches [*www.theportableclassroom.com*].

Multi-sensory Techniques

The more you can see it, hear it, say it and do it, the easier it is to learn.

When teaching a new maths concept teachers must relate it to something the student knows already so that he can build on that information. Teachers also need to use apparatus that students can touch and experience. Later, introducing a diagram to represent the information allows the child to make progress. Once the understanding is in place then a student can move from the diagram and begin to use symbols.

Figure 2 shows the steps taken by a student in progressing from the start of a new topic (step 1) to mastery of it (step 6). If a student begins to struggle then a teacher should investigate where the problem is located and go back to there. It is not always necessary to go back to the beginning level 1.

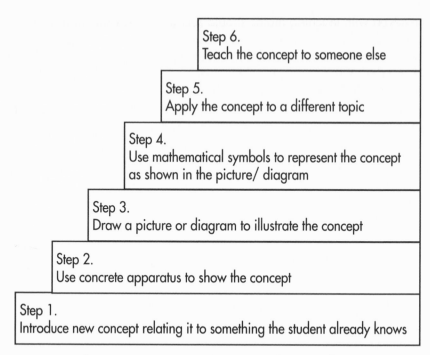

Figure 2. The steps in mastering a new mathematical concept

Conclusions

When teaching a new topic in maths we should try to:

- Relate new concept to past learning
- Prepare translations (English to Maths and Maths to English)
- Provide multi-sensory stimuli
- Work with each individual's learning styles
- Use mnemonics, mind maps, computers
- Set targets for improvement one at a time
- Provide handouts with notes for older students
- Encourage sharing (buddy system)

All learners need to be valued and none more than the dyslexic who is struggling in maths, often referred to as the dyscalculic. Everyone involved with teaching maths should recognise the value of making a mistake. If the ethos within the classroom encourages students to discuss their mistakes openly, then all will learn from the ensuing discussion. If learning is taught in manageable steps then there is a chance that the student will begin to understand and begin to make progress. Measuring against others often only makes him fail even more. We must encourage every small improvement perhaps with a sticker or badge to say: "I learned how to remember what + means," or: "I asked a good question". Teachers who promote self-esteem allow students to be positive in their approach to mathematics, which in turn enables them to make progress.

Useful books

Maths for the Dyslexic – A Practical Guide, by A. Henderson. David Fulton.
Basic Topics in Mathematics for Dyslexics, by A. Henderson & E. Miles. Whurr.
Dyslexia and Mathematics, by T.R. Miles & E. Miles. RoutledgeFalmer.
Maths and Dyslexics, by A. Henderson. University College of Wales Bangor.
Working with Dyscalculia, by A. Henderson, F. Came, & M Brough. Learning Works.
Building Learning Power, by G. Claxton. TLO.

Useful web sites

BEAM maths of the month   www.beam.co.uk
The Brain Buster   www.beam.co.uk
Think maths   www.beam.co.uk
Interactive Resources   www.interactive-resources.co.uk/
                                               indexmp1.html

Anne Henderson is an independent consultant in maths and dyslexia, based in North Wales.

Using existing and new technology to support dyslexic children

Victoria Crivelli

Information and Communication Technology (ICT) is widely used by children in school and home environments. As well as games and leisure activities, for many children ICT has become a key tool to access information and communicate, especially when using web-based technology. Children and young people with dyslexia often need no encouragement to use ICT and many acquire considerable skill in using it effectively. However, many additional features of ICT can help dyslexic children to overcome the barriers they face in learning.

The benefits of ICT

A typical example is using a text-to-speech facility to read information more easily and accurately. Another example might be easy editing of written information using common tools such as *copy*, *paste* or *undo* found in most word processing applications. Similarly additional tools such as speech supported word banks or predictive text can be helpful when writing. These advantages are not always obvious, so teachers, parents and supporting adults need to be aware and help find the appropriate tools, programs and options to maximise the full potential that ICT can offer to meet individual needs. These needs will change and develop over time, as children mature, gain confidence in using ICT and as literacy tasks become more demanding. So it is helpful to have regular reviews of what is working well and what is not.

Whilst 'high-tech' solutions may seem attractive, making the best of existing and 'low tech' facilities can be just as effective and supportive. Often simple changes in programs or one or two additional tools can make a huge impact on dyslexic learners. The ICT supplement to the BDA *Dyslexia Friendly Schools* pack contains several examples of such solutions in school [freely downloadable from the BDA website, www.bdadyslexia.org.uk]

Most schools would consider access and use of ICT to support the curriculum as an entitlement. The National Curriculum also ensures that developing key skills in ICT capability is a continuous process throughout all stages of education. Additional advantages ICT can offer in supporting dyslexic users are in providing a 'risk-taking' but nevertheless user-friendly environment that promotes independent learning. Good computer programs are patient, non judgemental and encourage the user to 'have a go'. Consequently, ICT can offer dyslexic users a real sense of independence and achievement, helping to create a level playing field for all.

Personalising the learning environment

A key feature for many users is creating a learning environment with a comfortable appearance that supports their needs and where the required software tools are readily to hand. Adjusting screen displays can be particularly beneficial in relieving visual stress often experienced by dyslexic users. Most computer systems and many individual programs offer choices in background colours, font styles, colours and sizes, including the appearance of toolbars, menus, web pages and folders. Word processors usually offer additional options in line spacing and margins to make reading onscreen text more comfortable. For example:

This text is written in Comic Sans font and has 1.5 line space with black text on a grey background.

There are commercial programs available that can offer such customisation with minimal mouse clicks, all of which can be saved for future use. Many of these programs offer other helpful facilities such as text-to-speech or predictive text tools. Examples include: *Claro Read* [www.clarosoftware.com], *TextHelp* [www.texthelp.com], and *Dolphin Easy Tutor* [www.yourdolphin. com].

Some users may already use a coloured overlay when reading a book or paper based text. There are ICT equivalents available, with a variety of colour choices and user options. They can be selected to appear over any screen display or program open. Some include an onscreen ruler option with the virtual overlay, to help the user follow text above, below or between the lines. Examples include: *Virtual Reading Ruler* [crossboweducation.com], *Claro View* (www. clarosoftware.com), and *Readable* [www.dyslexic.com].

Access to text and information

Text-to-speech programs enable all users to see and hear text simultaneously whenever they need support. Some users require all text to be read, while others may prefer the option to select individual words or phrases to be spoken. The latest programs will now read selected text in a choice of much improved synthesised voices. Some will identify easily confusable words such as homonyms, e.g. *their/they're/there*, offering helpful explanations. Some text to speech programs are freely downloadable from the web but may not work consistently or well in all programs or web pages. Latest versions of common programs, such as *Adobe Reader*, come with inbuilt options for speech, for documents in that format.

For continual and reliable access to text, the best option is to purchase a dedicated program with a text-to-speech facility. When considering any text readers that are on the market, important options to check for are: (a) whether the text is being spoken is simultaneously highlighted, and (b) that there are choices of voices, speed and pitch. Many programs enable these text-to-speech tools to be an integral part of the computer environment and not only facilitate visual formatting but also offer support for reading and writing text (see *Claro Read*, *TextHelp* and *Easy Tutor,* above).

Many younger users at school or home may already be using a dedicated *talking word processor* or have that available as part of another program. Examples include: *Clicker Writer* in Clicker 4/5 [www.cricksoft.com], *Textease* or *Inspiration* (both available from www.r-e-m.co.uk). Any text selected, such as from a web page, can be copied and pasted into such programs and then be read aloud as words, phrases, sentences or whole paragraphs. This facility could also read any instructions and help pages if required. Some programs used for different purposes, such as prediction, also include similar text-to-speech facilities, e.g. *Penfriend* [www.penfriend.biz].

Planning writing and presentation of text or information

The latest versions of common word processors such as *MS Word* have *insert diagram facility* (see Insert Menu) or similar, that can be helpful when either planning or presenting information in different formats. The *Table menu* is another useful option for organising text. There are, however, several dedicated programs that help **visual planning** such as concept or mind-mapping, with the essential integral speech support. Examples include: *Inspiration* [www.dyslexic.com] and *Spark Space* [www.barrybennett.co.uk]. These programs allow users to plan visually using text and graphics, often a preferred learning style of dyslexics. The visual plans can be converted at a single keystroke into linear text to be used for further writing or for importing into a preferred word processing program.

Many dyslexics may prefer onscreen *text predictors* with the essential speech option so they can make informed choices on words they might need to use, speed up the writing process, cut down keystrokes, and access accurate spelling. These programs are far superior to any predictions that people associate with mobile phones. They can be tailored to both individual need and different writing topics if required. Many can be used with standard MS word (e.g. *Penfriend*, *Co-Writer* [www.donjohnston.co.uk], *Claro Read* and *TextHelp*). *Penfriend* can also be embedded in the popular onscreen word banks of *Clicker 5*.

Onscreen *talking* word banks can often be of more use to young children or some older users who need dedicated and personalised lists of vocabulary. Some word banks can include pictures or symbols as well as text to aid recognition and understanding. Examples include: *Clicker 5, Wordbar* [www.cricksoft.com] and *Textease* [www.r-e-m.co.uk].

For those who have tried these tools and still need further support or who need to write at length, voice recognition programs may provide a solution, e.g. *Dragon software* [www.dyslexic.com]. For many users digital images and photos, inserted into writing or planning programs to help prompt, organise and sequence information, can be a simple and effective solution.

Improving specific skills

A wide range of programs is available to improve specific skills in literacy, numeracy or memory. Some tried-and-tested favourites have been upgraded to incorporate many new features. These can include more pupil options, improved content or options to add personal content such as specific spellings and detailed record keeping.

For example, *Wordshark 3S* has new phonics lists and activities, while *Numbershark 4* has additional content and teaching features (both products available from www.wordshark.co.uk).

Those choosing and purchasing software for any young person, where the purpose is to help improve skills need to look carefully at the breadth of content, pupil and teacher options, ease of use, speech support and value for money. A list of key features when choosing such programs is included in the BDA ICT supplement mentioned above.

Many dyslexics enjoy having interactive texts available on their computers. Some of the latest versions of these texts (fiction, non fiction or abridged classics) have wonderful graphics and good digital recordings. Many have additional activities and related games. Good examples can be found in books such as **Trackers** or **Find Out** and **Write About** for Clicker 5 [www.cricksoft.com] and many available titles from **Sherston** [www.sherston.com] and **Learners Library** (Neptune, available from www.r-e-m.co.uk).

Some of the latest programs to support reading skills enable the user to access talking books and choices to personalise the text such as highlighting colour. Recent developments that harness the full power of ICT are talking stories that have options to make a live digital recording of the user reading, so that the recording can be reviewed, progress and or any difficulties noted. This feature can be particularly helpful to the many older users who are often reluctant to read aloud to an adult or who want the opportunity to have a go on their own before doing so, e.g. **Rapid Reading Assistant** [www. harcourt.co.uk/rapid] and **Start to Finish** [www.donjohnson.com].

A useful development in harnessing new technology is the use of MP3 players. More commonly used to listen to music they can also be used to listen to digitally recorded text, key facts and information, or used as an organisational or revision aid, e.g. recording key science facts for revision in between favourite music tracks in a dedicated play list. A range of small memo microphones are now available for all important messages or essential daily information to help support memory and organisational skills [www.inclusivetechnology.com]

Assessment, diagnosis and practise activities

Since the introduction of synthetic phonics to the National Literacy Strategy and a keener focus on the teaching of phonic skills, there have been many programs offering a range of assessments in phonological awareness or activities to improve such skills. Some are separate programs targeted at specific age groups while others offer a combination with a facility to e-mail or transfer highly personalised programs of activities to other home or school computers, e.g. **Lexion** [www.lexion.co.uk]. Many of these skill-based programs keep detailed assessment records and a track of the user's attempts and progress. Such records are not only helpful to adults supporting them but also motivating for the users. Examples include: **Track Programs** [www.inclusive.co.uk], **Lexion** and **Wordshark**.

ICT can come in many formats and sometimes the simplest tools can be the most effective. Hand-held spellcheckers are often far more effective than any computerised spellchecker in suggesting the desired word. A reading pen that will scan text then say it aloud, can be a quick and simple hand-held solution for individual words and phrases, especially in longer demanding texts. A portable writing aid that offers access to word processing in virtually any environment can be a life saver to many young people. Current models include options for predictive text or activities to improve typing skills. Some offer speech support options as well. Any texts and saved files can be transferred easily to desktop computers or printers, via USB cables or infra red technology. All these tools are available from www.dyslexic.com and www.r-e-m.co.uk.

For all young dyslexics using technology on a daily basis, especially for writing activities, knowledge of the keyboard and an efficient typing speed, using two hands, will be essential. There are many programs that offer help and support with these skills depending on age and ability. (see www.dyslexic.com, www.r-e-m.co.uk , and www.2simple.com for examples of good programs). The BBC Schools web pages have a free dance mat touch-typing program available on line [www.bbc.co.uk/schools/typing]. Some are motivating and fun for younger users, others offer a daily program to increase skills as quickly as possible. Acquiring such skills is not dissimilar to learning a musical instrument and requires regular practice to improve accuracy and speed.

ICT will continue to improve, develop and change. It will affect all our lives. With appropriate use, it can make a real difference to enabling dyslexic children overcome barriers to learning, today and in the future.

Victoria Crivelli is an advisory teacher for SEN/ICT in Worcestershire and a member of the BDA New Technologies Committee.

Mobile technology to help the dyslexic learner

Sharron Butteriss and Ian Litterick

Demands on the learner are high. Students are asked to digest, present and recall information in a variety of environments throughout their learning life, usually with time pressure. The typical processing difficulties experienced by dyslexic students make these tasks all the more challenging. It becomes all the more vital to take maximum advantage of tools to simplify and enhance access to the written word and other resources. This article looks at a range of mobile technological aids to accessibility.

Away from base

For most students the home is their place of private study. However, they often need to read the written word or listen to the spoken word in a variety of other places. What are they studying? Where are they studying? For example, most students frequently visit lecture theatres and conference halls. Those with processing difficulties will find it hard to do multiple tasks. In such situations they are being asked to listen to a large volume of information, respond and contribute to the lecture, take legible notes, all without error and without missing salient points.

Travelling to and from destinations could be lost time or it could be valuable time for the dyslexic student who needs to maximise their learning programme. If they can use technology to recall information, to capture text and to support their literacy then they can gain precious study time to match that of their peers.

Navigation, whether of an educational site, a library or road network, can all be challenging to some people with dyslexia. Clear, uncluttered signage is important with pictorial maps or a guide to help find what they are looking for. Satellite navigation (GPS – Global Positioning System) could be a solution for those needing to travel by road as it can be set to give directions for car, bicycle or pedestrian. Within a library, the best resource is the centre staff and an efficient computer system with an advanced, speaking spellchecker.

Many educational courses will require students to go on work placements or to work a year in industry. Nurses, engineers or business students may need portable support. Safety and efficiency is likely be affected if the dyslexic on work placement is unable to understand posters or unable to read and deliver accurate instructions. These could be made easier with the right choice of mobile assistive technology.

All of these environments are implicitly affected by the need to organise and recall tasks, timetables and diary dates; so frequent and mobile reminders are often on the dyslexic student's wish list

Capturing audio

Students with auditory processing and/or multi-tasking difficulties need to re-examine, recall and summarise delivered speech. This may be verbal instruction, such as project tasks, or words delivered continuously throughout a lecture. Many find it difficult to recall people's names, telephone numbers or a short sequence of messages. If students can find a way to process and learn information then their understanding of the subject matter can be equal to that of their peers.

Recording devices have provided support and security to learners listening to speech for several years. Technology has evolved from reels and cassette tapes to digital media, such as mini-disk and, now, solid-state hand-held digital recorders. Digital recorders, like the *Olympus DS range*, have large capacity, in-built (or expandable) memory, replacing the need to label, turn-over or carry additional recording material. Portability is improved as they are small enough to fit in your pocket. Small, stylish devices, such as those currently provided by Olympus, have tens of hours of recording time, are easy to navigate and can upload recordings to a computer for later use. These features supply a mobile solution to recalling, editing and revising recorded speech; your own or another person's.

Digital recorders can record and play back compressed audio files (e.g. MP3) and podcasts but it may be necessary to capture the visual element of a demonstration as well, such as writing a lengthy mathematical equation on the white board or constructing engineering models. In this case even a camcorder with built-in microphone could be the answer.

Some students are willing to carry a notebook computer and, in principle, they can record directly into this device. With **Microsoft OneNote** software you can insert a recording immediately next to text within an on-screen journal. However, to record directly into a portable computer ideally needs a high performance external microphone and additional recording software to enhance poor sound quality. The notebook, therefore, can mean additional steps and distractions if recording on the move. If size counts, the digital recorder is ultimately much more portable.

Reading text on the move

Reading literature and other text when away from the normal study environment has always been problematic for dyslexic students. At home, on a desktop computer, the student is likely to have a text-to-speech program, such as **Read & Write** or **ClaroRead**. These will accurately read documents and web pages, assisting comprehension and proof-reading. Without the same software on a portable, notebook computer the student is disadvantaged when they are away from their desk. Fortunately, manufacturers have responded to the trend towards hot-desking (using whichever computer is available - which students have always done anyway) and now produce their text-to-speech programs on USB memory sticks. Thus your reading aid travels with you. Plug in the memory stick and your software is fully functioning with the ability to read back any electronic text on screen. This is a great solution for those on work placement or in the library and for shared computer users, as long as a USB port is available and enabled.

Hard copy documents, such as books, journals, lecture notes and letters, present another set of difficulties. For best results the institution should supply information in alternative formats or electronically, in advance. Failing that, for instant conversion, a good solution is a portable scanner with a notebook computer and text-to-speech software. Slim-line, flat-bed scanners, powered from the notebook computer, are light enough to carry. Once scanned, the text is stored electronically for immediate playback or editing. For those students without a portable computer, a hand-held scanner, such as the **Docupen**, can store whole pages of A4 text for later transfer to a PC - providing you have a steady hand!

If it is only necessary to decode the occasional word then a scanning pen such as the **Reading Pen** can be the answer. Hold this over-sized pen firmly, roll the end over a word or group of words and hear the sound and, if you wish, the definition. This also needs some dexterity so it is best to try it out first.

CapturaTalk

As James Bond and his gadgets move on so does assistive technology. There are portable tools which have more than one function and these continue to evolve. Mobile telephones are not just for making calls: a new piece of software called **CapturaTalk** has been released on a high specification Windows mobile **Smartphone**. Using the built-in high quality camera, the phone takes a photograph of inaccessible but printed text, e.g. a poster, letter or restaurant menu and instantly reads it back to you. There is no need to upload your photos to a computer, no need for additional text-to-speech software, **CapturaTalk** reads the text immediately and stores it for later use. As the software is built into a mobile telephone it is one useful tool that a student would always have to hand anyway, without adding to clutter.

Franklin

In recent years Franklin have excelled in their production of hand-held spellcheckers and dictionaries. Students facing difficult and new vocabulary could benefit from this discreet, mobile tool by tapping in a word they are failing to understand. Some dictionary models can read the definition back - an additional help for those with reading difficulties.

Capturing text and images away from your desk

Note-taking is the ability to capture text and images and is something a student has to do regularly. Those lucky enough to own a notebook computer have the means to type or dictate (using speech recognition software) almost anywhere. A student with good typing skills and minor auditory processing difficulties could take effective notes in a lecture environment, with a little practice. However, most dyslexic students won't be able to manage the multi-tasking needed. Speech recognition, with *Dragon Naturally Speaking*, for example, is possible on a portable notebook computer but external noise limits its use to quiet or controllable environments. A *Stenomask,* which covers your mouth and contains a microphone, allows you to dictate discreetly and apparently silently in a public lecture or conference. It is unlikely to be the answer for an individual student, but they are used by professional note takers and support workers.

Even with the advances in speech recognition, it is still unlikely that you will be able to get any usable results from recording a lecture and feeding the results into *Dragon Naturally Speaking*. The resulting sound levels are too inconsistent. Better to use a tool like *Audio Notetaker* to make notes from the recording afterwards. *Audio Notetaker* gives a visual representation of an audio file, and provides tools to make it easy to listen, edit, add notes, categorise them and copy them to a work file. If you really must have a verbatim copy of a lecture - which is usually a waste of time – it is usually best to re-dictate it whilst using *Audio Notetaker* or other good audio player to listen to it. It is also worth using a typing tutor program to improve typing skills to eliminate typing errors and speed up written work, because slow, inaccurate typing can cause as much lost time as reading or spelling difficulties.

P.D.A.s

Notebook computers can still be large or heavy and may not be usable in some situations e.g. on a nursing ward. Small-form replacements come under the name of P.D.A. – Personal Digital Assistant. These palm-sized devices provide the user with a screen (approximately 3.7cm corner to corner) and stylus for entering text, numbers and drawings. The art student who constantly has new ideas may sketch on the screen for later reference, or enter quick notes for later expansion or retrieval to relieve their short-term memory. You can load concept mapping software onto these mobile assistants but the screen and text size limit a global view of your ideas.

PDA's can take subject-specific dictionaries of, e.g., medical or legal terms. They can run satellite navigation mapping systems to ensure you get to your next destination without getting lost. Larger memory devices will also play back audio files to support the auditory learner. Synchronise the P.D.A. with your personal computer, via USB cable, to copy your remotely written notes without duplicating them. Share diary reminders with your P.C. to make sure you hand that work in, or get to an appointment on time. So PDA's can provide effective, mobile assistance for organisation, note-taking and as a reminder for the dyslexic learner.

Smartphones

The Smartphone combines the P.D.A. with a mobile phone – including the camera and recorder that most phones now have. So you can write notes, either by using a stylus or slide-out keyboard, take images with its built-in camera, make drawings, listen to audio, view emails or surf the internet, in addition to making telephone calls and texting. The function of a Smartphone is broad but, like the PDA, the small screen, method of text entry, navigation and multi-sensory tools are still limited to the strength of its battery and processing power. Importantly though, a mobile telephone is one piece of technology that a student would be loathe to be without. So it will normally be remembered and used.

Information doesn't always come in written form and image capture may be a requirement in study and work e.g. a picture on a wall or a 3-dimensional model. A learner could capture this image or text on camera. Digital cameras are commonly used due to their editing ability, remembering that a photo of text can usually be turned into electronic text by the use of OCR (optical character recognition) software. With the right quality device, an independent camera or one on a mobile telephone can provide an instant, portable way of capturing an image or text.

Conclusions

Assistive technology can speed up work-load, relieve the effects of literacy difficulties and give a multi-sensory approach to learning. All these features can help the hard-working dyslexic student. But learning is not tied to the desk and mobile aids may be required. As everyday portable technology develops, the choices for assistive technology become wider, more feature-rich and more convenient. Mass-market devices will not necessarily be user-friendly or disability aware. However, there is a welcome trend for designers to cater for the needs of people with disabilities in everyday products. With the *Olympus DS* range of digital recorders, for example, you can listen to the menus and distinguish the buttons by feel, as well as by sight. Good design for disability is often good design for everyone.

Sharron Butteriss is Account Manager for Iansyst Ltd, with a specific responsibility for mobile devices.

Ian Litterick is a volunteer member of the BDA New Technologies Committee and Executive Chairman of Iansyst Ltd.

A version of this article with links and occasional updates will be available on Iansyst's website at www.dyslexic.com/mobile-technology

Encouraging reluctant writers

Cheryl Dobbs

What is a reluctant writer?

Writing is a daily expectation in most students' lives, but what may seem easy to many is made more difficult by:

- planning difficulties
- processing problems
- poor spelling
- handwriting difficulties

Knowing how and where to start a piece of written text may cause immense frustration for some students, whilst others may begin to write or type but may only use simple phrases or sentences. They may avoid their usual spoken vocabulary and structure with the *safe* words that they know how to spell.

Others may be able to express their ideas well enough orally but then have difficulty organising these into a coherent structure. Some students simply forget what they want to say as soon as they try to place the words physically into print. Whatever the reasons behind these difficulties, the writing process becomes a laborious task creating reluctance and frustration for many dyslexic students.

Supportive software

There is no simple 'cure' available which will solve such difficulties, but the use of software that can help and support the individual, if chosen and used *appropriately*, does exist (for further information see www.bdadyslexia.org.uk/supportingwriting.html).

Specific software such as word prediction and planning tools can provide fantastic support, but one of the difficulties I have frequently encountered working with such students is actually *how* to motivate them to write in the first place. Motivation can so easily diminish with continued frustration and poor self-esteem. The student needs to be given the opportunity to try supportive tools, but reluctance or inability to create enough written text to make best use of the supportive software has to be overcome.

Many reluctant writers have found that the use of a talking word processor, or - better still - a talking desktop publisher, has helped to lighten the load but has also encouraged and developed confidence in their own writing ability. The software has to be easy to use, the key elements in its successful use being:

- the opportunity to read text back in a synthesized (robotic) voice with individual words highlighted as it is *read*

- the ability to record voices directly on to the page within the program

- the ability to allow text and objects (such as photos and other images) to be moved and resized around the page.

These elements have provided the opportunity to combine sound and visual imagery with photographs, video and art, which have created a motivation for the publishing process. It is important to introduce components of the software in successive stages. The development of the student's written skills can be facilitated by adding other supportive software (such as word prediction), gradually as the student's interest and confidence grows.

Getting started

The use of a digital camera with the software encourages even the most reluctant of students to create their own *talking* photograph album. These first attempts require little more knowledge than the ability to place a digital photograph onto a page, record a voice and then link one page to another. At this stage there is no requirement to add any written text. The student simply collects photos that are of personal interest. The more meaningful the photos are to the student's life, the greater their interest and motivation.

Adding words

The choice of software should allow text to be highlighted word-by-word and read back, either as it is typed, or at the end of the sentence by inserting a full stop. Showing most students this aspect has often led to a tentative desire to add some written text to produce a page which may look similar to a commercial talking book they may have seen and used. Initially, words are dictated by the student, and typed directly on to the page to illustrate the digital photo. Often these texts can display a use of vocabulary and language that is not usually apparent in their everyday writing.

As interest increases, students can quite frequently be encouraged to type in a few words of their own. This may only be the odd word in the middle of a phrase in the early stages but, over time, and with developing confidence, this can be increased. However, experience has shown that it is well worth taking time not to rush this stage but to allow interest and confidence to develop at the student's own rate.

This *softly, softly* approach has quite often led to an easy introduction to other useful software such as grids from **Clicker 5** (or **Wordbar** for older students) or a predictive typing package such as **Penfriend**. Many students may still need the opportunity to dictate some ideas as they often have insufficient stamina for a sustained piece of writing. To rely merely upon their own typed efforts without support at this stage, often does not reflect the quality of the language that they can actually produce.

Being creative

Each time the student uses the program a new aspect can be introduced which allows and extends a little creativity. Some students like to add scanned hand-drawn or painted images or use an on-screen painting program. Others like to arrange clipart to create a scene on the page and, if the program has the capability, to use animation as well. Others like to experiment with adding recorded music and speech. Over time, as more and more of these 'books' are created by different students, it becomes apparent that many of them are motivated, first, by seeing images on the screen, and then their spoken or written text grows from this creation.

Younger children are often encouraged to illustrate work after the completion of written text but as the child progresses through the school, greater value seems to be given to (and assessed on) the printed word. However, for these students, the opportunity to *think* in images sometimes helps them to use language in a printed format. Sometimes this appears in a very stilted style initially, perhaps only a word or phrase or two in the early stages – but certainly a start towards the writing process.

Using talking writing frames and prompts

This type of writing led to trying to find new and different ways for individual students to use their recorded speech to develop and encourage their writing. These included using the ability to record onto the page as a memory aid or prompt that could appear in the software as a small icon. The following three examples briefly illustrate the way that individual students were introduced to strategies but also began to adapt these to suit their own purposes.

Ben

Ben often had some great ideas but as soon as he began to commit these thoughts to the page they disappeared. Sometimes he knew and could initially write what he wanted to say but halfway through a phrase, the words would be lost. He was encouraged to record his thoughts into short individual segments. These were then moved around the page and ordered. He would listen to each segment and type what had been recorded. He sometimes used a word prediction package or a **Clicker** grid to do this. Not only did this prove to be an effective strategy for producing a coherent text but, as his confidence developed, he was observed devising his own strategies. Using his original recordings as a voice prompt, he would edit the spoken sentence and add or improve the initial vocabulary he had recorded. This ultimately developed and improved the structure of his sentences and overall content of his writing.

Beth

Beth responded to a verbal writing frame. Questions were recorded by an adult on to the page. She would listen to these and record her own response. Initially, these responses took the form of a single word or phrase and developed into a simple sentence. Over time, as she became accustomed to this method, the content of these questions altered until a prompt such as "can you think of a really good opening sentence" encouraged her to take on greater responsibility for the task.

Tom

Tom enjoyed making his own talking books and quickly became adept at using the software with many of its creative facilities with drawing, linking and animating tools. As he became more confident with writing and expressing his ideas orally, voice recordings could also be used to provide new and extended vocabulary. Occasionally he was also observed recording words that eluded his limited spelling ability. Rather than struggling and losing the flow of his ideas, would just verbally record the word that he needed. This certainly began to improve the quality of his writing and enabled him to escape the safe spelling and simplistic sentence structure seen in his earlier pieces.

Conclusions

The use of a talking desktop publisher was not something that achieved dramatic improved writing overnight with these students. It was part of an ongoing process that provided meaningful and enjoyable writing activities. As the students were able to increase the range of their writing, it also provided a reason to try new supportive software and compare them to discover the tools that were most appropriate for the needs of each individual student. Most importantly, it created enjoyable activities for developing confidence and creating opportunities for success, which they were keen to share with others. This should be at the heart of all education - to make learning fun!

Resources

TextEase CT [www.softease.com]
Clicker 5 and *Wordbar* [www.cricksoft.com/uk]
Penfriend XP [www.penfriend.biz]

For further information about supportive software visit
www.bdadyslexia.org.uk/aboutdyslexia.html

Cheryl Dobbs is an Independent ICT/SEN Consultant and member of the British Dyslexia Association's New Technologies Committee.

The role of recording and radio in language development for dyslexic learners and children experiencing language delay

Mark Sherin

The spoken word has a power all of its own

The role that speaking and listening plays in literacy development has been marginalised in the last decade or more. This situation is beginning to be rectified and the use of radio and recording materials to enhance the learning experiences of children is becoming increasingly recognised and accepted. The time is right for practitioners to take advantage of these changes and to look again at the opportunities available to support dyslexic learners and students with language delay.

At the Lyndhurst Dyslexia Centre in Southwark we are developing a program of study that improves our learners' language skills without the barriers that written convention imposes. Our aim is to allow them the opportunity to freely express themselves and show what they can achieve with an alternative way of responding and recording. Recording and using radio as a medium to record learners' successes and promote their achievements is, I believe, helping our dyslexic learners to find and own their voices and language. It provides alternative ways of recording what a child knows and can achieve, overcoming the barriers to learning presented by the conventions of handwriting, spelling and the written word.

There is a great freedom in recording ideas as opposed to writing them down. Many dyslexic learners respond better in a person-to-person situation rather than on their own with a piece of paper. Working with a person alongside allows them to be more expressive and whole-person communication encourages the learner to communicate more freely and individually. With support and encouragement, the teacher can help draw out language and vocabulary. The learner can feed off the nuances of body language, voice tone and rhythm, and feel the freedom in their own thoughts and expressions.

In this work we want to remove the fear of using words (incorrectly), so they can use their own words and language, and use them in a way they want. They are encouraged to be the craftsperson of their own imagination and voice. (Do you remember when you first heard 'bad' used to describe something 'good'?). We are fostering the idea that the learner owns their own language, particularly when spoken, but also when written down and that the learner is unique and expressive, their thoughts and language are valid and valued. We are using recording and radio to motivate and foster a liking (and ultimately, a love) of language and words.

Transcribing to written text

Usually the recorded work is an end in itself, and provides evidence of achievement for our students. Sometimes, however, with our recorded work, there is a need to move from the recording to the written word. This is usually achieved by transcription, which can be a daunting prospect and a time consuming one to less fluent typists. Possible solutions could include making links with the local business community or parent volunteers who could help with transcribing. E-mail them a sound file (with a thank-you from the child at the beginning!) and they can return a Word file to you. This enables the business community to help a local school/ child without leaving the office or home. Another possibility is to ask the child to write a sentence or two as a motivation for handwriting practice or leave gaps in the text for certain words targeted for spelling. As the child's touch-typing improves, a small amount of transcription may make suitable and meaningful typing practice.

When some of our dyslexic writers first saw a transcribed passage of their recordings, it was less a case of ownership, more one of rejection *"…oh no, look at all these words"*. To help them access their work we explained that this was already their language, owned by them and they were already capable of this (amount of) language and that they had already said it. It was about their thoughts and experiences and therefore valuable. We explained that there were treasures to discover in their own words, words to recognise and decode and patterns for them to spot and wouldn't it be great for them if they could read (and spell) their own words.

So we presented the transcripts in manageable amounts and played their recordings to them as they began to read the transcripts, stopping when necessary and highlighting difficult words and words they wanted to learn to read or spell. Using a combination of flashcards, precision teaching and phonic strategies, over time the students learnt to read (and spell) their own words. This process was a moving experience and powerful for our dyslexic learners. There is, I think, something magical for a child to see what they are thinking written down: *"I did that* (even at a stage when they can't read it all); *look at all these words!"*

Using personal experience

In similar ways we are able to scaffold literacy development at word and sentence levels. We always start from where the children are, and use their experiences (such as visits to art galleries, their journeys to school, their families, the built and natural environment, their responses to photographs, books and stories and to nature). Using these experiences, we model language, providing them with additional options and encouraging them to experiment and choose. We play their ideas back to them, discussing and editing along the way. We make collections of powerful words, adjectives, connectives, comparatives and sentence starters. The use of voice and expression here can really add meaning to the words and understanding for the learner.

There appears to be a lasting impact of dyslexic learners listening to themselves and working from their own experiences seems to aid memory. The successes of recorded work, the associated development of self-esteem and self-confidence will be taken forward to the next conversation or piece of work. Gradually, this leads to the dyslexic learner feeling less pressurised and fearful of language and writing, and, in time, developing an increased liking for words and language.

One thing we believe strongly in at the Lyndhurst Dyslexia Centre is the role that metacognition plays in supporting a student's learning. Recording our dyslexic learners, explaining how they get things right, saying which strategies they like to use to be successful in reading, spelling, writing or organising is very powerful. Playing these before starting a session is a way of priming them for success and reminding them of what will be needed. Sharing and listening to the other students' strategies is useful too.

Interviewing

Interview skills for our learners are broken into several elements. The first is the formulation of questions that will elicit interesting and informative answers. Looking at, and understanding, open and closed questions is important, as well as predicting and having to hand supplementary questions that allow the interview to flow and keeping it going. Our students soon discovered the benefits of pre-planning initial sentences, even when just to use as guidance.

Another skill is choosing suitable approaches and introductions to busy people. (Mentioning it's for a school project can be a great lever in this situation, though not always.) Supervised interviewing can be a thrilling and scary process. A small group of students sharing and rotating the roles of approaching, questioning and recording can be a powerful learning experience. It allows students to show their strengths and be supported when challenging themselves in less secure roles.

Interviewing allows experiential learning in a live setting, which students find meaningful, exciting and memorable. For dyslexic learners, this communication experience, complete with nuances of gesture, body language, facial expression and tonality, imparts understanding in a way that reading rarely can. The experience of getting live information – of living histories and story telling – shows dyslexic learners the variety of ways that people interpret and recall their experiences.

The differences and fluidity encountered in responses of voices to the same question, I believe, helps our students to validate their own experiences and the language they use to describe them. People answer the same or similar question in many different ways; the students learn that there is more than one way to answer a question while still remaining honest to yourself and about your experiences. In turn, this leads to thinking about the audience and informs the selection process when the students start editing.

Editing

Editing can be extremely liberating for our learners. It allows them to be brave with their choice of language and words. The ephemeral nature of the spoken word means that mistakes seem less important than if they were written down. Mistakes don't matter in the same way; they don't spoil the look or sound of their work. They are simply cut out or removed. Embedded in language acquisition is mistake making. The editing process simply and seamlessly removes the rejected attempts. Although the physical act of editing can be precise and time-consuming and learners may need a lot of support initially, with practice they can become proficient. For some of our learners it is a favourite part of the recording process and has given them a new skill, status and new teamwork opportunities.

There are additional finishing touches in editing that help make their work outstanding. Music and sound effects greatly enhance the finished work; whether used to illustrate comments, stories, poetry, interviews, jokes, magazine and news slots, sports reports or radio drama, the impact on atmosphere, meaning and mood is immense. It is also great fun and allows creativity that heightens the emotional involvement and enjoyment of the listeners.

SALT (speech and language therapists) and their programmes

Recording can play an important role in supporting dyslexic learners who present with an additional range of speech and language difficulties. There are several ways to use recording to support learning and to record achievements. For receptive and expressive language sounds, for social communication, matching intonation to sentence meaning, for personal narrative and the 'W' questions. Using the child's own voice is powerful, as is recording other voices (including the practitioner's), and modelling prepared sentences.

Asking a child to record their attempts of expressive language affords the practitioner the opportunity for the child to hear her/himself and make choices about their efforts. Recognising and selecting their best most accurate attempts highlights not only where errors are occurring, but also importantly where progress is being made. Sensitive record-keeping of sound production can provide tangible evidence to the student of their progress over time. This is a powerful and irrefutable sign of their success and a strong motivation to keep trying their best. What could be better for a child with speech and language difficulties than to hear himself getting it right? We are still learning about the range of possibilities that recording can provide to support speech and language therapists and our students.

Radio drama

There is a whole world of radio drama to develop and there is space for only a couple of ideas to be mentioned here. One is the use of actions to emphasise punctuation. As a text is read, a full stop is greeted with a jump, a comma with the right hand in the air, a question mark by standing on the left leg and so on You may need a bit of space, but it is fun. It also has an impact on children whose reading aloud has not yet reached the stage of taking account of punctuation. Another idea is changing a photo or story into a script, to help deepen empathy and understanding. Not all these methods may suit either you or your learners but I hope they provide some ideas and starting points.

Technical stuff: how much will it cost?

It's easier and cheaper than you think! As always there is a complete range of equipment from which to choose depending on your budget, requirements, aspirations and expertise. The following are suggestions to get you started:

- desktop or laptop computer
- internet connection
- external microphone
- free downloadable editing software (e.g. **Audacity** for PC; **GarageBand** for Mac)
- free podcast host (e.g. **iTunes** or **Gcast**)
- CDs to burn

There are free downloads for sound effects as well (e.g. www.a1**free**soundeffects.com; www.stonewashed.net/sfx.html; www.partnersinrhyme.com/pir/PIRsfx.shtml; www.grsites.com/sounds)

This set-up will allow you to record at the PC or where you position the laptop and edit the children's work. Other children, classes or interested parties will be able to listen to the recording if they have your address on the podcast host and an internet connection or if you burn them a CD.

If you have a little more money to spend, the addition of an MP3 player (£200-£250), headphones and a better-quality external microphone (£30 upwards) will allow great flexibility to record in any situation and to transfer recorded files computer. Spending more money will get equipment with better specifications, giving better quality recordings, more capacity and flexibility.

Sharing recordings with others

The whole purpose of recording children's work is, of course, to share it with others. Here are some possibilities for consideration. The internet; it is possible to upload your work to a podcasting host site which are free to access for your pupils and their parents/carers, friends and your national and international link schools. The following website describes how to create your own podcast: http://radio.about.com/od/podcastin1/a/aa030805a.htm

Another method of sharing would be to burn a CD. This can then be played in assembly, in other classes and sent home. Our leavers in Year 6 have recorded highlights of their time at Lyndhurst Primary School on CD as part of their Records of Achievement.
When written work is displayed on classroom walls you can set up a listening post (MP3 player or a CD player and headphones) underneath or nearby so that any curriculum work can be shared alongside the work of the rest of the class. A transcript also works well.

There has been considerable kudos for our dyslexic learners in leading the way in the use of technical equipment. They have become acknowledged experts amongst their peers and this is tremendous for their self-esteem and standing amongst their peer group (not to mention the staff and their parent/carers).

Conclusions

Clearly, much of our dyslexic students' work is concerned with the process of learning, language acquisition and development of skills and is not intended for broadcasting. This is stored on file and can be presented to the child as a CD of their work at the end of the academic year, along with the written report to parents/carers. Alternatively, it can be shared with parents/carers on open evenings. Although the finished recordings or broadcast are important for motivation and for the completion of work, the real benefits to our dyslexic learners are in the experience of the learning process and what they take from it to support their future learning.

GroveFM is the Radio Station of the Lyndhurst Dyslexia Centre and Lyndhurst Primary School. We have been broadcasting for one year. You can listen to our programmes on www.gcast.com/u/grovefm/main

Mark Sherin is manager of the Lyndhurst Dyslexia Centre and Grove FM. He is a specialist teacher in SpLD (Dyslexia) and a teacher trainer. He was awarded a distinction in the Regional Final (London) of Teaching Awards 2007 in the category of Special Needs Teacher.

Movement difficulties in the early years: a planned programme of support

Madeleine Portwood

Impairment of movement skills is a common theme running across the whole range of neurodevelopmental disorders. The co-occurrence of motor difficulties with other learning disorders appears to be the rule rather than the exception (Dewey et al, 2000; Kaplan et al, 2000). This research was carried out at the University of Calgary and the Alberta Children's Hospital, where 58% of children with ADHD displayed reading difficulties and, in addition, 27% of the children with ADHD also had problems with coordination. Of the children identified with developmental coordination disorder (DCD; sometimes known as dyspraxia) 82% displayed some other co-morbid disorder. Gilberg (1998) and Rasmussen et al (2000) have also identified autistic features, behavioural problems and depression as co-occurring with developmental coordination disorder.

Childhood developmental disorders are classified into discrete categories and in the majority of cases, children display the characteristics of several: co-morbidity is widespread (Dewey et al 2000). Research evidence suggests that between 50% and 80% of children with a diagnosis of DCD meet the criteria for at least 2 disorders (Biederman et al 1990). Children with coordination difficulties commonly have other conditions such as attention deficit/ hyperactivity disorder (ADHD), dyslexia and speech and language impairments (COT/NAPOT 2003). Substantive research connecting dyslexia with deficits in motor skills was published by Duffy and Geschwind (1985).

Dyslexia and motor skills deficits

The development of 'new' skills was the focus of much research undertaken by Fawcett and Nicolson in the early 1990's, particularly the automaticity of motor development, the point at which a skill is learned and can be completed virtually without thought. They discovered that children with dyslexia put more effort into 'planning' sequential movements when compared with 'controls' matched for age and ability. Nicolson & Fawcett (1990) assessed the performance of 23 thirteen-year-old dyslexic children using a series of motor tasks. A beam was constructed, using large building blocks, 6 inches high, 5 inches wide and a length of 8 feet.

Initially the tasks set were: -

- balancing, one foot on the floor, arms outstretched, for one minute
- balancing on one foot on the beam, leg straight, arms outstretched, for one minute
- balancing on the beam on one leg with bent knee for 30 seconds
- balancing on the beam on one leg with bent knee for one minute
- walking along the beam, with arms held out.

Error points for incorrect foot position, wobble, overbalancing and stepping off the beam were recorded. A secondary task was then introduced and the children were asked to count or press a button. The results for the dyslexic children were compared with a group of matched controls. Under the first conditions - 'just balancing' - the dyslexic children achieved as well as the controls. However, when 'dual' tasks were undertaken, the dyslexic children's performance deteriorated significantly, unlike that of the controls.

Later studies indicating that children with dyslexia have 'persistent and unexpectedly severe problems in skill' were presented in further research by Fawcett and Nicolson (1995). The study comprised groups of children with dyslexia and matched controls using two tests of motor skill (bead threading and peg moving) and one test of articulatory skill (speed of articulating well known words). The effect of maturation was monitored by using three age groups: 8, 13 and 17 years. The performance of children with dyslexia was consistently below that of their matched controls in every outcome measure. Depending on the task, between 40% and 100% of the dyslexic children in the study had a performance more than one standard deviation below that of the same-age control group.

To provide further evidence to support the idea that children and adults with dyslexia show signs of delayed automaticity of motor development and have difficulty processing sound sequences, Fawcett and Nicolson (1999) completed an additional series of experimental tasks involving 126 dyslexic and control children. The results indicated that more than 95% of dyslexic children showed evidence of deficits in postural stability and muscle tone. It was also noted that the degree of deficit was comparable in magnitude to the children's reading and spelling deficits.

There is other supportive evidence to link motor deficits and dyslexia. Ramus et al (2003) reporting on a study into motor control and phonology in dyslexic children, suggest that part of the discrepancy in motor skills is due to dyslexic individuals who had additional disorders ADHD and DCD (Dyspraxia). My own research (Portwood, 2000), involving more than 600 school-aged children with dyspraxia indicated that there was a co-occurrence with dyslexia in more than 50% of those studied

Moving forward

The evidence appears overwhelming that deficits in movement skills are common across the whole range of neurodevelopmental disorders. However, when I screened 400 3-year-olds in County Durham in 2005, it was extremely concerning to discover that 57% did not achieve the expected developmental levels for their age. Whilst it might be assumed that some of the children would 'grow out of it', many would not. With a colleague, Andrea Emerson, who had been appointed to work with me specifically targeting children in the Early Years (aged 3 – 5), a programme of 20 units of structured movement activities was developed to determine whether many of the youngsters were underachieving, simply due to a lack of opportunity to develop particular skills.

Pilot study

100 children in five nurseries in County Durham were assessed prior to the start of the programme and again after 12 weeks of intervention, using the schedule shown in Figure 1. Over half the children presented with difficulties planning and executing movements. For example, more than 20% of the group were unable to walk sideways without tripping over.

Then the nursery staff was provided with a structured programme of activities, which concentrated on the development of balance, movement and coordination skills. The children accessed the programme for 15 minutes a day on weekdays for 12 weeks. An example of the activities is as follows:

Unit 1.

Equipment needed – P.E. mats, beanbags and coloured spots for hands where necessary.

Skills – Crawling, balance and jumping.

1. Stand tall and stretch fingers towards ceiling – feet flat on the floor
and mouth closed.
Corrections; feet together facing forwards.

2. Kneel tall and stretch fingers towards ceiling – toes on the floor and
mouth closed. Count of 5. X5.
Corrections; toes of feet touching floor.

Name		Age	Date	
Gross Motor Skills		Comments	Yes	No
1	Crawl			
2	Walk Forwards			
	Backwards			
	Sideways			
3	Run			
4	Tiptoes			
5	Jump			
6	Climb			
7	Heel / toe			
8	Beam Balance			
9	Balance: Right Foot			
	Left Foot			
Fine Motor Skills				
10	Handedness			
11	Tower of Bricks			
12	Screw Toy			
13	Bead Threading			
14	Inset Puzzle			
Coordination				
15	Kick: Right foot			
	: Left Foot			
16	Throw: Right Hand			
	: Left Hand			
17	Catch (2 Hands)			

Figure 1. Record sheet for motor coordination in young children (Portwood, 2003)

3. On all fours, hands flat on the floor. Balance for the count of 5. (X5.)
   - Lift right hand off the floor and balance.
   - Lift left hand off the floor and balance.
   - Lift right knee off the floor and balance.
   - Lift left knee off the floor and balance.
   - Lift left hand and right knee off the floor – balance.
   - Lift right hand and left knee off the floor – balance.

   Corrections; hands facing forwards, toes of feet touching floor.

4. Face and hold hands with a partner, taking turns practise balancing
   on one leg. Count of 3.
   Corrections; feet together, toes facing forwards.

5. In pairs, face and hold hands with a partner, bounce from the knees,
   keeping feet flat on the floor, hold head high and keep mouth closed.
   Corrections; feet facing forwards.

6. In pairs, face and hold hands with a partner, hold hands and rock from
   heel to toe on the spot, hold head high and keep mouth closed.
   Corrections; feet facing forwards and together.

At the end of the term the children were re-assessed and 93% had developed their motor skills to the expected level of competence. The remaining 7% continued to exhibit movement difficulties – a percentage much closer to the acknowledged figure of 3 -6% used to describe the prevalence of developmental coordination disorder in the UK population.

Currently there are 83 Early Years settings (private, voluntary and maintained) in County Durham using the programme and, most importantly, it is completely inclusive and helps to develop the skills of all children – even the most able. It is proving particularly popular in the children's centres. The county has funded the purchase of core equipment and this is on loan to any setting that does not have its own resources.

The programme of 20 units is shortly due for publication by Durham County Council, entitled *Movement Skills in the Early Years – a Manual for Practitioners* by Andrea Emerson and Madeleine Portwood.

References

Biederman, J., Faragone, S., Kenman, K., Knee, D. & Tsuan, M.T. (1990) Family-genetic and psycho-social risk factors in DSM-III attention deficit disorder. *Journal of the American Academy of Child and Adolescent Psychiatry, 29*, 526-533.

College of Occupational Therapists, National Association of Paediatric Occupational Therapists (2003) *Children with Developmental Coordination Disorder: report on a survey of waiting lists and waiting times for occupational therapy services for children with developmental coordination disorder* London: COT.

Dewey, D., Wilson, B., Crawford S.G., & Kaplan, B.J. (2000) Comorbidity of developmental disorder with ADHD and reading disability. *Journal of International Neuropsychological Society, 6,* 152.

Duffy, F.H. & Geschwind, N. (Eds). (1985) *Dyslexia: a neuroscientific approach to clinical evaluation.* Boston: Little Brown.

Fawcett, A. J. (2001) Dyslexia and the cerebellum. *Patoss Bulletin,* November 2001, 2-5.

Fawcett, A. J., and Nicolson, R.I. (1992). Automatisation deficits in balance or dyslexic children. *Perceptual and Motor Skills, 75,* 507-529.

Fawcett, A. J., and Nicolson, R. I., (1995). Persistent deficits in motor skill of children with dyslexia. *Journal of Motor Behaviour* 27(3). 235-240.

Fawcett, A. J., and Nicolson, R. I., (1996). *The Dyslexia Screening Test.* London: The Psychological Corporation.

Fawcett, A. J., and Nicolson, R. I., & Dean, P. (1996). Impaired performance of children with dyslexia on a range of cerebellar tasks. *Annals of Dyslexia, 46, 259-283.*

Fawcett, A. J., and Nicolson, R. I., (1999). Performance of dyslexic children on cerebellar and cognitive tests. *Journal of Motor Behaviour, 31, 68-78.*

Gilberg, I.C. (1998) Neuropsychiatric disorders. *Current Opinion in Neurology, 11(2), 109-114.*

Kaplan, B.J., Crawford, S., Wilson B., & Dewey, D. (2000). Does pure ADHD exist? *Journal of International Neuropsychological Society, 6, 153.*

Nicolson, R. I. & Fawcett, A. J. (1990). Automaticity: a new framework for dyslexic research? *Cognition, 35(2). 159-182.*

Nicolson, R. I. & Fawcett, A. J. (1994). Reaction times and dyslexia. *Quarterly Journal Experimental Psychology* [A], 47(1), 29-48.

Nicolson, R. I., Fawcett, A. J., Berry, E. L. Jenkins, I. H., Dean, P. & Brooks, D. J. (1999). Association of abnormal cerebellar activation with motor learning difficulties in dyslexic adults. *Lancet,* 353(9165). 1662-1667.

Nicolson, R. I., Fawcett, A. J., & Dean, P. (2001). Dyslexia, development and the cerebellum. *Trends in Neuroscience, 24(9).* 515-516.

Portwood, M. M. (2000). *Developmental Dyspraxia: Identification and Intervention. A Manual for Parents and professionals 2nd Ed.* London: David Fulton.

Portwood, M. M. (2003). *Dyslexia and Physical Education* London: David Fulton.

Dr Madeleine Portwood is Specialist Senior Educational Psychologist with Durham County Council and Education Advisor to the Dyspraxia Foundation.

EDUCATION SERVICES

Mark College

A specialist school for students aged 10 - 18 with Dyslexia

Mark College has an international reputation for its educational work with dyslexics. Its goal is straightforward, to provide a top class education for pupils.

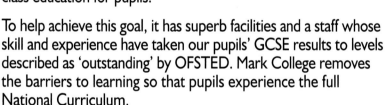

To help achieve this goal, it has superb facilities and a staff whose skill and experience have taken our pupils' GCSE results to levels described as 'outstanding' by OFSTED. Mark College removes the barriers to learning so that pupils experience the full National Curriculum.

The college is also recognised for its care. Work with pupils' self-esteem and self-confidence was the subject of a University study. Conclusions from this independent study have been presented at three international conferences. We are very proud of the findings from this research.

Mark College, Mark, Highbridge,
Somerset TA9 4NP

Telephone: 01278 641632
Fax: 01278 641426
markcollege@priorygroup.com
www.prioryeducation.com

A member of the PRIORY Group

DfES Approved.   CReSTeD 'SP'
DfES Beacon School
DfES 'Highly Effective School'
ISA 'Award for Excellence'
National Training Award
Sportsmark Award
'with distinction'

Lexion

Professional users:
SEN teachers, SENCOs, SLTs, Teaching Assistants, EPs and Teachers.

For students and patients with: Dyslexia, Reading and writing difficulties, Auditory processing problems, ADHD, ADD, Glue ear, Short term memory problems, Selective mutism, Delayed speech, ESL and Aphasia.

ASSESSMENT
Tests for ages 6-16 covering essential cognitive areas. Up to 10 tests per age group. All tests are standardised.

TRAINING
Consists of 94 different training modules and 1300 word lists with digital sound.

AFTER TESTING
If results are below average, the assessment part automatically generates appropriate exercises in the training part.

LEXION'S MAIN FEATURES
Cost effective and user friendly assessment, instant report on problem areas, instant entry to tailor-made remedial program, highly motivating for pupils with a wide range of difficulties, instant feedback on progress, linked to English Primary Literacy Strategy.

LEXION'S UNIQUE FEATURE
Exercises can be sent to pupils by email, USB or disk, enabling practice at home.

TESTIMONIALS

"Lexion is one of the most comprehensive and innovative pieces of software I have seen for many years. Lexion is being developed by a design team listening to pupils' and teachers' needs, based on sound practice and designed with attention to details."
Victoria Crivelli
SEN teacher and member of BDA new technologies committee

"Thank you for giving me the Lexion progam. I did it most days and everyone tells me how much I have improved. I wrote a story at school yesterday and it only had three spelling mistakes. I used to have lots and lots of spelling mistakes. I am much better with my English work now."
Sarah, a pupil of **Michael Jones** M.Sc, MRCSLT, PGCE, ADES

CONTACT
Annika Hallsvik
Phone: +447836504170, +46708342477
+4642124366
Email: lexion@euroguide.se

Lexion Ltd.
www.lexion.co.uk

Visual stress and dyslexia

Chris Singleton

What is visual stress?

Visual stress is the experience of unpleasant visual symptoms when reading and in some other visual tasks. The main symptoms include visual perceptual distortions (such as illusions of shape, motion or colour in the text); double vision; difficulty in focusing on the page; sore, tired eyes; and headaches. The condition was first identified over 25 years ago, when Olive Meares, a teacher in New Zealand, and Helen Irlen, an American psychologist, independently observed that some poor readers experience visual distortions when reading.

Visual stress is sometimes called 'Meares-Irlen syndrome' after its original discoverers but in the past it has also been known by other labels, including 'visual discomfort' and 'scotopic sensitivity syndrome'. Visual stress affects around 20% of adults and children, and is particularly common in dyslexics. However, the condition varies in severity so not all sufferers experience the same symptoms to the same degree.

Visual stress makes reading uncomfortable so it invariably hinders children's reading development. Once children have learned to decode words they need lots of experience of reading text in order to become fluent, proficient readers. Practice enables decoding to become automatic, reading eye movements to become smooth and disciplined, and the brain to cope with processing and understanding large amounts of text. If visual stress is not identified and dealt with early on, children are at risk of remaining weak readers. In particular, reading comprehension skills do not develop as well as they should, which can lead to lifelong problems. Many adults who suffer from visual stress tend to avoid reading as much as possible and they struggle to cope with any extended reading they have to do for their education or employment. At university, for example, visual stress is an increasingly common problem that interferes with students' studies.

Relationship between dyslexia and visual stress

Visual stress can occur in good readers but is more often observed in poor readers. Recent research has found that visual stress can be up to twice as common in dyslexics compared with the rest of the population. The term 'visual dyslexia' was sometimes used in the past (and may still occasionally be encountered today), but this term is misleading. Although visual stress is often associated with dyslexia it is <u>not</u> the same as dyslexia and the two conditions should not be confused. Most people who suffer from visual stress do not have dyslexia, and coloured overlays or tinted lenses (often used to treat visual stress) are <u>not</u> effective treatments for dyslexia (see Evans, 2001).

If dyslexia and visual stress are different conditions, why is visual stress much more common in dyslexics compared with non-dyslexics? One theory, suggested by Professor John Stein, is that both dyslexia and visual stress are conditions in which the magnocellular visual system is impaired, and that is why they are often seen together. However, there is not a great deal of scientific evidence to support this view at the present time.

The alternative view, put forward by Professor Arnold Wilkins (2003), is that the symptoms of visual stress are attributable to hyperexcitability of the visual centres in the brain, caused by pattern glare. It is known that striped patterns and flashing lights can evoke seizures in people with photosensitive epilepsy and can trigger migraine headaches. In normal people these stimuli can also produce perceptual distortions. The striped patterns created by moving the eyes across lines of print, especially where there is glare or strong contrast, generates similar physiological effects. Wilkins' theory is supported by the fact that children who benefit from coloured filters are twice as likely to have migraine in the family, and it is likely that the headaches often caused by visual stress are related to migraine. Like those who suffer from photosensitive epilepsy or migraine, people who suffer from visual stress also tend to be hypersensitive to fluorescent lighting, flicker on CRT computer monitors, and strobe lighting.

'Shifting the threshold'

On the other hand, as I have suggested elsewhere (Singleton, 2008), the link between dyslexia and visual stress may not necessarily be causal. Visual stress discourages motivation to practise reading, so this will progressively widen the gap between good and poor readers as a function of differences in reading experience (this is often called a 'Matthew effect'). It is likely that the dyslexic person's lack of automaticity in word recognition (e.g. due to underlying deficits in phonology or memory) necessitates them adopting a technique for processing text (e.g. detailed scrutiny of individual 'problem' words) that increases their sensitivity to the physical characteristics of the print. In turn, this will naturally tend to make symptoms or effects of visual stress worse.

Susceptibility to visual stress varies from person-to-person. The majority of the population is only mildly susceptible (i.e. they have a *high threshold*), but nevertheless most of us experience visual stress under certain conditions, e.g. when viewing a particular visual pattern or seeing flashing lights. At the extreme end of the spectrum, people who suffer from photosensitive epilepsy or from migraine tend to be highly susceptible to visual stress (i.e. they have a *low threshold*). This theory of the relationship between dyslexia and visual stress can be called *'threshold shift'*. The hypothesised impact of dyslexia is to shift the threshold for visual stress from higher to lower, increasing the person's susceptibility, in much the same way that people who suffer from migraine, for example, tend to be more sensitive to adverse visual factors and are more likely to have high susceptibility to visual stress. In a nutshell, this view is that dyslexia tends to increase a person's susceptibility to visual stress.

Treating visual stress

The unpleasant effects of visual stress can be eliminated or reduced in several ways. Meares and Irlen both discovered that symptoms were often reduced by using sheets of transparent coloured plastic (coloured overlays) placed on the page. Today, this is still the most widely used treatment for visual stress, although tinted lenses are also increasingly used.

Other solutions include enlarging print or using a reading mask that covers the lines of text above and below the lines being read. Anything that reduces the glare and high contrast that tends to arise when reading dark, black text on bright, white paper is usefully helpful. For this reason, it is generally better to use coloured paper rather than white paper. Background colours on a computer screen can be changed to reduce glare and make reading more comfortable. Lighting conditions – avoiding fluorescent or over-bright lights – make a big difference. Avoiding print that is a strain to read – e.g. because it is very small or not printed clearly (as with some cheaper or reprinted paperback books) – is also a good idea.

Coloured overlays

During the 1980s, Irlen and her associates regularly prescribed coloured overlays for people suffering from visual stress. At that time, however, members of the medical, psychological and educational professions were highly sceptical about the effectiveness of this method of treatment because it had never been scientifically evaluated. During the 1990s, however, Wilkins and colleagues carried out a series of rigorous double-masked randomised placebo-controlled trials. They found that coloured tints reduce symptoms of visual stress in most sufferers and improve reading speed, fluency, accuracy and comprehension. There was no direct impact of colour on reading ability; rather, the effect was indirect: by making reading more comfortable, readers are able to process text faster and with less effort. Wilkins also found that the most effective colour varies from person to person, although the reasons for this individual variation are still not understood. For further information on this research go to: www.essex.ac.uk/psychology/overlays

Coloured overlays are sheets of coloured acetate that can be placed over text while reading. Overlay testing kits for determining which colour of overlay would be most suitable for the child or adult are available. These comprise several sheets of acetate of different colours, which are placed over a page of text. In a straightforward testing procedure, pairs of colours are compared successively, the person being asked to judge which colour makes the text easiest to read. The text used for this purpose is usually meaningless, so that the person concentrates on the legibility and comfort of the text, not the comprehensibility. Wilkins developed a set of **Intuitive Overlays** that sampled the range of visible colours more systematically than the set used by Irlen. Intuitive Overlays are now the most widely used type and can be obtained (both as overlay testing kits and as packs of overlay sheets for regular use) from a number of suppliers (see list at the end of this chapter).

Research by Wilkins and his associates has shown that coloured overlays reduce the symptoms of visual stress and increase reading fluency in about 20% of school children. In 5% of children the increase in speed with overlays is greater than 25%. If those children who select an overlay are given it to use on daily basis, about half of them are still likely to be using it after 6–8 months. These findings have been independently replicated in numerous studies all over the world (see Wilkins, 2003, for review).

Reading rulers

Coloured overlays are normally supplied in A4 size, but these can be cut down if required. Recently, however, a range of inexpensive small overlays called **Reading Rulers** [www.crossboweducation.com/Eye_Level_Reading_Ruler.htm] has been introduced by Crossbow Education. These are about the width of an A4 page but only 60 mm high, with a black horizontal stripe across the middle to assist keeping on the line of text. Reading rulers have the advantage that they are conveniently sized and will fit easily into a pocket or pencil case, or can be kept in the pages of a book as a bookmark. They are more discreet than whole sheets of coloured acetate and hence may be more acceptable to older children and adults who might be embarrassed about using larger sheets of acetate.

Smith & Wilkins (2007) compared Reading Rulers with conventional overlays and found that children with visual stress did not show any significant increase in reading speed using Reading Rulers whereas using the conventional overlays they did. This effect was not due to the smaller size of the Reading Rulers but, rather, to the limited range of colours in the set which dramatically reduced the chances of coming close to the optimal tint for any given child. As a direct result of this research, Crossbow Education has now increased the range of colours available in Reading Rulers from five to ten, which should address this particular problem although unlike conventional overlays, Reading Rulers are only for use singly and are not suitable for use in combination.

However, there remain concerns about the way in which Reading Rulers may be used in the classroom, as children are often permitted to select colours by idiosyncratic preference on a day-by-day basis rather than by systematic pair-wise comparison in a screening situation so that the teacher can ensure that the most effective colour is being used by the child. There is a real danger that if, by chance, children choose a colour that is not effective for them, they may decide that colour, *per se*, does not help their reading when they have not had a proper opportunity to determine the most effective colour.

Tinted lenses

Although coloured overlays can be a satisfactory solution to visual stress, they are not always terribly convenient. An alternative solution is tinted lenses, which are easier to use (e.g. with white boards and when writing). Because the colour can be precisely prescribed from the full range of possible colours, the maximum benefit is likely to be obtained. Precision tinted lenses can be prescribed by an optometrist, who is likely to determine the optimal colour for lenses using an apparatus designed by Wilkins called the *Intuitive Colorimeter*. A few optometrists prescribe rival systems offering limited ranges of tints (e.g. Chromagen and Harris filters), but the effectiveness of these in comparison with precision tints has yet to be properly determined. The *Society for Coloured Lens Prescribers* [www.s4clp.org] supplies details of practitioners in the UK who subscribe to a professional code of conduct in the assessment and supply of tinted lenses.

Text size

A number of studies have shown that text size can affect reading fluency and efficiency. Adults and children tend to make more errors in reading errors as text size decreases and this effect is worse for those who suffer from visual stress.
Research indicates that most children of primary school age would benefit if the text size and line spacing of reading materials were increased slightly. As text size decreases, text increasingly takes on the appearance of a striped pattern that can trigger visual stress symptoms. If children are susceptible to visual stress then they will be particularly vulnerable to adverse effects of trying to read texts of smaller size. Enlarging text size should be especially beneficial for these children.

A number of products are available that will magnify text. The *Visual Tracking Magnifier* consists of a high-powered magnifying glass, with a central viewing strip about 7 mm wide. It can be easily tracked backwards and forwards across the text, and is particularly suitable for younger readers. The *VTM Line Reader* has been designed for users who have achieved a reading age of around 10 or above. The magnifier has shaded areas to mask pattern glare and has an overall length of 115 mm. This magnifier is also very useful for following lines of print in directories etc. [For details of both these products visit www.ic-online.co.uk/dyslexia/page2.htm.]

Computers and visual stress

People who suffer from visual stress often find that reading or writing on a computer can be visually irritating, leading to headaches and eyestrain. When children are writing using a word processor, they should be encouraged to work in a font size or viewing size that they are comfortable with. There are now several programs available that address this problem and which make using computers more comfortable. These products enable an easy choice of colours, fonts, size and spacing to be made. Examples include *Claro View* [www.clarosoftware.com]; *Readable* [www.dyslexic.com]; *Virtual Reading Ruler* [crossboweducation.com]; and the *Textic Toolbar* [www.textic.com].

Identifying visual stress

Until recently, the only techniques for identifying visual stress were subjective. They relied on the child or adult reporting symptoms of visual stress, or making a subjective judgment that text is easier to read with a certain colour rather than another. The snag with this approach is that most children as well as adults – given the choice – will choose a coloured overlay, even though the majority of them don't really need it. After a while most of them don't bother to use the overlay any more. For an adult that may not be of great concern – we can safely assume that they don't feel any real benefit (although if tinted lenses have been prescribed and then just left in a drawer this is a waste of money). But where children are concerned, parents and teachers don't know if the child has just forgotten to use the glasses or the overlay, or is just being lazy, or whether they simply don't need them after all

Children who suffer from the condition do not necessarily know they have a problem, and if they do report symptoms these may not always be reliable. Even some adults may not appreciate why they find reading so tiring, and fail to realise that this affects their work efficiency. A rate of reading test can be given to check that a chosen overlay makes a difference, but that only evaluates the impact on reading speed over a short time. None of these techniques establishes objectively that the person definitely has visual stress and therefore needs an overlay or other treatment.

To ensure that the children and adults who really need the treatment are identified and given treatment, objective evidence is required on whether the person actually suffers from visual stress or not. Recent research in the UK and elsewhere has revealed that children and adults who have visual stress are impaired in tasks involving visual search and this evidence has been used as the basis for a new computerised, objective screening system called *ViSS (Visual Stress Screener)*. ViSS is a word-search game that is carried out under two conditions – one in which the computer screen is visually stressful and one where it is normal. The program then works out whether the visually stressful condition made a significant difference to the person's performance. Extensive published research has shown that where ViSS finds a person to have significant difficulty on the visually stressful task we can predict that they will need an overlay or tinted lenses and that these will make a big difference to their reading. The objectivity of ViSS makes it more accurate than other methods currently available and it is suitable for use with dyslexics as well as non-dyslexics (Singleton and Henderson, 2007). ViSS is designed for user with children aged 7– 17, and there is a version for adults as well. For more information on ViSS visit www.visual-stress.com

Conclusions

Visual stress is a surprisingly common condition that has deleterious effects on the development of children's reading, particularly on reading fluency and comprehension. The impact of visual stress gets worse as the demands placed on the person's reading increase. At college and university, visual stress and the legacy of the failure to recognise and treat the problem earlier, can be a serious hindrance to successful studying. In many careers, untreated visual stress can be a considerable barrier to advancement. There are efficient ways of identifying the condition that can be used readily in the classroom and elsewhere. Once identified, the effects of visual stress can be alleviated using colour, a solution that is both cheap and easy to apply. The challenge today is to ensure that all teachers are informed of the condition and that effective steps are taken in every school to make sure that students who need this treatment have access to it. There is a good case to be made for screening all children for visual stress, but the arguments in favour for screening are especially strong for those with dyslexia, who are 75% more likely to suffer from visual stress than the rest of the population.

References

Evans, B.J.W. (2001). *Dyslexia and Vision.* London: Whurr.

Singleton, C. (2008) Visual factors in reading. *Educational and Child Psychology,* 25(3).

Singleton, C. & Henderson, L.M. (2007) Computerised screening for visual stress in children with dyslexia. *Dyslexia,* 13, 130-151.

Smith, L. & Wilkins, A. (2007) How many colours are necessary to increase the reading of children with visual stress? A comparison of two systems. *Journal of Research in Reading,* 30, 332-343.

Wilkins, A.J. (2003). *Reading Through Colour.* Chichester, Sussex: Wiley.

Suppliers of coloured overlays

Crossbow Education

01785 660902; www.crossboweducation.com

I.O.O. Sales

020 7378 0330; www.ioosales.co.uk/html/education/edu01D.html

Cerium Visual Technologies

01580 765211; www.ceriumvistech.co.uk/Overlays.htm

Dr Chris Singleton is Senior Lecturer in Educational Psychology at the University of Hull, Research Director of Lucid Research Ltd, and Associate Editor of the Journal of Research in Reading.

Dyslexia and self-esteem

David Pollak

What is self-esteem?

We all have an overview of ourselves, which includes two parts: our self-image (how see ourselves) and our 'ideal self' (how we would like to be). Self-esteem is made of the contrast between the two parts, so our self-esteem is likely to be poor if we see ourselves as falling short of the ideal. What influences these two parts of our self-concept? Other people. For example, if a dyslexic child finds it harder to read and write than her classmates, the reaction of other children, teachers and parents is crucial. My research and that of Barbara Riddick and her colleagues both found that many dyslexic university students believed that significant people in their lives (such as parents and teachers) thought they were incompetent and unintelligent.

At whatever age a person is assessed as dyslexic, the process is likely to have an enormous effect on his self-esteem. The label has great power. It can serve as an explanation of experiences, a link with others and a gateway to accessibility arrangements (both in education and at work). But the way dyslexia is presented or explained is the key. Is it a 'neurologically-based disorder', or are the indicators of dyslexia simply signs of a kind of brain which is not well matched to a literacy-based society in which linear thinking dominates? In other words, is the dyslexic person told: "you've just got this little thing wrong with you" (as one of my research interviewees put it), or: "now we know more about where you fit into the neurodiversity spectrum"?

We cannot talk about the self-esteem of dyslexic people without mentioning the topic of intelligence. Over the years, many students have said such things to me as: "I'm dyslexic but my brother is very bright". Parents have often spoken of their children in similar terms. Adults are frequently hesitant about being assessed because of fear of being found not dyslexic but unintelligent, and children can be cruel about the 'dyslexic = thick' equation. There are two parts to the intelligence issue: when arrangements are not dyslexia-friendly, dyslexic people can feel stupid, and it is widely known that many psychologists favour a model of dyslexia based on a contrast between IQ and other test results.

What can improve the self-esteem of dyslexic people?

Terminology

It is essential for dyslexic people and those working with them to avoid medical terms, which give dyslexic people the message that they are sick. Words to avoid include 'condition', 'disorder', 'defect', 'symptom', 'syndrome' and, worst of all, 'comorbidity' (which means having more than one disease at once). The word 'diagnosis' is less straight-forward. Although many people associate it with a medical context, it literally means 'a critical analysis of the nature of something', and can thus be seen as acceptable. The expression 'specific learning difficulties' could be replaced by 'specific learning differences'. That may seem a small change, but it is very significant. The central question has to be: Is dyslexia a problem within individual people, or is its existence a challenge to society as a whole?

Family life

The Dyslexia Teacher website [www.dyslexia-teacher.com] recommends that parents should "…make sure the child knows he is loved for himself, and that this love is not dependent on how well he does at school". It is important to encourage a child to take part in activities where she can use her strengths, which may be in sport, music, drama, art or computers, but also in verbal creativity such as oral story-telling. But the main thing parents can do is to counter-balance medical images of dyslexia. It is a bad idea to encourage negative attitudes towards teachers, but the notion that 'the school isn't as dyslexia-friendly as could be, yet' can be presented in a supportive manner. In other words: 'it's not that there is something wrong with you, but rather that you need to be taught in the right way'.

If a parent is a linear, verbal thinker, s/he may struggle with navigation across a town or assembling a complex toy. The dyslexic child will probably find these things quite easy. Relying on him for this not only boosts his self-esteem, but is also an opportunity to point out that we all have neurodiverse strengths to contribute. Home is also the place where personal organisation skills can be developed. The short-term memory aspects of dyslexia can lower self-esteem if a person is not proactive about it. Habits such as the pictorial 'things to take today' list stuck to the door-frame can be learned in childhood and be helpful for life.

School

The single most effective thing a school can do for its pupils' self-esteem is to follow the advice in the BDA's *Achieving Dyslexia Friendly Schools Information Pack* (available on the BDA website). The principles behind this advice can be summed up as: If children don't learn the way we teach, we will teach them the way they learn. This does not always mean overt differentiation. For example, compare: "Here is a copy on cream paper for John because he is dyslexic" with simply providing everyone with cream paper. Schools can also do a great deal to promote social inclusivity. Assemblies can be used to showcase dyslexic achievers. Anti-bullying policies must include the clear message that picking on children because of neurodiversity is unacceptable.

Michael Thomson describes how academic self-esteem can come from successful strategies. Dyslexic children who have developed good self-awareness, study skills and determination at GCSE level can do better at A level than non-dyslexics who found GCSE easy, but are not ready for the higher standard and harder work of A level study.

College and University

Students' self-esteem can be lowered by two factors: the classification of dyslexia as a disability and the remedial model of learning support. The first is not something over which institutions have any control; funding for learning support is currently delivered by the government via the disability system. University students who are UK citizens can claim the Disabled Students Allowance (DSA), for which they need two assessments; this confirms their sense of 'otherness'. However, staff working with them can use this system as an opportunity to discuss their self-image and the relationship between their natural thinking style and academic conventions. The remedial model of learning support can be confronted. This requires an effort on the part of academic staff, for whom the choice is clear. They can say to the student: "You have a problem. Please go to the learning support department and get help" – or they can say to themselves: "There are dyslexic students on my course. How can I make it more accessible to them?"

The existence of neurodiversity challenges lecturers and all examination boards to justify their assumptions. Why is the ability to write three-hour exams essential? Why is a 3000-word linear essay the only way to assess a course? The self-esteem of dyslexic students is affected by the fact that in so many ways, education is what Morgan and Klein call a 'non-dyslexic world'. They are expected to work in ways that do not suit them; they are effectively disabled by the system.

Employment

Key4Learning [www.key4learning.com] is an organisation that visits workplaces and facilitates planning for the successful integration of dyslexic (and other) staff. There are also several other companies that offer this service. This can include what should be an essential contributor to the self-esteem of a dyslexic worker: a 'disclosure document' which describes the person's strengths and challenges and sets out the reasonable adjustments which should be made. This agenda sums up the key issues for dyslexic people in the workplace: self-knowledge and disclosure.

Positive self-knowledge leads to confidence about telling people you are dyslexic, because you have belief in your working approaches. You are not apologetic about having dyslexia. For example, instead of saying: "I'm so sorry, my note-taking is so bad, I need to use this sound recorder", you say: "I use a sound recorder instead of a note-book", or: "This team will work more effectively if I use my sound recorder". There are several useful books about dyslexia in the workplace; one of the best of them (Goodwin and Thomson, which is about life in general) models good practice by including a CD containing the whole book and supplementary materials.

Social life and relationships

This area is different from the rest. So much of it is about personal confidence. Years ago, when Richard Branson first 'came out' as a dyslexic person, a mother told me how she had overheard her daughter saying "I'm dyslexic, like Richard Branson". Dyslexic people have a lot of public figures nowadays who are role models (even though not many are women). A test for anyone in the dating or friend-making 'market' involves the ability to say: "If I forget to turn up at the pub, or even forget your name, it doesn't mean I don't want to know you. It's just part of dyslexia."

This may be different from the previous topics, but it is strongly influenced by them. People who have been crushed by their educational or employment experiences are unlikely to find it easy to achieve such confidence. Richard Branson can afford to employ a PA to remember things like the names of people he has appointments with, but for those who have to rely on human support from parents or partners, the potential threat to self-esteem is obvious. Why is this? The answer is connected with the old British issues of status and snobbery. However many of your friends rely on you to mend their appliances or fellow electricians need you to tell them where all the circuits start and finish, if you need help to write an essay or a letter, you may feel like a failure.

The way forward

The concept of 're-framing' has been around for some time, and involves re-interpreting (in this case, dyslexia) in a more productive and positive manner, as Gerber and his colleagues have put it. The increasing numbers of dyslexic millionaires show how a holistic, global thinking style is an asset, and the same could be said of dyslexic architects. Society still attaches great status to the printed word, but these people and many others like them do not admire it. Giving a lift across the city to a dyslexic colleague one day, I was following her instructions as she occasionally pointed that way or this way (no need for the words 'left' or 'right'). At one point, I noticed a road name and said: "Ah, we're in Dysart Way". "Huh, those are words," she said, "I don't use those". I, on the other hand, with my lack of sense of direction or mental overview of the city, have to rely on road names, and frequently get lost.

Disabled people coined the expression 'nothing about us without us'. Dyslexic people are showing increased self-confidence by setting up their own organisations. A good example is EDEN Skills (Education, Dyslexia and Electronic Needs), a training service for dyslexic learners in further and higher education that combines study skills strategies with assistive technology [www.edenskills. co.uk]. It is the use of such technology that provides independence with activities such as writing letters and academic assignments.

Conclusions: the inclusive society

The concept of assistive technology brings us to the notion of a truly inclusive society. If a wheelchair user is confronted by a flight of steps leading to a library, s/he is not a disabled reader but a potential reader disabled by the building. Likewise, if a dyslexic person who finds reading slow and laborious is confronted by shelves of printed books, s/he is disabled by the fact that audio versions or digital versions are not available.

The relevance of this to self-esteem is that people should not have to claim labels such as 'disabled' or 'dyslexic' for accessibility to be provided. Recent legislation, such as the Disability Discrimination Act 2005, is moving society in that direction, and there have been improvements. Just as level access to buses helps people with child buggies and walking aids as well as wheelchair users, dyslexia-friendly teaching methods help all students.

The self-concept can be sub-divided into academic and non-academic aspects; the latter includes social, emotional and physical views of the self. As we all know, dyslexia is about much more than reading and writing. When we have a truly inclusive society, dyslexic people will not have to be assessed by psychologists and given labels that mark them out as different. They will then have access to true self-esteem.

References

Gerber, P., Reiff, H. et al. (1996) Reframing the learning disabilities experience. *Journal of learning disabilities*, 29(1), 98-101.

Goodwin, V. & Thomson, B. (2004) *Making dyslexia work for you*. London: David Fulton.

McLoughlin, D., Leather, C. & Stringer, P. (2002) *The Adult Dyslexic: Intervention and outcomes*. London: Whurr.

Morgan, E. & Klein, C. (2000) *The dyslexic adult in a non-dyslexic world*. London: Whurr.

Pollak, D, (2005) *Dyslexia, the self and higher education: learning life histories of students identified as dyslexic*. Stoke on Trent: Trentham Books.

Riddick, B., Farmer, M. and Sterling, C. (1997) *Students and Dyslexia: Growing up with a specific learning difficulty*. London: Whurr.

Thomson, M, (2001) *The psychology of dyslexia*. London, Whurr.

Dr David Pollak is Principal Lecturer in Learning Support and Dyslexia Studies at De Montfort University, Leicester.

Access arrangements for dyslexic students in GCSE and 'A' level exams

Caroline Read

Access arrangements have been made available to candidates who have difficulty accessing exams and assessments in their normal format for a number of years. Awarding bodies that assess general qualifications, as well as trade and professional qualifications, alongside the National Assessment Agency (NAA – a subsidiary of QCA) all offer a range of similar arrangements, though the criteria and requirements for application vary between qualifications and assessments.

For the purpose of this article we will be focusing on access arrangements for general qualifications (GCSE, GCE 'A' level, GNVQ, etc.), which are republished each year in September by the Joint Council for Qualifications [1].

Why are access arrangements needed?

Access arrangements are made available to candidates who are able to access the content of an assessment, but due to some disability or difficulty cannot access through the format in which the assessment is presented. For example, a candidate with a visual impairment may need the help of a practical assistant to carry out a physics experiment because he is unable to see the equipment sufficiently well, even though his understanding of physics would warrant him an A* grade. Perhaps a pupil with a specific learning difficulty has an excellent command of geography that he can demonstrate verbally, but struggles to read the paper, and consequently needs the help of a reader.

The aim of an access arrangement is always to remove a disadvantage, while not giving a candidate an unfair advantage over his or her peers. For this reason the criteria and application procedures are rigorous. Professionals carrying out assessments need to be certain that a candidate is genuinely disadvantaged before an arrangement is requested. For example, unless a candidate genuinely works at a slower pace than others of his age, to give him extra time could put him at an unfair advantage over his peers.

Arrangements should never undermine the assessment criteria. For example, a reader is not allowed in papers where reading is the focus of the assessment (e.g. English literature) otherwise a candidate would be gaining marks for a skill that had not been demonstrated, thereby undermining the validity and integrity of the qualification.

The main arrangements available include:

- **Extra time**, for candidates who work very slowly

- **Rest breaks**, for poor concentration or extreme stress

- Use of a **bilingual dictionary**, for candidates whose first language is not English, Irish or Welsh, subject to the regulations

- **Readers**, for very poor readers with decoding or comprehension difficulties who cannot read by themselves

- **Reading aloud**, for those who have reading difficulties and can concentrate better if they can hear themselves read

- **Scribes**, for very poor or slow writers who cannot write by themselves

- **Word processors**, for poor or slow writers who are used to typing

- **Transcripts** of candidates' writing which may be hard for the examiner to read

- **Prompters**, for candidates who lose concentration easily

These arrangements can be separated into two types: those where an application must be made to the appropriate awarding body (often referred to as type A), and those which can be allowed within the centre as long as appropriate evidence is available on file (type C). Readers, scribes and word processors are all type A arrangements. Any of the listed arrangements might be appropriate for a candidate with specific learning difficulties, depending on their particular difficulties and needs.

Who might need access arrangements?

Before we look in more detail at individual arrangements it is important to understand that a significant change has taken place over the last few years in terms of who qualifies for access arrangements. In the 1990s the focus was on *diagnosis* or label – if a candidate has been diagnosed as dyslexic s/he would qualify for extra time or perhaps a reader, where as someone with moderate learning difficulties would not.

The focus is now on *need*. For example, to be allowed extra time an assessor needs to demonstrate the need for extra time, perhaps by using a test of reading or writing speed, or a rapid naming test to show deficiencies in processing speed. It is no longer sufficient to diagnose dyslexia – the assessor must make clear why this diagnosis leads to the candidate working slowly. A common misconception is that if a discrepancy between a student's IQ and their reading or spelling ability exists they should be allowed extra time. In fact any assessment would need to show why that discrepancy leads to the candidate needing the extra time, and how allowing the time will help to demonstrate their knowledge or skill.

How can arrangements benefit dyslexic candidates?

Up to 25% extra time might well benefit a candidate with dyslexic difficulties. Perhaps s/he reads slowly, needing to re-read text two or more times before the meaning has been grasped sufficiently to answer questions. Maybe the problem is with writing. Often dyslexics struggle with the organisation of writing and extra time to plan or to check through after writing can make a real difference. The problem could be with underlying processing speed – thought processes taking longer than usual. Extra time can help to put dyslexics on a level playing field with their peers.

Rest breaks are an underestimated and underused arrangement. In some cases a rest break would be a more appropriate arrangement for candidates who are instead given extra time. Many dyslexics would benefit more from one or two short breaks during a long exam than they would from spending longer completing the paper. It is generally agreed that a quick walk in the fresh air, perhaps followed by a drink is more beneficial than staying in the exam room. If a candidate needs a break then why not allow them a proper break. Time taken for each break is added to the end of the exam, so there is no disadvantage for the candidate.

Candidates whose first language is not English, Irish or Welsh may benefit from using a *bilingual dictionary.*

Readers – either individual or shared (i.e. one adult can be available to read the odd word or phrase to a group of candidates at each one's request) – can be requested for very poor readers with decoding or comprehension difficulties who cannot read by themselves. An assessor needs to demonstrate a standardised score of below 85 on a reading test for a candidate in order to request a reader for a candidate.

Some dyslexics with reading difficulties do not qualify for readers but may benefit from *reading aloud*. Many people can concentrate better if they can hear themselves read.

Various arrangements are designed to help those with *writing difficulties*, and of course slow writers may find up to 25% extra time or rest breaks sufficient to overcome their difficulties. *Scribes* can be requested for very poor or slow writers who cannot write by themselves. A scribe might take different forms. A candidate might dictate to an adult to writes or types word for word. Voice activated or word predictive software can be used as an alternative.

A candidate with poor writing or organisational difficulties but with good keyboarding skills might be granted permission to use *word processor.* Spelling and grammar checkers must be disabled. Careful thought should be given to whether extra time should be allowed for those using word processors. Some candidates can type much faster than the average writing speed, which is approximately 17 words per minute for Year 11 students [2]. There is a real danger that candidates using a word processor could have an unfair advantage if extra time is also allowed.

Where a candidate's only problem is writing legibly – particularly where only the odd word or phrase is difficult to read – *transcripts* can be produced by someone in the centre who is familiar with the candidate's writing.

Prompters, often the exam invigilator, can tap the table if necessary in order to help candidates who lose concentration refocus on the paper.

History of need and provision

The regulations make very clear that arrangements must <u>not</u> be put in place simply for exams. They should be a continuation and reflection of work and support that has taken place in the centre throughout the candidate's course of study. This can cause problems for centres when candidates or their parents arrange last minute reports from independent professionals recommending access arrangements without reference to the perceptions of the centre.

Occasionally a genuine exception to the required history of need and support may be acceptable. Some students are so bright that they are able to cope throughout secondary schooling, and sometimes even into 6th form without help, but their learning difficulty becomes apparent as the academic demands of their studies increase. In such cases if genuine evidence can be gathered to show that, for example, the candidate needs extra time to process a paper and demonstrate their true potential, then extra time could be granted even though no history exists.

Failure to comply with the regulations

Not following the regulations can carry serious penalties. Putting into place arrangements not agreed by awarding bodies, permitting arrangements within the centre which are not supported by appropriate evidence or the failure of reader or scribe to abide by the regulations could all be considered to be 'failure to comply'. Malpractice may impact on the candidate's result or even lead to their disqualification.

Special Consideration

Occasionally a candidate who has been fully prepared to take part in an assessment encounters an unexpected exceptional circumstance that affects their performance, or even leads to them missing part of that assessment. In such cases it may be appropriate for the exams officer to apply for special consideration. Common causes for special consideration include illness, bereavement, accident or serious disturbance. A very small number of marks – in very serious cases a maximum of 5% additional marks – can be added if the paper was completed. If sufficient evidence of a student's performance can be provided to the appropriate awarding body it might be possible to make an award even if part of the exam was missed for genuine reasons. Special consideration cannot compensate for poor preparation on the part of the centre or the candidate, even if this was through no fault of their own.

Conclusions

It is not possible in every case to remove the disadvantage caused by learning difficulties, physical impairments or medical problems. However, the provision of access arrangements by the awarding bodies is a genuine attempt to make a level playing field for candidates without undermining the integrity of the qualifications they offer.

References

[1]   The Joint Council for Qualifications *Regulations and Guidance Relating to Candidates who are Eligible for Adjustments in Examination.* This document is published on the JCQ website [www.jcq.org.uk] in early September under 'Publications & Common Documents'.

[2]   Allcock, P. *Group and Individual Assessment of Writing Speed.* [Downloadable free from www.patoss-dyslexia.org]

Caroline Read is a specialist teacher who provides training in the field of special educational needs, particularly for teachers assessing students who require exam access arrangements [www. communicate-ed.org.uk].

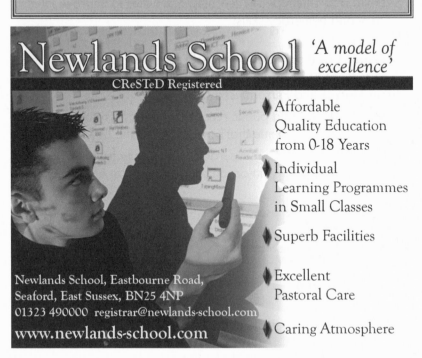

BDA Quality Mark

Jennifer Owen Adams

The BDA Quality Mark continues to reach out to schools, colleges, children services and, increasingly, to employers to celebrate and accredit best practice in these sectors of society. As a reminder to readers of the BDA Handbook, the BDA Quality Mark:

- Helps deliver the BDA's vision to develop a dyslexia-friendly society that enables dyslexic people to achieve their full potential.
- Helps teachers to help children and young people in schools with dyslexia and other specific learning difficulties to improve their literacy and numeracy skills.
- Is a template of good practice for schools and other centres of learning as it provides a practical roadmap to meet the requirements of government educational initiatives such as *Every Child Matters* and *Personalised Learning*.
- Provides external and public recognition for organisations registered on the scheme that have achieved the BDA standard.
- Affords a tangible and measurable opportunity for the BDA to work collaboratively with organisations to inform and change practice.
- Helps public service providers to meet the requirements demanded of them by the *Disability Discrimination Act* and the *Special Educational Needs and Disability Act*.

BDA - QUALITY

Recent developments

- Consolidating the developmental work that had taken place in refining the design and the delivery mechanism of the BDA Quality Mark accreditation service. The aim has been to ensure that future plans are built on a robust structure that can assure the quality of dyslexia-friendly provision offered by the BDA Quality Marked organisation.

- Building on the success of the BDA Quality Mark pilot project by expanding its remit to work with schools as well as to embrace the requirements of emerging children's service departments within local authorities.

- Working towards making the BDA Quality Mark accreditation service self-sustainable through income generation. Evidence from our work in the education sector suggested that the potential for growth is enormous – as a national authority in dyslexia and related specific learning difficulties, the BDA has the scope to reach out to every school and other centres of learning across England, Wales and the Northern Ireland.

- Establishing a fully-fledged BDA Quality Mark office. In early 2007, a mid term review of the Quality Mark team took place as a result of staff changes. The newly established team undertook a mid-term review of systems and procedures and, as a result, a more customer-centred system has been established.

From local education authorities to children's services

Following re-organisation of local government in England and Wales, a number of local authorities realigned their social and education services for children to form children's service departments. This development took the BDA Quality Mark into new arenas that required further development work regarding how dyslexia-friendly good practice should be defined, particularly within social care and non-educational settings. A BDA Quality Marked children's service department requires the demonstration of dyslexia-friendly good practice by all members of that department, not just within the education team. This went beyond the remit and scope of the previous set of quality standards for local education authorities. As a result, quality standards for local authority children services are now available and are beginning to be implemented following a nationwide consultation programme with the regional BDA Quality Mark forums.

From dyslexia friendly to inclusion friendly

An unexpected outcome of the original pilot was the emergence of a new slant to the dyslexia-friendly standards. Inclusion friendly status (as opposed to just dyslexia friendly) was a strong message coming from partner authorities in the field. The educational professionals were looking beyond being dyslexia friendly to being inclusive friendly. Recent research (as evidenced at the BDA 7th International Conference in March 2008) suggests that dyslexia co-exists with a number of other specific learning difficulties such as attention deficit hyperactivity disorder and developmental coordination disorder. Hence individuals with dyslexia may also have characteristics associated with these other types of specific learning difficulties. Educational professionals were therefore seeking a code of good practice and associated accreditation scheme that could support the learning of all of these young people. These changes in perspective meant that the BDA needed to consider expanding the quality mark standards to embrace the whole inclusion agenda. With dyslexia being the most common of all the specific learning difficulties, and in the knowledge that what is good educational practice for dyslexic learners is generally good practice for all learners, irrespective of what specific learning difficulty is evident, the BDA considered developing a set of quality standards for inclusive-friendly settings.

The opportunity for the BDA to be the lead-player in driving forward the inclusion agenda for hidden disabilities via an *Inclusion Friendly Quality Mark* is recognised. However, a strong message emerged from our membership of the danger of 'losing' the dyslexia agenda within the broader inclusion debate. The Quality Mark team considered this view and decided to embark on a feasibility study to look at the issues and implications of developing a Quality Mark that addresses the broader inclusion angle. The issue of the BDA accrediting inclusive good practice in non-dyslexia fields is an interesting one. In the meantime, our aim is to make links with other SpLD interest groups to build a *pan-SpLD forum* that may, as a start, wish to build on the examples set by the BDA Quality Mark for dyslexia. We are currently seeking partnerships with other national organisations to explore the feasibility of developing this work.

Adult and young offender custodial settings

Building on the work of two previous BDA projects and on BDA research working with adults and young people who were either offenders or at risk of offending, the BDA wanted to establish a set of quality standards and an accompanying BDA Quality Mark to identify and verify dyslexia-friendly good practice in prisons, young offender institutions and other organisations working with offenders. The high incidence of dyslexia amongst this section of society is well documented. The aim was to support these settings to ensure that dyslexic offenders, or those at risk of offending, had an opportunity to break the cycle of offending by being in a dyslexia-friendly environment where there was an empathy for dyslexia and where dyslexia was identified, understood and supported.

For this area of activity, we are working in partnership with City College Manchester, which is the biggest providers of offender education nationally. The aim is for each prison education service, managed by City College Manchester, to register on the Quality Mark programme and achieve Quality Mark status. This initiative is closely linked to changes in offender learning criteria such as the implementation of the *Offender Learning Journey* document that outlines the specific standard of education and training expected within secure settings. Dyslexia is specifically mentioned in this document, with clear targets regarding the required level of support that should be available to offenders. Achievement of the Quality Mark enables the providers of such education to evidence and demonstrate not only that the standard has been achieved but also exceeded.

Post-compulsory education and training

Reducing the number of NEETs (those **N**ot in **E**ducation, **E**mployment or **T**raining) is a government priority. Transition from compulsory education to further education and training opportunities is a challenging time for dyslexic learners. Retaining dyslexic learners within FE and training is an additional challenge. In 2005-6 the BDA established and led a national working party in further education which looked at the feasibility of establishing a BDA Quality Mark with accompanying standards for the post-compulsory education and training sector. Quality standards for post compulsory education and training settings were agreed and the BDA ran a pilot programme to trial these standards in a range of FE colleges in England, Wales, Northern Ireland and the Channel Islands. To date, six FE colleges have received the Quality Mark Award.

Other BDA Quality Mark achievements

- Quality standards for individual schools have been designed, approved and launched.
- Quality Mark standards for schools have been submitted to Department for Children Schools and Families to contribute to the DCSF's Inclusion Development Programme for educational practitioners in schools.

- Closer links have been established with the BDA Training Department to ensure that Quality Mark promotion follows on from BDA Training Department events.
- Expressions of interest have been received from other organisations outside the education sector, including Liverpool Police Authority, the Home Office, various Health Trusts and the prison service. In addition, links have been formed with Liverpool Community College to engage with Work-Based Learning Providers. A pilot group of these employers will be formed to work towards achieving the BDA Quality Mark for dyslexia-friendly organisations and employers.

Future Plans

Our current key priorities are to:

- Expand the BDA Quality Mark for Schools programme. This was a new development and is beginning to be very popular. The BDA feels this is the correct approach as it is easier to assure the quality of best practice at the school level particularly as local authorities are increasingly delegating SEN budgets to individual schools.
- Launch the BDA Quality Mark for Employers. The BDA has already published an *Employers Guide to Dyslexia* and a *Code of Practice* and has developed a set of quality standards against which employers can benchmark their dyslexia best practice.
- Respond to approaches for a BDA Quality Mark from local authority leisure services, libraries, transport, websites, e-learning platforms, and training organisations in the UK and Europe.

For more information about the BDA Quality Mark, visit www.bdadyslexia.org.uk or contact Katherine Dumas at the BDA on katherined@bdadyslexia.org.uk or telephone 01344 381 560. We look forward to picking up your enquiry and telling you more about the BDA Quality Mark.

Jennifer Owen Adams is Education and Policy Director of the British Dyslexia Association.

Dyslexia in different languages

Cross-language comparisons and multilingualism in dyslexia

John Everatt, Gad Elbeheri, Christine Firman and Dina Ocampo

In this short paper, some of the issues related to differences across languages that may be important for dyslexia research and practice will be considered in terms of their implications for multilingual contexts. The primary cross-language comparison will be between the English and Arabic languages. The similarities and differences between the spoken and written forms of English and Arabic present examples of the factors that need to be incorporated into views of dyslexia, as well as into assessment and intervention procedures, if they are to be applicable across languages. We will then consider two multilingual examples, one in the Philippines and the other in Malta. These will be discussed to provide insights for the development of appropriate support for children and adults in any multilingual context.

Dyslexia is a worldwide condition that affects children and adults in many countries, who speak numerous languages. Research suggests that dyslexia is related to specific cognitive and/or neurological differences, which are associated with language skills but not intelligence in general. Informed early assessment of potential areas of difficulty and strength should allow appropriate support to overcome the difficulties, allowing the abilities to come forth. In the area of literacy difficulties, early identification typically leads to more effective intervention outcomes, whereas a failure to recognise difficulties can often lead to an individual becoming anxious or depressed and suffering losses in self-esteem, confidence and motivation. However, an assessment of dyslexia often involves a consideration of educational achievement, such as literacy attainment levels, which requires the assessment process to wait until the child starts to fail before support can begin.

Predicting difficulties in literacy

Understanding the factors that predict future literacy problems can be of use to educational practitioners who support children with dyslexia. Screening and assessment tools have been developed to aid the process of identifying or predicting learning problems; however, most assist in the identification of the needs of the monolingual, predominantly English-speaking child and there is a need to consider the appropriateness of these test measures/ materials across language contexts. Even in the UK, the child whose first (or home) language is not English may show different results on these measures compared to the first language English child (though see Everatt et al, 2000; Frederickson & Frith, 1998). Such considerations seem particularly important when identifying literacy deficits. The main predictors of future literacy problems are based on characteristics of the language – typically the sounds within the language. These characteristics may vary across languages in such a way that they do not provide the same level of prediction about literacy learning problems across those languages. Similarly, the way the written form represents the language may vary in such a way that literacy learning involves different skills and a measure of an underlying skill in one language may not be entirely appropriate in another.

The differences between English and Arabic may help explain some of these ideas. Both languages are spoken by a large number of individuals as first or additional languages. Both are highly influential in terms of their economic, political and religious importance for indigenous and immigrant populations. The sounds used by the two languages show similarities but also obvious differences, so that the additional language learner whose first language is English will have to learn new sound forms when attempting to learn Arabic, and vice versa. When acquiring literacy skills, the additional language learner will also notice major differences between the written forms despite the commonalities of the concepts underlying the two scripts. Both derive from the idea of representing basic sounds within the language by written symbols. Hence it is possible in both Arabic and English to translate a written word into a meaningful verbal form by associating letters with their corresponding sounds (sometimes referred to as phonological decoding). This allows the writing system to represent the language in a relatively reliable way and requires the ability to recognise and manipulate basic sounds within a language, a skill often referred to as phonological processing. Recognising that two words rhyme involves phonological processing, for example. Based on research primarily in English, such phonological processing skills seem to be a good predictor of future literacy learning problems and have formed the basis of the majority of assessment tools developed specifically to identify dyslexia.

Phonological decoding in Arabic

Consistent with the English language work, research in Arabic has also indicated that such phonological processes are predictive of reading levels amongst Arabic children and that poor Arabic readers show weak phonological decoding and low levels of phonological awareness in comparison to matched normal readers (see Abu-Rabia et al, 2003; Elbeheri & Everatt, 2007). Arabic literacy acquisition starts by using a writing system that is relatively consistent in its relationship between written letters and language sounds. This can be contrasted with English, which has a relatively inconsistent relationship between letters and sounds. When cross-language research looks at this variation in simplicity of the relationship between letters and sounds, differences occur in the prediction provided by phonological processing measures. Certain measures of phonological processing are less predictive of future literacy levels in languages with a simpler relationship than in languages with a more complex relationship. Hence, at least in the early years of learning, phonological processing measures may not be as predictive of literacy learning in Arabic as they are of literacy learning in English.

Studies of Arabic literacy have found that the level of prediction provided by phonological processing skills may be less than expected from previous research in other languages (Elbeheri et al, 2006). Thus, although phonological measures can provide the basis on which to identify and predict literacy learning difficulties in Arabic, additional measures may provide more precise levels of prediction that may be more specific to Arabic literacy learning. Therefore, measures of phonological processing may need to be supplemented by additional measures that focus more on the specific features of the writing system. In the case of Arabic, the formation of letters within a cursive writing system, or morphemic patterns, may be important aspects that the child needs to understand to become a skilled reader. Therefore, measures of these skills may be required when predicting additional levels of literacy achievement across different grades.

Differences in orthography

The use of a regular orthography (i.e., one that has a simple relationship between letters and sounds) also leads to increased accuracy in literacy in the early years of acquisition. Assessments of literacy skills within regular orthographies, therefore, often focus on rate/speed of reading rather than reading accuracy (see discussions in Goswami, 2000; Smythe & Everatt, 2004). Therefore, the assessment of Arabic literacy skills may have to consider measures of reading speed. Arabic also has the feature that, after initial learning, the relationship between letter symbols and verbal sounds becomes more complex due to the removal of markers that provide clues to pronunciation. Due to this, texts experienced by older readers often contain a large number of words that sound alike (homophones), which means that the context within which a word is written becomes the key to understanding its meaning as well as its correct pronunciation. As the reader becomes more experienced, therefore, the need to use the context within which a word is written becomes more important. These two features (early regularity and later contextual use) mean that measures of early literacy levels may have to focus on rate of reading, whereas more skilled literacy levels may have to be measured by tasks that require reading within context. Therefore, simple measures of word reading accuracy, typically used in studies of English-speaking children, may not be as appropriate to assess literacy levels amongst Arabic children.

Multilingualism

For the assessment of children learning to be literate in more than one language, these factors are also important. A child who has learnt to read and write in one language may have to learn a new set of strategies to be competent in reading and writing in another language. Similarly, assessment of literacy and literacy-related skills may need to consider language background to ensure that appropriate measures of these skills are used. For example, Everatt et al (2004) found that monolingual English children with good and poor English literacy skills could be distinguished by English-language measures of phonological awareness. However, these same measures did not distinguish bilingual children with good versus poor English literacy skills, even though English was one of the languages in which these children were competent. When the same skills were assessed in the bilingual children's home language, those with good and poor English literacy skills could be distinguished. Hence, although an assessment in the language of literacy was not informative of underlying phonological awareness problems, an assessment in the child's home language was.

This is not to say that assessments in one language may not be informative of problems in another. Work with bilingual Tagalog-English speaking children within the Philippines suggests that skills in one language are highly predictive of skills in the other. Hence measures in the one language (English) should be predictive of skills levels in the other (Tagalog). This bilingual context is fairly unique in that the children experience the two languages side-by-side, both prior to and within school. This reduces the need to learn one of the languages during schooling. However, even when the two languages are experienced side-by-side in every-day life, there may still be an emphasis for one of the languages to be more dominant over the other. In Malta, for example, the different school systems mean that children in one sector are likely to be more competent in Maltese compared to English, whereas the reverse is true in another sector. As suggested by the cross-language data above, the best set of predictors of literacy skills varied across these groups. In both bilingual contexts, regularity of the orthography was important, but so too was experience of the language. Both script and language experience factors may need to be taken into account to identify the optimum assessment process for a particular group.

Conclusions

Clearly, there is a need for more cross-language and multilingual research to identify the most appropriate assessment procedures for such children. However, some basic conclusions can be derived from the work already conducted. The first is that there are probably more commonalities between languages and writing systems than differences. Thus assessments can be cross-language or focus on the language of literacy. If an assessment in English is all that is available, then it is probably best to use that assessment than wait for an alternative to be developed. For the majority of cases, the assessment will probably produce the right results. Such assessments would seem to be most successful if they focus on phonological processing skills and incorporate measures of phonological awareness, phonological memory and the rapid access of phonological labels. For older children, with some literacy experience, measures of phonological decoding that assess both accuracy and rate also would seem appropriate for cross-language tools.

However, differences between languages/scripts mean that optimal assessment procedures may need to take into account the features of the writing system to be learnt, as well as the language background of the child. For example, assessments used with more regular orthographies than English may require measures of phonological processing that combine an awareness of sounds with speeded access or manipulations in memory; that is, tasks that are more complex than those used in typical English-language early literacy assessments. Alternatively, a child attempting to be literate in English who has learnt English as an additional language may be better assessed by tools that include measures in their first language as well as in English. These more comprehensive assessment procedures are still to be developed fully. However, the findings are relatively optimistic about our current procedures and should not be used as an excuse for depriving children of necessary support.

References

Abu-Rabia, S., Share, D. & Mansour, M. (2003). Word recognition and basic cognitive processes among reading disabled and normal readers in the Arabic language. *Reading and Writing,* 16, 423-440.

Elbeheri, G. & Everatt, J. (2007). Literacy ability and phonological processing skills amongst dyslexic and non-dyslexic speakers of Arabic. *Reading and Writing,* 20, 273-294.

Elbeheri, G., Everatt, J., Reid, G. & Al Mannai, H. (2006). Dyslexia Assessment in Arabic. *Journal of Research in Special Educational Needs,* 6, 143-152.

Everatt, J., Smythe, I., Adams, E. & Ocampo, D. (2000). Dyslexia screening measures and bilingualism. *Dyslexia,* 6, 42-56.

Everatt J., Smythe I., Ocampo D. & Gyarmathy E. (2004). Issues in the assessment of literacy-related difficulties across language backgrounds: A cross-linguistic comparison. *Journal of Research in Reading,* 27, 141-151.

Frederickson, N. & Frith, U. (1998). Identifying dyslexia in bilingual children: A phonological approach with inner London Sylheti speakers. *Dyslexia,* 4, 119-131.

Goswami, U. (2000). Phonological representations, reading development and dyslexia: Towards a cross-linguistic theoretical framework. *Dyslexia,* 6, 133-151.

Smythe, I. & Everatt, J. (2004). Dyslexia – a cross linguistic framework. In Smythe, I., Everatt, J. & Salter, R. (Eds) *International Book of Dyslexia,* Part 1. London: Wiley.

Dr John Everatt is a senior lecturer in psychology at the University of Surrey.

Dr Gad Elbeheri is director of the Center for Child Evaluation and Teaching, Kuwait.

Dr Christine Firman is head of the Unit for Learning Difficulties at the Ministry of Education, Malta.

Dr Dina Ocampo is a lecturer at the College of Education, University of the Philippines.

Prosiect Dyslecsia Cymru / Welsh Dyslexia Project

Michael Davies

Prosiect Dyslecsia Cymru / Welsh Dyslexia Project (PDC / WDP) was set up as a registered charity in April 2001, with the aim of being an organisation offering advice and support to dyslexic individuals (whether they are children, young people or adults) in Wales, and especially those having dyslexic difficulties when using the Welsh language [www.welshdyslexia.info]. This chapter reviews the achievements of the project since its inception.

CD for parents

One of the earliest projects developed by PDC/ WDP was a CD for parents. The idea was to use pictures and sound to allow parents to access information in every school in Wales. This meant that from the beginning PDC /WDP was making a proactive attempt to provide audio presentation of information, thus overcoming any literacy difficulties the parents may have. But the organisation also wanted to extend the reach and therefore re-packaged CD slightly and put it on the web. And just to make it interesting, it was also developed in Romanian, Hungarian, Polish, Portuguese and German. And it has inspired similar projects based on the PDC / WDP format and script in Hong Kong and Sweden. The Hong Kong version was made available in every school, with staff given training on its use. It thus became an early version of the e-learning WDP subsequently developed, and again introduced into Hong Kong. The Swedish version, also based on the PDC / WDP script, was given to parents of all children starting school in a municipality, and it will extend across Sweden later this year.

Screening

Due to the lack of a Welsh language screening test for use in schools in Wales, PDC / WDP made a grant application to the National Assembly for Wales in 2002, and with that being successful, commissioned the University of Wales Bangor Dyslexia Unit and Psychology department to develop a new screening tool. The aim was to provide a resource that classroom teachers could use, to help them recognise those children at risk of being dyslexic, and assist in schools developing appropriate learning and teaching strategies to meet the individual's need. This screening tool (standardized in Wales, is now available free of charge from PDC/ WDP's web site: www.welshdyslexia.info

European projects

When it comes to European Projects, PDC / WDP has led some of the most innovative dyslexia projects. The first was *Provision and use of ICT by dyslexic students in university in Europe.* Originally designed to include just five countries (Wales, England, Sweden, Greece and Hungary) the project expanded, with the project meetings also having participants from Austria, Egypt, Japan, Poland, Spain, Bulgaria and Romania, the latter two going on to form national dyslexia associations. Russia also attended the second workshop, and subsequently the Russian Dyslexia Association was formed.

The other major EU funded project is **Dystrain**, whose goal was to evaluate the difficulties of the dyslexic student in an e-learning environment. We developed an e-learning course on supporting the dyslexic child, which was accredited by Open College Network (Wales) at the end of 2005. This course has contributors from as far as Australia and Canada, and is now available in English, Welsh, Swedish, Romanian and Hungarian. This project was briefly outlined to the Department of Special Education in Brazil in February 2006 and they immediately saw its potential to teach the teachers in a country where there are few qualified to provide the specialist training in this country of 170 million people. Since the end of the Dystrain Project in July 2005, PDC / WDP has developed a further on-line e learning course on teaching and supporting children or young persons with dyslexia, the assignments for which can be undertaken through the medium of either Welsh or English.

Along the way, PDC / WDP has also had funding for other projects which have impacted in other areas. Among these is the idea of webcam support and remote diagnosis. This was pioneered by the PDC / WDP as a proof of concept thanks to support from the Welsh Council for Voluntary Action. The work was subsequently included in the WDP project Dystrain.It is also being considered in Canada, where an assessor may need to make a three-hour flight even in the same education authority.

Other initiatives

PDC / WDP was also responsible for funding the development and adapting **Ed-Word**, a free talking word processor, which enabled it to work with the Welsh language with Welsh menus and a Welsh voice. PDC / WDP acknowledges the support given by Canolfan Bedwyr, Bangor University as far as allowing us to have the use of the Welsh voice that they developed. This software program, available on CD free of charge, was launched by Helen-Mary Jones (National Assembly Member for Llanelli) at the National Assembly in January 2007. Since then, a large number have been given to schools who have asked for them, and to parents of children who receive their education through the medium of the Welsh language. As a by-product, it has now been adapted to provide the first such program in Brazil, again demonstrating the impact of the PDC / WDP approach to ensure wide access and support for the dyslexic individual. No doubt it will also be adapted for other languages in time, thereby helping even more dyslexics.

PDC / WDP runs regular conferences open to both the general public and those professionals interested or involved in dyslexia. It also produces a regular quarterly newsletter, downloadable from the web site. We also appreciate the contributions made by those prominent people in the field of dyslexia who have come to Wales to share their expertise, knowledge and advice with us. These include Gavin Reid, Lee Pascal, Neil Mackay, Ian Smythe, Anne Henderson, Kate Saunders, Lindsay Peer, Mike Jones (NESSY), Jackie Stordy, and the Staff from the Dyslexia Unit at Bangor University, all of whom who have certainly enlightened parents of dyslexic children in Wales.

PDC / WDP also developed a mission statement to guide development of resources. This included policies, resources and training. This model has been used as a point of reference for many colleagues worldwide, including Hong Kong, Kuwait and Brazil, and was the only such statement of its kind in the *International Book of Dyslexia*, which included information on 53 countries.

The future

All in all, it is possible to reflect that PDC / WDP has made an impact not only in Wales, but is helping change the face of support for dyslexics around the world. But this is not to say the job is done: not until every dyslexic child is given the support they need to have the opportunity to develop to their full potential. So let us celebrate not only the success of the last six years, but look forward to the innovation and developments that PDC/ WDP hopes to bring about in the future, when we will be aiming for the following goals:

- Welsh language Assessment test for Students entering Further Education, Colleges and Universities

- A National Advice and Resource Centre for Wales

- Free Telephone advice line for parents, carers , dyslexic individuals

- A Welsh language Predictive Text (with speech) Word Processing program

- A new or revised Welsh medium Reading Test

- The creation/ setting up of a number of Parent Support Groups across Wales (run and managed by parents)

- Securing funding to enable PDC / WDP to undertake specific projects in Wales

- Research on dyslexia and the Welsh language, with specific attention to dyslexia in Welsh as a second language, and identification and assessment of dyslexia in bilingual children in Wales.

- Securing core funding to enable PDC / WDP become a truly National Dyslexia Support organisation in Wales.

Michael Davies is a trustee of Prosiect Dyslecsia Cymru / Welsh Dyslexia Project.

Project INCLUDE: supporting dyslexic adults in Europe

Ian Smythe

The new European Dyslexia Association definition of dyslexia (March 2007) says that it "...is a difference in acquiring reading, spelling and writing skills, that is neurological in origin." It goes on to say: "The cognitive difficulties that cause these differences can also affect organisational skills, calculation abilities etc. It may be caused by a combination of difficulties in phonological processing, working memory, rapid naming, sequencing and the automaticity of basic skills." That is, dyslexia is not specific to any one language. Indeed, whatever the language, country or cultural context, there will always be some children in a class who have diverse neurological differences, and some of those differences will lead to reading and writing difficulties, and may be called dyslexic.

However, while dyslexia occurs in all languages and scripts, the nature of the language construction and script will affect the way it manifests itself. Thus the difficulties of dyslexics in English, Hungarian and Polish may be very different, even though they all use a Roman alphabet. Similarly, Bulgarians and Greek dyslexics using the Cyrillic script will also have diverse difficulties that are influenced by the language in question and its specific construction. In turn, the difficulties in the Roman alphabet languages and Cyrillic alphabet languages may be very different. These differences are due to many factors, including sound-letter correspondence, the use of prefixes and suffixes, importance of word order, grammar, orthographic similarities and general 'regularity'.

Why highlight these countries? Because they are the languages of the partner countries of an exciting EU-funded project led by the British Dyslexia Association that provides an online tool for identification of difficulties of the dyslexic individual, as well as providing support for them. However, before going into details, let us consider how we can still create a framework for testing across languages having said that there are such diversities across languages as well as between individuals in any one language. We can do this by looking at a case study. Consider the following difficulties of a young man:

- Driving illegally as could not pass the theory test

- Has problems in decoding the questions in driving theory

- Work includes telephone reception, which he finds difficult

- In work, has creative ideas but lacks confidence to share.

- Left/right confusions in production but not reception

- Poor memory to recall recent facts or multiplication tables.

- In writing, sentence construction was poor

- In writing, vocabulary was simpler than spoken

- Handwriting was CAPITALS, not cursive.

- Reading: without fluency

- Reading: making visual errors

- Has to re-read paragraphs repeatedly for understanding

The question is: What is his first language? The answer is that it is not clear from this, but the pattern of difficulties is familiar enough to say that his difficulties are consistent with somebody who is dyslexic. (His first and only language was Romanian.) It is this commonality of issues that allows us to create a common framework for assessment of strengths and weaknesses, as well as a (relatively) common support system.

About Project INCLUDE

If you were to count the number of adult dyslexics identified and supported in the UK, it is probably less than 10% of those who are dyslexic. Therefore it would be inappropriate to say that dyslexics are well catered for in the UK. However, at least the issues are being addressed at some level, and it is possible to look up services in this Handbook, BDA Dyslexia Contact and on the internet. However, if you consider that there are almost no books, services or identification tools to support the dyslexic adult in any of the languages of these partner countries, you will appreciate that the UK is comparatively well served but there is still much to be done in other languages.

Project INCLUDE was developed out of the identification of this need to provide support for the dyslexic individual in different languages, and particularly for those entering vocational training. The partnership identified two potential routes: a) development of a support system which involved training support workers for ongoing support, and b) to provide as much support as possible through a self-supporting mechanism. In the circumstances it was realised that the latter was more sustainable, and did not burden partners with ongoing administrative costs. The finance provided by the EU was therefore able to help develop a website that provided the focus for a support system. This was seen as a way to empower the dyslexic individual, and provide support in many of the areas seen as difficulties.

Assessment of needs

The two main types of assessment are: (i) to understand difficulties, strengths, weaknesses and needs, and (ii) to establish the likely existence of dyslexia. The label 'dyslexia' is usually needed to access funding for the provision of services and resources for the individual. However, in most cases in the project partner countries, the label does not make any difference, since there are no services to be accessed. Furthermore, even with the label, it does not indicate what exactly is required. With this in mind, the concentration here was on the identification of the needs of the individual.

There are many areas that can be assessed. However, not all of them provide information that can be acted upon. As part of the consultative process, the development team consulted dyslexic adults and service providers, as well as researchers across Europe. It also took into consideration recommendations made in *Assessment of the dyslexic adult: A framework for Europe* a book chapter by Smythe and Siegel for another EU project. This led to the development of an 'assessment' tool, which included a questionnaire and a brief series of 'tests' that could be easily implemented into an internet-based tool for identification of both strengths and weaknesses.

Careful consideration was given to the terminology used to ensure that all users were clear that at no point would the results say that somebody is dyslexic. That requires a) a more in-depth assessment by a specialist, and b) a clear set of criteria, which currently do not exist across Europe. However, it was possible to say that the tool could identify those whose profile was consistent with those individuals diagnosed as dyslexic. In other words, the tool was tested with those who had been assessed as dyslexic as well as non-dyslexics and had been found to provide a good indication not only of dyslexia, but also some of the specific needs.

The test was made a brief as possible, without compromising the ability to help the individual. It includes a checklist, a brief spelling test, a memory test, a sound discrimination task, a 'parallel processing test' and a visual spatial task. These tests have all been used in the identification of the dyslexic individual across Europe. The tasks were chosen in an attempt to show not only 'traditional' difficulties, but also to address areas often seen as strengths in dyslexic individuals. The list is far from exhaustive, but may be considered by many as a starting point for a more in depth assessment. In many languages across Europe this will be the first opportunity they have to understand their difficulties.

Support

Most people assume that the support of the dyslexic individual will be specific to each language. To some extent that is true. If you are teaching phonics in Greek it will be different to phonics in English due to the nature of the language. However, in this project there is no attempt to teach the basic skills themselves, since the users will already be in vocational training and therefore have basic literacy skills.

However, consider the advice given on how to study for an exam: 'Take time to read the question carefully' is the same advice no matter what the language! It is this similarity that should allow Project INCLUDE to have a major impact across Europe, because the advice offered to the dyslexic adult is largely the same across countries, languages and cultures. Or to put it another way, what is good for the English dyslexic adult is also good for the Polish, Bulgarian, Hungarian and Greek dyslexic adult. The level and nature of additional support may vary, e.g. access to basic skills support. But how to study, how to support yourself, and how to acquire life skills are similar for most dyslexics irrespective of the language.

There is an old Chinese expression that says: 'Give a man a fish and he will have enough for a day. Teach him to fish and he will have enough for life.' It is this philosophy that the project uses by providing self-help rather than individuals who will provide long-term support. However, this was not to ignore the importance of understanding the role of personal support. As a result, a three-pronged approach was developed, which included: a) basic support literature; b) a CD of the support material; c) access to support advisors.

Support literature and CD

It would be unfair to give an individual with reading and writing difficulties a 100 page book on how to overcome their difficulties! But the information has to be provided in some format, and alternatives such as human or computer support have severe financial implications, particularly in some of the partner countries (e.g. in Bulgaria a teacher earns around £150 per month but computers cost the same as in England!). For this reason, the project took two approaches: a) develop the support material as a conventional book, and b) adapt the material to a CD with audio presentation using real people. This allows all individuals to access the material. The book is provided to all those who are assessed, and the CD is provided with the book. This ensures full accessibility.

The book includes chapters on an understanding of dyslexia, education and lifelong learning, life skills, employment, and understanding strengths and weaknesses, with contributors coming from Poland, Hungary and the UK.

Support advisors

While the emphasis was on self-help, each partner in the project also trained individuals to provide support through email and telephone to give personal advice to those who needed it. Although this proved to be of minimal need, it does ensure those using existing support services are well trained. This is an extension of the existing work of the BDA Helpline, but with other partner countries this was the first time such Helplines had been made available to dyslexic adults.

Conclusions

This project does not claim to have all the answers, but the positive response indicates the long overdue need in Bulgaria, Greece, Hungary and Poland as well as the UK. With partnerships now forming between the BDA and service providers such as Rathbone, it is clear that an easy to access system is appreciated as a good solution to providing a low cost support system that can have a real impact on the lives of many. If you want to find out more, check out the website at www.includedyslexia.eu

Reference

Smythe I and Siegel L (2005) Assessment of the dyslexic adult: A framework for Europe. In Smythe, I. (Ed.) *Provision and Use of Information Technology with Dyslexic Students in University in Europe.* Welsh Dyslexia Project. Cardiff. www.welshdyslexia.info/minerva/book.pdf

Dr Ian Smythe is an independent dyslexia consultant who specialises in dyslexia in different languages.

Dutch dyslexia policies: the 'Dyslexia Masterplan'

Tom Braams

Introduction

Over the last twenty years, the policy of the Dutch government has been to try to reduce the number of children referred to special schools. In a developent that is similar to the inclusion movement in UK education, teachers in mainstream schools were encouraged to increase their knowledge of how to teach children with special educational needs, and children diagnosed with dyslexia were not admitted to special schools anymore.

However, as a consequence of this policy, many children with severe reading and writing problems did not receive adequate help because the knowledge of primary school teachers and remedial teachers in mainstream schools was inadequate for the job. Furthermore, there was no general plan how to deal with these problems. This has led to an increasing demand for specialised assessments and treatments outside the schools, paid for by the parents of these children. Because of the very labour-intensive and specialised nature of the dyslexia assessments and treatments, this extracurricular help was only within reach of parents who could afford it. Many children, therefore, did not get proper treatment.

In 2003, increasing pressure on the Dutch government led to the establishment of an organised body with the remit to instigate appropriate intervention for dyslexic children within mainstream primary and secondary schools. Because of the very persistent nature of reading and writing disabilities in some dyslexic children, it was realised that specialised provision outside of mainstream schools was also necessary. So two goals were set: a well organised and efficient 'first line of care' for dyslexic children in mainstream schools and a cost-effective 'second line of care' in specialised dyslexia institutes, subsidised by the government.

Content and goals of the Dyslexia Masterplan

During the last ten to fifteen years a lot of instruments and materials have been developed for screening children for dyslexia at an early age, and for preventing and remediating reading and writing difficulties. The *Masterplan Dyslexie* body was formed to collate these programs, to fill the gaps and to implement all necessary procedures and knowledge. The main projects were:

1. Development of a procedure to recognise and remediate dyslexic children in primary and secondary education.

2. Implementation of this approach and increasing the expertise of teachers, remedial teachers and special educational needs coordinators (SENCos) about treating dyslexia in primary and secondary education,

3. Increase in knowledge on dyslexia of students at teacher training colleges.

4. Advancing dyslexia policies in schools, with boards of governors, and in 'cooperations' (clusters of schools).

5. Refining the support provided for dyslexic children at school, at home and by remedial teachers and specialists.

Although the Dyslexia Masterplan has not yet been fully implemented, most of it was evaluated in 2006. In the following part of this article I will give a summary of the projects, the evaluation and some personal critical remarks. Because of the wide scope of the Masterplan, a lot of the content will not be addressed in this article. For more details please see *Projectgroep Masterplan Dyslexie* (2004) and Ledoux et al (2006).

Developing the instruments

Protocols for ways of identifying students with dyslexic problems and ideas about effective and ineffective remediation, prevention and early recognition were developed for several levels of education, from the first years of primary school up to professional schools and university. A lot of emphasis was placed on monitoring the progress children make in reading and writing (and, in kindergarten, in oral language abilities). Inspired by English and American examples, remedial reading methods were developed for use with small groups of poor readers.

Primary schools in Holland are organised in 'cooperations', with one or more special schools. Schools can ask for advice and extra remedial teaching for students with very persistent problems from remedial teachers and psychologists working for this cooperation. These cooperations usually were the starting point for spreading knowledge to the schools. Conferences and workshops held by the Masterplan team were very well attended by co-workers of these cooperations. Instruments for monitoring and remediation were well accepted. The general feeling now is that this project was quite successful.

Implementing procedures and spreading knowledge

A high percentage of the primary schools started working with the dyslexia monitoring procedures. Most schools are very motivated, others are motivated by the Education Authorities in Holland. Increasingly, the Education Authorities require schools to make a dyslexia policy part of their educational reforms. In evaluating the Masterplan, many interviewees believe the sharing of knowledge has not penetrated well enough into the classrooms. My personal guess is that less than a third of the teachers use special reading techniques that are up to standard. The forefront of the teachers are doing well, the 'trend followers', however, will need more training and persuasion to follow in the next few years.

The situation in secondary education is more problematic, because most subject teachers have very limited knowledge of dyslexia. Teachers of foreign languages (Dutch students learn English, German and French) are aware of dyslexia, but often lack guidelines what to do. Few teachers are aware that dyslexia can also cause problems with maths, geography, history, music and other subjects. School directors have the right to allow dyslexic students the use of all kinds of ICT aids and facilities, but sometimes they do not use these powers to the full. Some of them fear a negative response from Education Authorities; others don't consider facilities as 'rights' for dyslexic students. Dutch law is not very helpful: it gives the power of decision to school directors, which can lead to great inequality between schools.

Because of these limitations of knowledge and procedures in secondary education, parents of dyslexic primary school children choosing a secondary school are advised to obtain extensive information about the dyslexia friendliness of schools in their neighbourhood. Reaching all the subject teachers, to get them to teach in a dyslexia-friendly way is still a huge challenge.

Teacher training colleges

Although dyslexia is the most common disability in primary and secondary schools, until recently the management of most teacher training colleges felt no urgency to make dyslexia an integral part of the training curriculum. Consequently, most of the recently qualified teachers lack adequate knowledge of recognising, monitoring and working with dyslexic children. The evaluation results of the teacher training colleges by the Education Authorities and professionals in the field of education have not been very positive in the recent past.

In my opinion the poor professional status of teachers (compared with some decades ago) also plays an important role. Hardly any A-level students go to teacher training colleges anymore. In the summer of 2007, 25% of the students in teacher training in Holland failed an exam on arithmetic that was at 6th grade level! So while education is getting increasingly complex, and students have to be trained to become qualified teachers in the space of only three years, the intellectual level of the aspirant teachers is declining. If the desire of politicians in Holland is to have a well-educated population, steps have to be taken to upgrade the status (and wages) of teachers. The question 'what makes a teacher an excellent teacher' also requires much more careful study.

Advancing dyslexia policies in schools

Almost all primary and special schools, and all secondary schools, now have a dyslexia policy. As this is more or less required by the Education Authorities, and because dyslexia has been a hot topic in Holland in the last few years, this is not surprising. In particular, most SENCos (in primary school usually teachers who received a supplemental training, in secondary education often remedial teachers or psychologists) are up-to-date in their knowledge of the items developed within the framework of the Masterplan.

Collaboration with parents and other professionals

When a dyslexic child gets professional treatment outside school, it is very important that there is close cooperation between specialist and teacher. However, the way that dyslexia institutes work together with schools varies and, as yet, there is no standard in which information is transferred from school to the institute and vice-versa. Protocols are needed to deal with this systematically, particularly once dyslexia institutes have been formally appointed as 'second line of care' and have an official role in assessment and remediation of children with very persistent dyslexia.

Second line of care

Preparations for specialist care of children with dyslexia outside schools, were made alongside the Masterplan. In 2002, a proposal by the Health Care Insurance Board (CVZ) was made to add specialist dyslexia care to the *Cure Insurance Act*. In Holland there is system of private insurance companies, which have to provide a minimum health care program for everyone. The basic content of health care is laid down in the *Cure Insurance Act* but companies are allowed to compete on provision of additional extra care and on premiums charged. At the time, however, not all the problems concerning which children were to be admitted to this specialist dyslexia care were solved. In subsequent years, key questions arose, such as how many children will qualify (the estimate is around 3.5%), and how to assess children with dyslexia in a scientifically sound way. Nevertheless, most professionals concerned are confident that specialised dyslexia assessment and treatment will be part of the *Cure Insurance Act 2008*.

Conclusions

The Dyslexia Masterplan body played a very important role in integrating all efforts and in making sure that all the elements necessary for a comprehensive dyslexia policy were in place. In my opinion, excellent work has been done in devising procedures and in developing materials for prevention, remediation and assessment of dyslexia. The transfer of information to SENCos and other dyslexia specialists has also gone well. The most difficult part of the process is (always) to reach all teachers in primary schools and subject teachers in secondary schools. To get them to apply all the recommended methods of good practice will only happen if they receive additional training. A statutory obligation for teachers to have a certain amount of additional training each year would be a step in the right direction.

References

Ledoux, G., Peetsma, T., Emmelot, Y., Boogaard, M., & Emans, B. (2006). *Evaluatie Masterplan Dyslexie*. Amsterdam: SCO-Kohnstamm Instituut van de Faculteit der Maatschappij- en Gedragswetenschappen, Universiteit van Amsterdam (SCO-rapport nr. 747), projectnummer 44507.

Projectgroep Masterplan Dyslexie EN/WSNS+/KPC Groep (2004). *Masterplan Dyslexie*. Z.p.: EN/WSNS+/KPC Groep.

Important websites about the *Dyslexia Masterplan* and about procedures and materials:
www.masterplandyslexie.nl
www.steunpuntdyslexie.nl/sitemanager.asp?pid=771
www.taalonderwijs.nl/dyslexie

Tom Braams is an educational psychologist in Holland who specialises in learning disabilities. He is director of one of Holland's leading dyslexia institutes. He has written many books and articles on dyslexia and has produced Dutch versions of the well-known UK programs Wordshark and Numbershark.

Tintin helps dyslexic learners

Judith Sanson

Tintin helps dyslexic learners is a CD produced by the BBC for *Dyslexia International – Tools and Technologies* (DITT), a non-profit international all-volunteer organisation based in Brussels that works with leading experts to create and promote tools and technologies that enable young dyslexic learners to succeed in a competitive world. The story on the CD is *The Mystery of the Lost Letters – an adventure on the Road to Success.* In this story you join Tintin, the intrepid boy reporter and his trusty dog Snowy. They are there, ready to assist you, along with all dyslexic learners worldwide, and their mentors, too.

Development of the project

When BBC producer Gail Block first came to Brussels to meet DITT members, she was still scribbling down notes in her book until way past midnight, hearing one story after another from dyslexic learners of all ages and their parents. The themes were the common ones: failure and frustration. Rising to the challenge, DITT set out to look for partners to make an innovative tool to make a difference. The Levi Strauss Donor Advised Fund at Charities Aid Foundation, Cable & Wireless, and Microsoft all gave their much appreciated backing. By then DITT had already been granted permission by the Hergé Foundation for Tintin to take part.

Under the direction of Andrew Law, head of BBC Worldwide Interactive Learning, a unique new CD ROM, fun and interactive, was planned. This was to be an educational tool specifically designed, first to counteract the debilitating loss of self-esteem and to get dyslexic learners past the first hurdle of feeling worthless; second, to give the learners a chance to get a grip over how they learn, and third, to provide scientific evidence for dyslexia and how it may be handled not only to the sympathetic mentors but to the non-dyslexic sector – the 90% or so – for whom dyslexia still means 'getting the letters the wrong way round, or something.'

Throughout production, the BBC regularly consulted a focus group of dyslexics – adults and children - who critiqued and added their views on font, colour backgrounds and preferred designs for icons. Whilst BBC settled on 8-13 years as the target age group, in different part of Europe the CD has been used successfully by learners of all ages, helping them tap into their individual talents.

What is on the CD?

How was the CD designed to address these issues? As they go in, users are first welcomed and directed on how to join Tintin on a quest to find Professor Calculus who is hidden in castle, collecting clues as they go.

1. Raising morale

In the first stop - *Hall of Fame* - by playing a game of hide-and-seek, seven successful dyslexic celebrities can be discovered. In short filmed interviews they tell how they overcame their feelings of worthlessness and despair and how they dealt with their dyslexia at school and got on with their lives to develop their gifts. The interviewees included architect Lord Richard Rogers, poet Benjamin Zephaniah, eight-time world memory champion Dominic O'Brien, and famous French singer Hugues Aufray as well as a famous furniture designer and a well-known television presenter.

The spoken text can be read on screen as each one speaks and biographies are there too – a treasure trove of material for teachers or parents to discuss with their dyslexic learners alongside.

2. Discovering individual learning styles

In the *Hall of Mirrors* users explore how they learn best through a series of colourful quizzes. The questions give rise to discussion points that make for a lively exchange whether the CD is being used in a group setting or simply by the user and his or her mentor.

In the *Dangerous Dungeons* users face up to their challenges and are given tips on overcoming their difficulties, before scaling the *Tower of Triumph* to win a print out of their profile that offers positive feedback on how to build on strengths and advice on how to cope with weaknesses in addition to a certificate of completion.

Dr Gavin Reid is the mind behind the *Hall of Mirrors* and *Dangerous Dungeon*. The games-like approach of these sections masks a sophisticated diagnostic tool which builds a profile of how the user learns best, cognitively, socially and environmentally.

3. A mine of information

The bookcase in the *Main Hall* is a mine of information. Articles by twelve leading experts, including members of DITT's Scientific Advisory Committee, provide information on the brain, diagnostics, teaching methods, technologies, giftedness, vision, parenting, multilingualism and other key aspects of dealing with dyslexia. These may be read online or printed out (40+ pages).

Going global with Tintin

In Belgium, where DITT has its offices, Tintin is a national hero. But he is also loved throughout the world, translated into more than 60 languages with over 200 million copies of his adventures sold. In 2009, when Steven Spielberg is due to start work on the films of Tintin, his fame will spread even wider.

Thanks to Tintin, DITT teams were invited to the prestigious *Microsoft Government Leaders Forum* in Rome in 2003, and in 2004 to give a presentation on dyslexia at a meeting attended by members of the Education Committee at the European Council of Ministers - Europe's highest legislative body. The launch of the CD, with full television coverage, was held at the Royal Palace in Brussels in the presence of Her Majesty Queen Fabiola and DITT Patron, Her Royal Highness Princess Margaretha of Liechtenstein.

DITT has already sent complimentary copies with promotional literature of *The Mystery of the Lost Letters* to British Councils and Goethe Institutes across the world. Complimentary copies of the CD will be also given to over 400 delegates from 193 member States attending the World Dyslexia Forum in 2009.

DITT has many links with the British Dyslexia Association, including sharing film sequences in making the BBC film *Language Shock – Dyslexia across cultures.* Judith Stansfield of the BDA New Technologies Committee acted as consultant on the CD and the accompanying website. Her support and encouragement and that of Sue Flohr of the BDA continue to be invaluable. Reviewing *The Mystery of the Lost Letters* Susan Tressman, former Education Director of the BDA said: "I thoroughly enjoyed working with this material, which I found to be innovative, engaging, with a clear audio facility and excellent use of colour options and graphics. It was user friendly and sustained my interest throughout. This CD is a valuable and novel addition to teachers and all those involved with extending learning opportunities for students with dyslexia and other literacy needs. It will assist learners in understanding the way they learn and how to develop strategies to enable them to realise their full potential."

DITT's website offers many free resources for dyslexics, their parents and teachers, including the film *Language Shock – Dyslexia across cultures,* a 28-minute video by the BBC in which DITT was involved [www.ditt-online.org/Pack/Video.htm]. It is about dyslexic young people in Europe, showing the devastating effects on the individual and society when the problem is ignored, and offering key principles for remedial help. This film with its accompanying guide in five European languages has been distributed to ministries of education across Europe. At the World Dyslexia Forum at UNESCO Paris in 2009, it will be offered to ministries of education in over 190 countries and their television circuits.

Further information may be found at www.ditt-online.org, including a powerpoint presentation and information on the linked website www.ToSuccess.org. This, with Tintin illustrations, contains a catalogue of recommended resources put together by young dyslexic learners and their mentors, called the *Winners Team*. They select and recommend tools and technologies that help dyslexic learners with reading, writing, spelling, keyboard, maths, memory, organisation, and languages.

So what counts as 'success' for dyslexic learners and their mentors? For many young people it is no more than 'to be like the others'; to able to work and study like their classmates, without struggling helplessly. For the mentors success may mean greater understanding, finding empathy and cooperation in those non-dyslexic parts of society that fail to understand dyslexia and therefore offer little support.

Judith Sanson is Executive Director of Dyslexia International – Tools and Technologies (DITT).

Dyslexia in adulthood

Dyslexia and dyspraxia: assessment for adults

Sylvia Moody

In recent years information on dyslexia and dyspraxia in adulthood has become more widely available and, as a result, adults of all ages – from twenty-something to eighty-something – are now coming forward in ever greater numbers to request assessments. Some people need an assessment because of difficulties with their work or studies; others simply want a better understanding of themselves. It can take some courage to have an assessment, but it is very rare to hear of anyone who has regretted the decision to do so.

It may be that the reader of this article is at this moment wondering if s/he would benefit from an assessment. If this is the case, I would advise you to inform yourself about dyslexia and/or dyspraxia by consulting the websites of the *British Dyslexia Association* (BDA) [www.bdadyslexia.org.uk] and the *Developmental Adult Neuro-Diversity Association* (DANDA) [www.achieveability.org.uk].. On both sites you will find information sheets and checklists. If you find you tick a lot of items on the checklists, then perhaps you should consider a full assessment.

You may also have the opportunity to take a screening test. However, you need to be aware that screening tests have limitations: they do not always pick up milder types of dyslexic difficulty and, conversely, they can sometimes suggest that difficulties are more severe than they really are. The only way to be absolutely sure if you have dyslexic/dyspraxic difficulties to any significant degree, and to fully understand the nature of them, is to have a full diagnostic assessment. In this article three types of assessment will be described: 1) diagnostic assessment, 2) needs assessment in further or higher education, and 3) workplace needs assessment.

Diagnostic assessment

A diagnostic assessment must precede either of the two types of needs assessment.

Where can I find an assessor?
Contact the local branch of the BDA or DANDA for a recommendation.

Can I get funding for an assessment?
A diagnostic assessment usually has to be done privately. Fees currently range from around £300 to around £500. If you have private medical insurance, these organisations may sometimes fund the assessment, and a limited number of bursaries are available from the main dyslexia organisations. If you are in further or higher education, there is a good chance that your college will provide funding, and if you are in the workplace, then your employer may do so.

What happens in the assessment?
The assessor will talk with you about your perceptions of your strengths and difficulties, take a relevant history, and administer a wide variety of tests which will give indications of dyslexia and/or dyspraxia. The tests fall broadly into two types: (a) cognitive tests, which look at abilities such as phonology, memory, reasoning, perception; and (b) literacy tests. In adult assessments, it is vital that the literacy tests include not just tests of basic reading skills (single word reading and spelling) but also tests of higher-level skills, such as reading with comprehension and recall, note taking and structuring written work.

What should I expect from the assessment report?
At the end of the assessment, the assessor should clearly explain to you the results of the assessment, and the recommendations

he/she has made. However, this same information should be presented again clearly in the report. In particular, there should be detailed recommendations for an individual tuition programme, IT support and other study aids. If you are in FE/HE, there will be also recommendations about concessions for examinations and coursework. If you are in the workplace, there should be *general* recommendations for an individual training programme, IT support, and ways in which an employer can be helpful. It is important to note, however, that the recommendations made in the diagnostic assessment report will be very general, and will act only as pointers to the more detailed recommendations which will be made in a subsequent HE needs assessment or workplace needs assessment.

Needs assessment for the Disabled Students Allowance (DSA)

If you are in higher education, or if you are in further education but planning to go on to an HE college, you will need to follow up your diagnostic assessment with a needs assessment. The needs assessment is funded by your local education authority (LEA), and is usually done at a centre, and by an assessor, specified by the LEA. This assessment does not involve further tests. Rather, you will discuss with the needs assessor the general recommendations made in your diagnostic report, determine exactly what your needs will be in terms of tuition and equipment, and get these needs costed, so that the LEA knows how much funding they are being asked to make available.

You will receive a copy of the needs assessment report, and it is important that you take this back to your college and discuss it with your dyslexia support advisor. If you and the advisor feel that the needs report is deficient in any way, you can request that the report be revised accordingly.

If you are planning to go up to university, it is preferable to go through this process of having a diagnostic and needs assessment before you begin your university course; otherwise it could be well into your second term before funding for support is available to you. For this to happen, one of the following three things must apply:

1. You are willing to fund the initial diagnostic assessment yourself.

2. Your future university is willing to fund the diagnostic assessment once they have given you a definite place.

3. You already have a diagnostic assessment (done since your sixteenth birthday), which the LEA is happy to accept.

Workplace needs assessment

If you are in the workplace and have had a diagnostic assessment then you need to follow this up with a workplace needs assessment (WNA) in order to receive appropriate help and support. The WNA looks in greater detail at the support you need in the form of training and equipment, and also makes recommendations for help that your employer can provide.

Sources of funding

Funding for the support you need could come either directly from your employer or from the government's *Access to Work* scheme. To begin the application process for the latter, you need to personally telephone your local *Access to Work Business Centre* and request an application form. Although you fill in this form yourself, your employer needs to know that you are making the application, as they will be asked to make some contribution to the expenses involved.

Arranging a workplace needs assessment

There are two ways of arranging an assessment, each of which has advantages and disadvantages. The first way is to arrange the assessment through *Access to Work*. The advantage of this route is that *Access to Work* will pay for the assessment. Possible disadvantages are that your assessment may not be carried out by a dyslexia specialist and, consequently, an individual dyslexia tuition training programme may not be specified.

The second route is to go through a *private dyslexia organisation* which specialises in carrying out workplace needs assessments and in writing reports in a form required by *Access to Work*. If you do approach a private organisation (or practitioner) to get a needs assessment, it is essential that you check that they are qualified to offer this service. Your local dyslexia association should be able to help you find a suitable assessor. The disadvantage of the private route is that you or your employer will have to fund the assessment. The advantage, however, is that the assessment will certainly be carried out by a dyslexia expert, who will be able to specify a detailed training programme.

Whichever route you go on for assessment, you can still apply to *Access to Work* for the funding for the help you require.

Workplace needs assessment report

Your assessment report should include recommendations for *all* of the following:

- A detailed training programme which covers all aspects of literacy that are directly related to your work – e.g. research skills, writing reports, reading technical manuals. General work skills should also be covered, e.g., dealing with job interviews or work reviews, contributing to meetings, understanding instructions, time management, organisational skills. An initial training programme should ideally be around 30 hours spread over a period of at least three months.

- A list of IT recommendations and specific recommendations for how the IT training is going to be carried out. It is not useful for training to be delivered in just one day, or one half-day; rather it should be spread out over several short sessions. The trainer should be knowledgeable about dyslexia and deliver the training in a manner and at a pace suitable for a dyslexic learner.

- Detailed recommendations to the employer about what actions they can take to support the programme, for example, giving time off for training, providing a quiet workspace, etc.

- If the report you receive does not include *all* of the above recommendations, you should take up the matter with the assessor, or with the organisation that has provided the assessor, and request relevant additions to the recommendations. It is important to stress this point, because it frequently happens that dyslexic employees, after going through the long process of diagnostic and needs assessments, do not get the training provided in a manner which enables them to make efficient use of all the help that they are given. Adequate training can make all the difference between keeping and losing a job.

More detailed information about assessments at all levels from 16+ can be found in Dr Sylvia Moody's *Lifetime Dyslexia Guides*:

- *Dyslexia: A Teenager's Guide* (Random House)
- *Dyslexia: Surviving and Succeeding at College* (Routledge)
- *Dyslexia: How to Survive and Succeed at Work* (Random House).

Dr Sylvia Moody is an educational psychologist working with the Dyslexia Assessment and Consultancy in London. For further information visit www.dyslexiaassessmentandconsultancy.co.uk

Dyslexia at work

Katherine Kindersley

Frequent questions from employers

- Is dyslexia covered by the Disability Discrimination Act (DDA)?
- Is dyslexia only about literacy?
- Why is the workplace difficult for those with dyslexia?
- Can people's skills improve?
- How can an employer help?
- What are dyslexia friendly workplaces?

It is encouraging that many employers are asking these questions and there is a growing awareness and understanding of dyslexia at work. This is important because without support, many dyslexic adults are unable to work to their potential. "It can be really frustrating," explains Jeff from BT, "it's like trying to unscrew a jar. You know it can be done, and that you are capable of it, yet you're still unable to do it. The frustration can be enormous, and the more frustrated you get, the worse your dyslexia can become." Many dyslexic adults have high levels of anxiety about areas of work performance and report a mix of the following.

- going to untold lengths to conceal their difficulties
- living in fear of being 'exposed'
- feeling a lack of confidence and self-esteem

With the right information and answers to the above questions, employers can bring about changes in the workplace, helping to create an inclusive environment where differences are welcomed, abilities recognised and difficulties are supported. Such environments can bring about significant improvements in work performance. The whole organisation can become more productive and successful and a happier place to work.

Is dyslexia covered by the Disability Discrimination Act?

Yes. The DDA protects those with dyslexia (and other forms of learning difficulties) and employers are expected to make 'reasonable adjustments' so that dyslexic people are not significantly disadvantaged at work. The legal framework covers all organisational processes, from initial recruitment and interviews, to terms of employment, to promotion and training opportunities, to dismissal and redundancy procedures. For example, interviews, testing and assessment cannot be organised or conducted in a way that will discriminate against those with dyslexia. Even if a person's difficulties are not thought severe enough to earn the protection of the DDA, many employers are willing to meet their responsibilities and to support all their employees in a fair and reasonable way.

While it may be very difficult for an employee to talk to a manager about dyslexic difficulties, it is also hard for an employer to provide the right kind of support if dyslexia is kept hidden. Jeff confides: "When your self-esteem is low, you are reluctant to put your head above the parapet, in fact it is the last thing you feel like doing. You just want to get on, head down, unnoticed." However, once Jeff decided to talk about his dyslexia openly, he received 'fantastic' support from his managers. An assessment led to him receiving one-to-one training and assistive software, allowing him to dictate to his computer and hear text read back to him. He now encourages others to share their concerns with their manager.

Is dyslexia only about literacy?

No. Dyslexia is characterised by weaknesses in short-term and working memory, processing speed, phonology (sound processing skills), and sometimes visual processing problems. These affect reading and writing efficiency, but also a range of other activities, particularly those where memory and organisational skills are important.

Difficulties are commonly seen in the following activities at work:

- **Reading:** emails / letters / reports / instructions / technical manuals

- **Writing:** spelling, grammar and punctuation / emails / letters / reports / taking notes / completing records and forms

- **Memory and concentration:** following spoken instructions / writing down telephone messages / names / remembering where things have been filed / concentrating for long times / thinking in a focused way

- **Organisation:** organising the day's activities / forward planning / time management / files/ papers / meeting deadlines / working efficiently / doing things quickly enough

- **Data:** working with numbers / entering information into databases / making calculations

- **Sequencing:** filing / putting things into order / prioritising tasks

- **Visual and motor skills:** activities requiring manual dexterity / analysing tables / graphs / proof-reading / skimming text / following directions / finding one's way

- **Other difficulties at work**: spoken language situations / following and contributing clearly to discussions / organising thoughts clearly / explaining things

Why is the work environment difficult for those with dyslexia?

There are many reasons why workplaces can be unfriendly, or even hostile for those with dyslexia. In recent years, changes in work cultures have often made things more difficult. In general, there is an emphasis on strong and speedy written and verbal communication skills. A significant change is that all jobs now seem to require literacy, with record keeping, form completion, email and written correspondence. Henry, for example, is a successful locksmith working for a big organisation, but he knew he was not doing as much as he could, particularly in training young locksmiths, because he was afraid of writing things down. "A workmate laughed at a word I got wrong on an email, and when he told me why he was laughing, I felt really embarrassed." Fortunately, Henry has now been assessed as dyslexic and is getting support. With assistive software, he is currently developing a training manual to help a young team of locksmiths.

Other causes of difficulty at work:

- Workplaces can make particular demands on memory and organisational skills, commonly specific areas of difficulty for adults with dyslexia

- Timescales are short and deadlines are tight

- There is an emphasis on multi-tasking

- Work processes and systems are often rigid and there is little opportunity for manoeuvre or to do things differently

- There is more performance management, more surveillance, job intensification, long hours culture, more short-term contracts, less representation from, for example, trade unions, more stress

Dyslexic difficulties are sometimes uncovered by a change in circumstances. There may be a change in the job description, a role change, or a new manager. It might be a promotion, which demands a greater reliance on written communication. It may be that some strategy for support has been taken away – perhaps a friendly colleague who always helped has moved on – or there are changed circumstances at home that leave the individual without a support system.

Can people's skills improve?

Yes. Appropriate specialist training can help adults with dyslexia improve their skills in all areas of employment. The particular needs of an individual employee will be identified at the assessment stage and a good report will highlight where the focus of the training should be.

A skills development programme might include specific training in:

- Ways of holding onto and recalling information
- Organising thought
- Planning activity and time
- Understanding new information, and applying new knowledge
- Following spoken and written instructions
- Different reading strategies – to support more accurate and more efficient reading
- Managing and taking control of incoming information
- Spoken language situations: conversations, discussions, meetings, presentations
- Developing confidence and self-esteem
- Ways of managing stress

The specialist trainer will be able to tailor make an appropriate programme to help the individual employee meet the specific requirements of the particular job. The trainer will work with real tasks, introducing basic level skills where necessary, but using material appropriate for an adult. He will normally be able to give advice on IT and electronic and technical aids. He will be able to liaise with the employers, advising on any further helpful measures that they could take to support the programme.

Many adults regard individual training as the most valuable element of a support programme because of the way it can improve skills and increase confidence. It is important that the workplace needs assessment specifies this training and recognises that the needs of dyslexic adults are unlikely to be met by short intensive courses. Michael, who works in a housing association said: "After some months of training, I was managing much better and it was great when the people I worked with really began to notice a difference in what I was able to do."

There is also much support available from equipment and assistive software. The particular IT support will be identified at the needs assessment stage, and may include digital recorders to record discussions and meetings, voice recognition software, software to read text aloud, programs to help organise and prioritise ideas and activities.

How can an employer help?

It is hard for individuals to succeed in isolation and the most successful outcomes are where the employer and the organisation are working together and the workplace culture is a supportive and inclusive one. Employers operating in an increasingly competitive commercial world may feel it is not easy to create dyslexia-friendly work environments, but it can be done. Many adjustments are relatively easy to introduce and are not expensive. General recommendations might be that managers become informed about dyslexia difficulties and their effects, both practical and emotional, and accept that individuals may need to work in different ways.

Flexible working practices can provide good support:

■ Provide a quiet work room so employees can have times of working without interruption

- Allow employees to come in early or stay later to find quieter work times

- Allow more time than usual for tasks to be completed if needed (not all tasks are urgent)

- Allow absence from work for training

- Modify procedures for testing / assessment

- Allow adjustments to processes, or redesign jobs to take into account employees' strengths

- Focus on outcomes, not methods (e.g. minutes of meetings to be taken from a tape-recorder)

Consideration of the way information is presented can be important for an employee with dyslexia. Good practice guidelines are to:

- Give simple and direct instructions and supply written back up

- Present information in clear and/or in different formats

- Give advance notice of tasks whenever possible rather than setting sudden deadlines

- Provide reading material in advance of meetings

- Summarise main points at end of discussions or meetings

- Keep emails succinct and to the purpose; use bullet points whenever possible

- Try to avoid frequent or mid-task interruptions

- Give help with prioritising tasks as necessary

- Allow employee access to note or reference material

It may be helpful to provide printed material on coloured paper, adjust the colour or contrast of computer screen background colour, adjust the lighting in the office, check the employee's position in relation to entrances, exits, photocopier, kettle, lift lobbies etc. There are countless numbers of small and specific adjustments which can make a difference to an employee's performance and which can be identified through careful analysis of the work environment and work practice.

What are dyslexia friendly workplaces?

They are workplaces where the organisation as a whole understands that people with dyslexia can provide a valuable contribution, but that they may need to use different approaches or different processes. They are organisations prepared to put in appropriate support, and show a positive engagement with promoting the skills of all employees. They recognise that people with dyslexia may have special strengths. Dyslexic adults are often hard-working and determined. They may be creative and innovative, good at problem solving, able to find solutions with an intuitive insight. They may have particularly strong powers of visualisation.

The good news is that as awareness of dyslexia in employment grows, more and more companies and organisations are engaged in promoting good practice and are willing to develop anticipatory measures to support diversity in the workforce. If – as is estimated – approximately 10% of any workforce has dyslexia, it is important for there to be a partnership between employer and employee so we can move forwards.

Further information

Moody, S. (2006). *Dyslexia: How to survive and succeed at work.* Random House.

www.workingwithdyslexia.com for information on workplace issues, adult dyslexia assessment; training for individuals; courses for dyslexia specialists and awareness training for employers.

http://www.jobcentreplus.gov.uk/JCP/Customers/ Helpfordisabledpeople/Accesstowork/index.html click on 'Access to Work Team Addresses' for regional contact details.

Katherine Kindersley specialises in provision, training and support for people with dyslexia in the workplace. She is based at the Dyslexia Assessment and Consultancy and Dyslexia Teaching Centre, London.

New technology to support adults with dyslexia

EA Draffan

New technologies appear and disappear rather too quickly to make this article as up-to-date as one would wish. However, various gadgets and software that can be useful for adults with dyslexia have appeared over the last few years. I have reviewed these under the headings: communication, recording, planning, reading and writing. The last section includes spell checking on the web when filling in text fields in a browser like *Internet Explorer (1)* and *Mozilla Firefox (2)*. (The numbers refer to internet addresses that are listed at the end of the chapter.)

Communication

It is said there are more mobile phones in the UK than there are people (3) but how many of us spend time squinting at the screen or mis-reading messages? It is possible, especially on the latest Windows mobile operating system (4) phones, to enlarge the text through the Accessibility options. These are often found under the settings menu.

If you want to remove patterns or pictures from the home screen of your Windows mobile phone and make the text more readable, try linking (synchronising) the phone to a computer and adding a small picture that you have made of a plain colour, in my case dark blue. This can be added to the home screen menu under background image and can increase the contrast between text and background.

When writing messages or SMS, it is possible to speed text input with various predictive systems. Most phones now have what is called a T9 option or similar software. This means you do not have to press a key several times to reach each letter. The software works out what the word is likely to be and attempts to finish it by offering a possible next letter or even word in some cases. Beware – you need to look at what you have written or 'home' becomes 'good', 'gone', 'hood', 'hoof' or even 'goof'!

It is also possible to add speech to your mobile phone depending on the make – **Smart Hal (5)** from Dolphin is one option. Other phones such as Nokia, Panasonic and Samsung have **Nuance TALKS (6)** and **ZOOMS(7)** that offer magnification. The RNIB produces a useful fact sheet that discusses these programs and other accessible mobile phones (8). The **Nokia 5500 (9)** is an example of a phone that has text-to-speech for messaging as part of the system and the new **Emporia Life (10)**, offers simple menus, easy buttons, a flashlight, emergency number button on the back, good volume control, an alarm function and substantial vibration if silent mode is needed but a reminder is still necessary. It may not be the all-singing and dancing **iPhone (11)** equivalent, but it is an easy-to-use mobile phone with a large screen and keypad!

Sadly, the cost of good quality synthesised voices, whether on a computer or phone, makes some of these options expensive and phones that can be used on any network such as the Emporia Life tend to cost more.

Handheld organisers

Most mobile phones and personal digital assistants (PDAs) can help with planning and time management. Some use Microsoft operating systems and the company offers some hints and tips (12) on how you can organise you life! Many of these devices have alarms, memo recording facilities and a camera for snap shot reminders. You can link up with a computer to set up task lists, appointments and phone books, so that numbers and addresses need only be added once and a back-up is kept on the computer just in case.

There are two main operating systems for handheld organisers. The table below offers some broad comparisons.

Pocket PC Handhelds	Palm OS Handhelds
■ faster Processor ■ multimedia (video/ audio) ■ familiar Windows interface ■ native MS Office integration ■ multi-tasking ■ shorter battery life ■ more expensive	■ slower processor ■ multimedia (limited) ■ extensive additional software ■ simpler interface ■ uni-tasking ■ longer battery life ■ less expensive

Both systems offer the colour and text size options. On the Pocket PC this is possible through the themes offered and many free programs. The Palm operating system also comes with some changes but not with the flexible options offered by programs such as *Butterfly (13)*,which allows you to set a variety of colours for different elements.

The onscreen keyboards or thumb keyboards tend to be small but text input can be speeded through letter- or word-prediction. It is possible to download programs such as *Dasher (14)* or *WordLogic (15)* for Pocket PC handhelds and *Quickwrite (16)* for the Palm OS.

Magnification, text-to-speech and many other utilities are available for both systems. It is best to browse through websites such as www. PocketGear.com, www.palmgear.com or www.mobilesystems.co.uk. There are also office packages, dictionaries for many languages, spell checkers, calendars, planners, mind mapping, and many other items available.

TechDis (17) has some useful notes for those using PDAs for learning. It is often possible to record notes on a PDA, just as you can on some mobile phones, but for lengthy meetings it is best to use digital voice recorders.

Recording

Many digital recorders have become easier to use with more tactile buttons and links to computers for storing audio files. The *Olympus DS-30, DS-40* or *DS-50 (18)* are good recorders, with quality speech output and ease of use, with a clear, readable screen and voice or sound feedback for the actions. The main difference between recorders is the amount of storage space offered by the flash memory. They all use DSS player software to link to a computer and can be used with speech recognition. That is when the user records messages or dictates notes. The trained speech recognition software such as Dragon Naturally Speaking can transcribe the audio file directly into a text window. Other recorders such as Sony and Philips offer similar systems. Sadly, good results are not always possible when you try to record someone else's voice and they have not trained on the speech recognition software.

These recorders tend to save files as .WMA, .WAV or MP3 and if you want to make notes about the recording this cannot be done within the software that comes with the devices. However, there is a software program called *Audio Notetaker (19)* that not only allows you to make notes by the recording, but also to see the audio file in a series of dashes and spaces representing the spoken phrases. It is possible to colour code these for importance and to change their size and spacing. Text and background colours can also be changed. If a collection of phrases all about one topic is needed from several recordings, it is possible to make up projects with the collection. Copy and paste the sections, date, title and summarise them and they become searchable for use later.

Recorders provide good audio reminder tools for those who like to listen rather than read memos. After they have been downloaded onto a computer, audio files can be linked to calendar applications or mind-mapping programs.

Planning and organising tools

Both Mac and Windows computers come with diaries and calendars. If you have XP you need Microsoft Office to have a diary/calendar that is linked to e-mails, task lists and notes in the form of Outlook. Vista has its own calendar so you can get away with a free office suite such as *OpenOffice (20)*.

It is possible to use programs such as Microsoft PowerPoint or Keynote 3 for Mac as a way of planning events or projects as the slides can be shuffled in any order with pictures, text and links to websites. A free option as part of the OpenOffice is *Impress*. The outline view offered by these programs can be exported to a word processor to provide headings or the main points when writing articles etc.

If you prefer diagrams and working in a graphical way then there are a number of mind-mapping or concept-mapping programs available. In fact, the number available has expanded to such an extent that it is hard to choose which one provides the best support for chosen tasks. *Inspiration (21)* now offers a Tony Buzan (22) type format, as well as the usual layout of lines leading to shapes that have text, pictures and can be used with different colours to aid the memory as well as set priorities.

Tony Buzan has his own mind mapping tool called *iMindMap* but there are many free versions of mapping programs such as *Freemind (23)* and even online versions such *MindMeister (24)*. Most of these programs allow you to take the diagram into an outline view that can provide a basis for a report or assignment.

Reading and writing

Whether reading web pages or items that have been saved to the computer it is usually the file format (e.g. plain web page, Word doc, Adobe PDF, or Excel spreadsheet) that dictates which program is most suitable for reading the text. However, there are programs such as *TextHelp Read and Write (25)* or *ClaroRead 2007 (26)* that will cope with all these types of files as long as they have been made in an accessible way. Sometimes it is possible to check this by running the mouse cursor over the text to see if it highlights.

There are also many free text readers available, such as one designed specifically for Microsoft Word called **WordTalk (27)** or **NaturalReader (28)**, which can cope with accessible web and Adobe .PDF pages. They do not offer spell checking, dictionaries or scanning support and tend to use the clipboard function for accessing the text.

When reading or writing on the computer it may help to change the background colours. Programs such as **Readable (29)** and a free option called **Colour Explorer (30)** offer this function and **ClaroView (31)** provides a virtual colour tinted overlay for the whole screen. Most operating systems also offer background colour changes through their control panels. This is also possible in Internet Explorer and Mozilla Firefox and it may help to follow guidelines provided by the **BBC My Web, My Way (33)**.

Text layout and font or letter changes are possible in Word processor packages such as Microsoft Word, Apple Works and OpenOffice. It is also possible to use freely available on-line writing and spreadsheet packages such as those offered by **Google (33)**, although a good internet connection is needed. If you are working through a browser and spelling is an issue, there is a free option for Internet Explorer called **ieSpell (34) Mozilla Firefox (35)** also has several add-ons, including dictionaries and an **Accessibar** that offers text to speech, colour and font changes.

If typing is slow or finding the right words is a problem **TextHelp Read and Write** and **ClaroRead** offer word prediction as does **Penfriend (36)**, but it may be enough to use **Autotext** in Word to complete a short form or predetermined sentence rather than need every word finished. **Dasher**, which has already been mentioned for the PDA also works on a PC and finishes words in a rather different way. The program zooms into a suitable next letter, when it has been selected, it continues in this fashion until the word, and then phrase or sentence is complete.

Where complex vocabulary is an issue, Autotext can be used but there is also a program called *Wordbar (37)* that provides a selection beneath the text being written. This can be useful where several words that sound and seem the same need to be used, as text to speech is also available. It is also possible to add your own database of words.

The world of speech recognition, where the user dictates a document or notes, has really improved over the last few years. *Dragon NaturallySpeaking (38)* for the Windows computer, is so much more accurate and involves virtually no training, although obviously with a good headset microphone and using the guides offered by the program results can be improved. *IListen (39)* is available for Mac users and if you have ventured into the world of *Microsoft Vista* you will find the operating system has a free speech recognition application. It may not be as accurate as *Dragon NaturallySpeaking* or have all the user options with speech feedback, but it is worth a try.

Finally...

It is important not to forget the older technologies, such as *Franklin* handheld spell checkers, that have improved with easier to read screens and British English dictionaries and reading pens for complex words with better scanning capabilities. There are also watches with alarms and many off the shelf technologies that can be extremely useful, such as cooker timers for setting time limits for tasks, talking thermometers when reading numbers is an issue and finally perhaps speaking navigational system when roadmaps cause confusion.

If you are finding all these technologies are too much in one go, why not return to your computer – relax and sit back to watch you favourite program from last week via the *BBC's iPlayer (40)*!

Resources

1. Microsoft Internet Explorer http://www.microsoft.com/windows/products/winfamily/ie/default.mspx

2. Mozilla Firefox http://www.mozilla.com/en-US/

3. http://www.vnunet.com/vnunet/news/2127294/uk-mobiles-people

4. Windows Mobile phone systems http://www.microsoft.com/windowsmobile/articles/default.mspx

5. Smart Hal from Dolphin http://www.yourdolphin.com/productdetail.asp?id=26

6. Nuance TALKS http://www.nuance.com/talks/

7. Nuance ZOOMS http://www.nuance.com/zooms/

8. RNIB accessible mobile phone fact sheet http://www.rnib.org.uk/xpedio/groups/public/documents/publicwebsite/public_mobphonesfactsheet.hcsp

9. Nokia 5500 http://www.nokia.co.uk/A4221004

10. Emporia Life http://www.comm8.com/html/emporia_life.html

11. Apple iPhone http://www.apple.com/iphone/

12. Mobile organisation hints and tips http://www.microsoft.com/windowsmobile/articles/organizebusiness.mspx

13. Butterfly http://software.palminfocenter.com/product.asp?id=10164

14. Dasher http://www.dasher.org.uk/

15. WordLogic http://www.wordlogic.com/

16. QuickWrite http://www.palmgear.com/index.cfm?fuseaction=software.showsoftware&PartnerREF=&siteid=1&prodID=19093

17. TechDis M-Learning http://www.techdis.ac.uk/index.php?p=9_5_32_2

18. Olympus DS-30, DS-40, DS-50 http://www.olympus.co.uk/

19. Audio Notetaker http://www.dyslexic.com/audio-notetaker

20. OpenOffice http://www.openoffice.org/

21. Inspiration http://www.dyslexic.com/inspiration

22. Tony Buzan http://www.buzanworld.com/

23. Freemind http://sourceforge.net/projects/freemind/

24. MindMeister http://www.mindmeister.com/
25. Texthelp Read and Write http://www.texthelp.com/
26. ClaroRead 2007 http://www.clarosoftware.com
27. WordTalk http://www.wordtalk.org.uk/
28. NaturalReader http://www.naturalreaders.com/index.htm
29. Readable http://www.dyslexic.com/readable
30. Colour Explorer http://www.microlinkpc.co.uk/downloads.php
31. ClaroView http://www.clarosoftware.com/
32. BBC My Web My Way http://www.bbc.co.uk/accessibility/
33. Google docs and spreadsheet http://www.google.com/google-d-s/intl/en/tour1.html
34. ieSpell http://www.iespell.com/
35. Mozilla Firefox add-ons https://addons.mozilla.org/en-US/firefox/recommended
36. Penfriend http://www.penfriend.biz/products/
37. WordBar http://www.cricksoft.com/uk/products/wordbar/
38. Dragon NaturallySpeaking http://www.nuance.co.uk/talk/
39. iListen http://www.dyslexic.com/itemdesc.asp?ic=4382&eq=&Tp=
40. BBC iPlayer http://www.bbc.co.uk/iplayer

E.A. Draffan is with the Learning Societies Lab at the University of Southampton, where she specialises in assistive technology; she is also a member of the BDA New Technologies Committee

Reasonable adjustments in the workplace: the role of information technology

Andi Sanderson

Many dyslexics entering the workplace – whether for the first time, or straight from university, or starting a new job – are faced with an environment that exacerbates their dyslexic difficulties. The *Disability Discrimination Act 1995* and the *Disability Equality Duties 2006* (for those publicly funded), require employers to remove, where possible, those barriers which reduce the efficiency of, and frustrate, their disabled workers. Most employers are happy to make what the legislation refers to as 'reasonable adjustments' as there are many benefits in terms of increased output, more effective team-working, and a better motivated workforce, resulting in increased staff retention and reduced training costs.

In some instances, the required 'reasonable adjustments' can be funded via the *Access to Work* scheme operated via *Job CentrePlus* offices. This scheme may meet some of the costs incurred, whether these are mentoring, one to one support, training, dyslexia awareness sessions, software solutions, but it does not usually extend to covering the cost of business hardware. Alternatively, some employers (usually larger international/national organisations) prefer to put in tailored support packages that can more precisely meet the needs of individuals within the context of their organisation.

There is no doubt that appropriate 'reasonable adjustments' for dyslexic employees can turn a hostile work environment into a place where the individual feels enthused, valued and able to succeed. Below is a case study showing how good practice can overcome the difficulties experienced by many employees. As the case study demonstrates, it is important that 'reasonable adjustments' are a package that include information technology (IT) solutions – not in isolation, but in partnership with other support – without which the IT may not be effective.

Background

Daniel Fairchild is employed as a sales manager responsible for a small team of eleven people, based in the East Midlands. He has been recently promoted and is finding difficulties with managing priorities and ensuring his paper work is in order. In his previous position as a sales representative for the same company, Daniel excelled at his job, but now he is feeling demoralised and unable to cope. His line manager, aware of Daniel's difficulties and his dyslexia, approached a specialist company to assess Daniel's difficulties in the work place and make suggestions for 'reasonable adjustments' with the aim of alleviating some of Daniel's difficulties.

The assessor requested Daniels assessment report and established that Daniel is: '...a person of above average intelligence, but has difficulties with short-term auditory memory, organisational and sequencing skills. He also experiences difficulties with reading comprehension, and reading at a speed commensurate with ability, difficulties with writing and spelling.'

Difficulties experienced in current role

The assessor visited Daniel at work and discussed with him his role, his difficulties and potential solutions. Meetings were also arranged with Daniel's line manager and the IT department. The assessment concluded that, as a result of his dyslexia, Daniel was experiencing difficulties in five specific areas in the course of his work. These are outlined in the table shown on the next page:

Task	Difficulties	Consequences
Reading reports	• Poor word recognition • Slow rate of reading	• Requires additional time to re-read • Unable to read material in meeting sufficiently quickly to contribute to discussions
Writing letters/ reports	• Poor punctuation • Poor spelling • Poor proof reading skills • Slow rate of writing • Poor word finding	• Requires addition time • Omission of words, or use of wrong word • Errors remain undetected
Taking minutes	• Poor auditory sequential memory • Poor (illegible) handwriting	• Unable to take meaningful minutes in meeting
Organising work priorities	• Poor sequencing • Inability to organise	• Time limits often exceeded • Irritating others • Generating additional stress
Recalling detail from telephone conversations	• Poor auditory sequential memory • Poor spelling • Poor (illegible) handwriting	• Unable to recall telephone numbers, names etc

Recommendations

The assessor made the following IT recommendations:

1. **TextHelp Read and Write Gold** software to assist Daniel with many aspects of reading and writing. In particular TextHelp will read text on his PC (including text on the internet), which will ensure that when he proofreads his work the correct words have been used. This software will also support Daniel with reading as this particular version of TextHelp contains **Abbyy Fine Reader**, an OCR software package, which will allows Daniel to scan text into MS Word and have this read back to him. This should enable Daniel to access text much more quickly and accurately. In addition, the package contains a spell checker, a homophone checker and a thesaurus, all designed for dyslexic users. This should assist Daniel with writing tasks. This package should be supplied with a pair of headphones to facilitate working confidentially.

1. An **Olympus DS40** digital recording device to facilitate the accurate recording of meetings, etc., hindered by Daniel's poor auditory sequential memory. This recorder will reduce the strain experienced in such situations where he is concerned that he will forget necessary detail. The recorder comes with software that allows recordings to be downloaded and stored as auditory files to be replayed at a later time. This recorder will help Daniel with recalling specific detail following meetings. This device should be supplied with a microphone (**Sony ECMZ60**), a small directional microphone that will improve the quality of the recording.

2. A copy of **Audio Notetaker**. This software will work with the **Olympus DS40** digital recorder and will enable Daniel to record meetings as required and later 'see' a visual interpretation of a recording. He will then be able to divide recordings up into manageable chunks, add notes and edit to his requirements.

4. **Retell 957** pro call recording software to facilitate the recording of telephone conversations directly onto Daniel's PC where they may be stored indefinitely for later referral. This software will allow Daniel to have conversations on the phone without the

worry that he may forget or incorrectly record some important details. The software also notes the time, date and duration of the call. Notes can also be attached to individual files if required. This software will need to be used with consideration for confidentiality and data protection issues.

5. *Mind Genius*. To enable Daniel to produce concept maps and using the tools in this software programme turn them either into word documents containing a copy of the map and a linear text interpretation, or into a PowerPoint presentation. The former will allow Daniel to use his visual conceptual strengths for planning/ structuring and in using the software produce paragraph headings ready for writing so reducing some of his difficulties.

6. A copy of **Visual Thesaurus.** This piece of software will provide Daniel with a visual map showing groups of alternative words. It is much more than a traditional thesaurus as it will allow Daniel to map strings of words and simultaneously review these rather than seeking single one-word alternatives with no reference to previous suggestions.

Other reasonable adjustments

1. Provision of an appropriately **qualified dyslexia specialist to work one-to-one** with Daniel for five, two-hour sessions. During these sessions Daniel's work processes can be reviewed and recommendation/suggestions made. These sessions should aim to address Daniel's difficulties with organisation to improve efficiency and reduce stress. The use of Outlook calendar and task list and the use of some templates for writing structured reports should be considered.

2. Provided with a **room to himself** to enable Daniel to focus on work without distractions or interruptions.

3. Provided with some **secretarial support**. Access to approximately four hours secretarial support per week will allow Daniel to have important/long reports to be typed. This will

allow Daniel to focus on content rather than on writing at speed further reducing errors in his work and stress.

4. That there should be no requirement for Daniel to take *minutes* during meetings. This will allow Daniel to concentrate on discussion, rather than attempting to record outcomes and action points for individuals. Daniel should be permitted to record meetings he attends.

5. Wherever possible, to distribute paper-based *information electronically*. This will allow Daniel to use TextHelp Read and Write and features in MS Word, to set an appropriate font, font size, line spacing and have information read by his computer. This will improve Daniel's rate of reading and reading comprehension.

6. *Additional time* is permitted for reading/writing tasks, whilst Daniel is adjusting to a new way of working. It is suggested that a period of four months is permitted, to be reviewed on conclusion.

7. Colleagues and managers are provided with some *dyslexia awareness* training so those who work with Daniel are better able to understand his difficulties and how they may reduce additional stresses that they and Daniel may experience.

Outcome

The employer implemented all of the suggested 'reasonable adjustments' and purchased the recommended IT hard/software. This resulted in:

1. **Daniel** feeling much **more productive and motivated** in his work. He now feels able to enjoy the satisfaction of doing a good job. In particular, Daniel feels that the digital recorder and TextHelp Read and Write in conjunction with the specialist IT training and one-to-one sessions made a huge difference

to the way he works. Daniel no longer feels demotivated or despondent.

2. Following the dyslexia awareness sessions, many other colleagues identified difficulties they were experiencing similar to those associated with dyslexia. In response, the company purchased **Lucid LADS screening software** as a means of identifying those with possible dyslexia [www.lucid-research. com].

3. In addition Daniel's employers, having seen the positive result of investing in Daniel as a valued employee, have implemented a series of **dyslexia friendly initiatives across the company**. For example, using Arial as the company font instead of Times New Roman; agendas for meetings together with papers are distributed electronically; some open plan offices are being redesigned to create small group offices with some areas specially designated for individuals requiring a quiet area.

Daniel's employers are continuing to work with the original specialist company to devise a disability-friendly policy.

Conclusion

From this short case study it is clear that the role of IT can be liberating for the individual transforming a situation from a struggle to success. However, it is equally important that IT is seen part of a range of 'reasonable adjustments' and not in isolation. Daniel would not be enjoying the clear success he is currently, without the other support mechanisms being implemented, in particular the one to one support.

For further details of reasonable adjustments in the workplace and employer duties please consult the following website www.re-adjust. co.uk Details of the software mentioned here, together with other appropriate workplace software can also be found on this website.

Dr Andi Sanderson is an assessor and trainer working with Iansyst Ltd.

Dyslexia in the dock

Melanie Jameson

Appearing before the courts is generally a demanding and stressful experience but if the individual has dyslexia or related specific learning differences (SpLDs), the challenges can appear almost insurmountable. We may come before the courts in a number of roles: as witness, appellant, respondent, plaintiff, or defendant. It could be a driving offence or as a witness to a crime. Perhaps it is a family issue, such as custody of children or a dispute with neighbours. Other possible scenarios include employment tribunals or benefits appeals. Sometimes the courts direct people to undertake procedures such as a psychiatric or psychological assessments. People with SpLDs appear in all these settings on a daily basis. Unfortunately the failure of the courts to recognise and accommodate their difficulties is demonstrated again and again. In my experience, these judicial and legal shortcomings can constitute a barrier to justice.

Courtroom skills

If we consider the skills and abilities that make for a successful court 'performance', they read like an inventory of what people with dyslexia find particularly difficult:

- Concentration and freedom from distractibility
- Understanding the import of questioning and responding appropriately
- Focused listening
- Rapid information processing skills
- Ability to locate and respond to written information (on the spot)

- Good oral skills
- Accurate recall
- Consistency
- The ability to cope with stress

Since dyslexia affects the processing of information – both written and spoken – dyslexic people are clearly disadvantaged by conditions that place heavy demands upon them in terms of language and working memory. Your credibility is on the line if you are hesitant or inconsistent and you can appear evasive by missing the point of questions – this is all too easy when questions are oblique or compound in nature.

Although many adults with dyslexia may appear to have compensated for various problem areas, they are obliged to divert energy into the operation of their coping strategies. Therefore, when a situation arises which impacts directly on key areas of weakness, they have no extra resources to call on because they are already operating at full stretch.

Dyslexic people before the courts

An example of a high profile figure 'coming unstuck' in this way is Richard Branson during his complex libel and counter-libel action in January 1998. Although his dyslexia was not public knowledge at the time, his performance gave many clues. The report of the case in *The Times* describes Branson as 'um-ing and ah-ing', 'struggling to recall events and dates' and drying up completely at one stage. He could only stutter: "I'm sorry, my mind's gone blank…what on earth…I can't remember what the, what do you mean, meant at the time". The contrast between this hesitant and confused person and the competent businessman who had set up and run at least two hundred businesses could not have been more pronounced.

As an expert witness, I have had opportunities to observe adults with dyslexia and/or related SpLDs in the courts. I will never forget

M, who had been charged with driving whilst under the influence, but claimed that the substances were legitimate medication allowed by his doctor. (Later in the proceedings his doctor had the opportunity to back him up, confirming that the drugs he was on were to help alleviate his long-standing depression and would not affect his driving.) M seemed too big for the dock in Croydon Magistrates Court. He was unable to get his words out without flailing his arms and striding in and out of the dock area. His voice came out overloud and his responses tended to be rambling and often inconsequential, as though he were trying to avoid the question. In fact he was struggling to answer the points with precision, an experience he found so frustrating that he was reduced to tears. Hopelessly he kept getting out the notes he had prepared but was unable to make sense of them.

Documentation on M included his assessment, which identified the literacy and memory difficulties typical of dyslexia but also recorded dyspraxic characteristics; these included weak visuospatial skills, clumsiness/poor motor coordination, disorientation and poor posture. Many of these factors became relevant in evidence relating to M's failure to pass the test of sobriety for drivers. The doctor at the police station required M to bring his finger from a distance in front of him to touch his nose. He was also asked to walk along a thin line, placing one foot in front of the other. In his report the doctor recorded that M was *"unable to accommodate his vision"* – a well known correlate of dyslexia – and that he was *"ponderous and slow, asking for all instructions to be repeated"*. The latter failing was taken as a further indication that M was under the influence of alcohol or some other substance, but it could also be interpreted as the struggles of someone with a weak short-term memory and tendency to misinterpret information to ensure a correct grasp of what was required.

It only took a few minutes for me to establish that M was unable to pass these tests under any circumstances. His was one of the many cases in which stress played a part. Stress is a well documented factor in the exacerbation of dyslexic and dyspraxic difficulties –

Professor Tim Miles has edited a book on the subject, now in its second edition. In Chapter 6 of this book I illustrate, through a combination of case studies and literature on dyslexia, how stress can be an additional handicap. I have also brought these issues to the attention of district judges through their professional journal.

Legislation and the courts

Is there any legislation which relates to issues of disability and the courts? As the courts are regarded as providing a service to the public, they come under the provisions of Part III of the Disability Discrimination Act (1995) and are therefore obliged to make *reasonable adjustments* to accommodate difficulties arising out of a disability. However, the issue of disability is not straightforward where dyslexia is concerned: the Act defines disability as follows: *a person has a disability if he has a physical or mental impairment which has a substantial and long-term adverse effect on his ability to carry out normal day to day activities.* Section1(1). *Substantial* implies severe dyslexia and this must be shown to have an adverse effect on *normal day to day activities.* The issues of stress and the undermining of coping strategies are also mentioned in the notes for guidance that accompany the Act: *In some cases people have 'coping strategies' which cease to work in some circumstances (for example, where <u>someone who stutters or has dyslexia is placed under stress</u>). If it is possible that a person's ability to manage the effects of an impairment will break down so that the effects will sometimes occur, this possibility must be taken into account when assessing the effects of their impairment.* (Section A8).

Another piece of pertinent legislation is the European Convention of Human Rights, Article 6 of which covers the right to a fair trial and has been incorporated in UK law through the Human Rights Act. Although both laws should protect people with SpLDs, neither has been 'fleshed out' sufficiently through test cases.

On a number of occasions I have drawn up and submitted documentation that itemises the particular difficulties of an adult with SpLDs in the context of the courts and proposes *reasonable adjustments* by court officials and legal professions. Unfortunately

I have found that the courts still fail to take account of these disability-related problems. In the only instance where the judge did acknowledge receiving my materials, the client was informed that he was "using his dyslexia to present himself as a victim". This would appear to be a Catch 22 situation: either you struggle in the courts with your difficulties unacknowledged or they are documented but it is inferred that you are using them as an excuse.

Employment Tribunals

People with dyslexia often report discrimination in the workplace; this may take the form of bullying, mockery, lack of promotion or failure to provide *reasonable adjustments*. Unfortunately prolonged difficulties at work can lead to stress-related illness, it is therefore doubly debilitating that the (ex-) employee may also have to face the additional stress of appearing before an Employment Tribunal. Having your competence probed and your areas of weakness exposed is a distressing experience, aggravated by the protracted nature of some hearings. For all these reasons, it is greatly advisable to try and resolve complaints through the *Questions Procedure* (DfEE 1998) whereby the complainant fills out a questionnaire to which the respondent must reply within a given time limit.

L had a disastrous experience preparing for a tribunal case, described in extracts from a letter, dictated to her partner:

I have found the whole legal & medical process in connection with my accident and unfair dismissal claims extremely complex and stressful. I have tried to make my solicitor aware of dyslexia and how it affects me, but I have found that my dealings with her, and especially the medical examinations and interviews by specialists, extremely distressing. Attempts to explain my dyslexia have often been met with examples of successful celebrity dyslexics such as Duncan Goodhew or Richard Branson – look how well they've done.

One of the specialists (who claimed to know about dyslexia) enquired of me early in our meeting 'I gather you have a dodgy memory?' I found this very offensive. When required to fill in forms, I have pointed out that I am dyslexic and find them extremely intimidating and very difficult to fill in. It has now become clear to me that due to my dyslexia, some responses on my forms were not accurate reflections of my experience, because of misunderstandings on my part.

L concluded: *There seems to be little or no recognition that difficulties stemming from my dyslexia (especially overload, memory, putting myself over, low self esteem and lack of confidence), affect my ability to make my case. Moreover I have found the manner of some of the specialists at times both unprofessional and patronising.*

This lack of understanding on the part of legal and judicial professions is a key issue. Another growing concern is the decreasing availability of legal aid, forcing some people with SpLDs to represent themselves.

Supporting documentation

When people with dyslexia come before the courts, documentation must be prepared by experts with a sophisticated understanding of dyslexia, in addition to knowledge of legal procedures, and usually under the instruction of a solicitor. This is a specialist area. In my expert witness work the starting point is providing evidence that the individual is dyslexic; this usually comprises a diagnostic assessment report. If protection under the Disability Discrimination Act is an issue, it has to be shown that the individual comes within the definition of disability (mentioned earlier).

In many cases, the assessment report does not bring out key factors relevant to the case or document the effects of stress, which may well have affected the person's actions. It may be necessary to show how the effects of stress can be more severe in dyslexics compared with non-dyslexics; this can be done in part by referring to specific learning difficulties literature. I have often quoted a remark by Dr

Harry Chasty (formerly of Dyslexia Action): '*A dyslexic appears completely incompetent in situations of stress*'. One may need to argue that difficulties inherent to specific learning differences are responsible for a certain incident, rather than criminal behaviour (as in the case of M).

Provisions and good practice

Since the Ministry of Justice is now responsible for the courts, their website should be the ideal place to locate information on accessibility. However, provisions currently relate principally to physical disabilities and the visually/hearing impaired. Alternatively, the direct.gov.uk website contains a section: *Going to court if you have a hidden impairment*, which actually mentions dyslexia but this is equally inadequate. A disability helpline is in place but this simply advises callers to contact the customer service officer at the court where the case is to be heard. However, in the case of SpLDs, they will generally meet with ignorance. An example of this was the response to my enquiry to Her Majesty's Court Services (HQ): I was told that they could supply "alternative formats to aid people with dyslexia such as Makaton signage"!!

Better understanding is shown by the Equal Treatment Advisory Committee (ETAC) of the Judicial Studies Board. Their document *Fairness in Courts and Tribunals* underlines the duty placed on service providers to take *reasonable steps to change any practice which makes it impossible or unreasonably difficult for people with disabilities to make use of a service which they provide to other members of the public.* The ETAC has also revised the disability section of the Equal Treatment Bench Book (ETBB), which provides guidance to the judiciary. It is suggested that specific needs should be considered on an individual basis and ideally ascertained before the hearing so that helpful procedures can be in place: *...each person with a disability must be assessed and treated by the judge as an individual so that their specific needs can be considered and appropriate action taken.* (ETBB 5.1.1)

The key pronouncement is one that I endorse wholeheartedly: *The overall aim must be to ensure that the disability does not amount to a handicap to the attainment of justice* (ETBB 5.1.4) but until guidelines are comprehensive, adherence to them 100% and training obligatory, this will remain merely an aspiration.

It is worth considering provisions made for other vulnerable groups. A *Litigation Friend* can conduct court proceedings on behalf of someone with a mental disorder; *Witness Intermediaries* can be available to assist vulnerable witnesses to communicate during police investigations and trials. ('Vulnerable' people are defined as young people under the age of 17 and people with physical, mental or learning disabilities / disorders and those who have communication difficulties.) Video links may also be set up for this group. Under the provisions of the Police and Criminal Evidence Act an *Appropriate Adult* can support juveniles and 'mentally vulnerable persons' in police custody.

I believe that adults with SpLDs are indeed vulnerable, but not in the same way as the groups above; their solutions may draw on these models but will differ in key respects. Fortunately a way forward on several fronts has opened up at the time of going to press: namely, the chance to work with the ETAC and the Developmental Adult Neuro-Diversity Association (DANDA) – which includes dyslexia – to update the Equal Treatment Bench Book. We also hope to produce a booklet on specific learning differences in a court context and contribute to Judicial Studies Board training materials. The aim is to enable people with dyslexia in the dock to have a better opportunity to access justice.

References

DfEE (1998) *The Disability Discrimination Act 1995 – Employment Provisions: The Questions Procedure.*
Disability Discrimination Act *Definition of Disability* Section 1 (1995).
Evans, B.J.W. (2001) *Dyslexia and Vision.* Whurr Publishers.
Jameson, M. (2001) Dyslexia in the courts. *Law Bulletin,* vol. 13(2).

Judicial Studies Board: *Fairness in Courts and Tribunals* (2004) and
Equal Treatment Bench Book, Section 5 (revised 2006)
Miles, T.R. (Ed) (2004) *Dyslexia and Stress*. Second edition, Whurr
Publishers.

*Melanie Jameson is an adult dyslexia specialist who has taught in
prisons and trained prison staff. She has also worked as an expert
witness and undertaken consultancy for the Law Society and the
Colleges of Law. Her current priority is to promote an understanding
of specific learning differences within the legal system.*

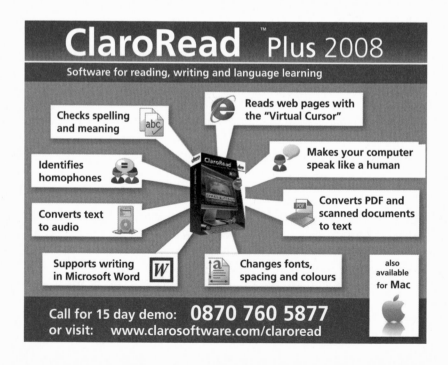

Offending and dyslexia: closing the revolving door

Melanie Jameson

Escalating prison numbers often hit the headlines; the subsequent over-crowding puts a great strain on the prison service, undermining 'purposeful activity'. As spare capacity appears and disappears, prisoners may be moved from one institution to another at short notice – or no notice at all, disrupting education, training and rehabilitation work. Among the more vulnerable prisoners are the mentally ill and those with learning difficulties and specific learning difficulties (SpLDs). Despite reviews, investigations, new initiatives and considerable investment in certain areas, it is obvious that prison 'doesn't work' – this is illustrated by the re-offending statistics, which remain high, leading to what has become known as the 'revolving door'.

So, what can be done to close the revolving door – at least for some offenders? One way could be to look at the issue of dyslexia and related SpLDs in the context of offending behaviour.

Is there a link between dyslexia and offending?

Jo Matty, magistrate and dyslexia expert, described an <u>indirect</u> link between <u>unaddressed</u> dyslexia and offending:

"When dyslexics experience lack of appropriate support from the early years of education, this can lead to

- *poor literacy and numeracy skills*
- *lack of confidence and low self esteem*

- *boredom, disaffection*
- *frustration, anger*
- *behavioural problems*
- *truanting or exclusion from school*
- *poor employment prospects*
- *all of which play their part in the climate of offending."*

Recent research points to high numbers of people with hidden disabilities in the offending population – a recent project carried out by Dyslexia Action reported that 20% of prisoners in the study were found to have a 'hidden disability' affecting learning and employment, such as dyslexia, dyspraxia or attention deficit disorder. This currently amounts to roughly 16,000 prisoners, and when offenders on non-custodial sentences are included, the numbers more than double.

The implications of thousands of offenders with SpLDs are far reaching for National Offender Management Service (NOMS) and Ministry of Justice targets for getting ex-offenders into work-based training and employment. This huge cohort is unlikely to encounter sustained success unless their difficulties and learning differences are taken into account.

How are people with SpLDs identified in the prison system?

Every aspect of support for offenders is laid down in the publication *The Offender's Learning Journey* (OLJ), which is jointly produced by the various sections of government concerned with offenders. Organisations, such as colleges and training providers, compete for contracts to deliver a range of services; their performance is measured against stated performance indicators. Section 2 of the OLJ, *Assessing the Learner's Needs*, states: *Potential dyslexia indicators should be identified and formal dyslexia assessments should be carried out if required. An effective system for identifying potential dyslexia should be in place and in use.*

Unfortunately, my experience leads me to conclude that this is not routinely taking place. Contracts for initial assessment work may be won by organisations without an education background and lacking awareness of SpLDs. Moreover there seems to be no accountability or penalty for failure to identify specific learning needs.

Useful screening tools have been around for a number of years, but even where these are used and learning needs are flagged up, the next stage – diagnostic assessment – is rarely accessible. In a volatile prison environment it is unwise to flag up an issue and then do nothing about it. To get round this problem I developed and piloted an 'unobtrusive' dyslexia checklist nearly ten years ago which screened for dyslexia without it being apparent, taking the approach: *Help us to help you.* In this way an establishment can obtain information on the likely prevalence of dyslexia (hopefully in order to advance the case for proper provision) and the needs of those coming on to educational or training programmes.

The situation for dyslexia may be patchy but those with SpLDs such as dyspraxia, attention deficit disorder or dyscalculia are even less likely to be identified and supported appropriately. For this reason materials produced by the Dyscovery Centre, Cardiff are of particular interest. They have developed the Dyscovery Profiler, a tool that identifies barriers to learning across the spread of SpLDs rather than screening for a particular condition. It is available in a computerised version with tailored feedback for individuals, relevant to their specific environment (one of these is prisons). Linked support materials are also available – an invaluable resource when so few staff have SpLD training.

What are the issues in supporting offenders with SpLDs?

Those offenders who are found to be dyslexic experience a range of emotions such as bewilderment, shock, anger and frustration.

Lacking the support of an adult dyslexia group or trained counsellors, they have no-one to turn to so education staff may well be drawn in at this time. Offenders with SpLDs need to feel 'safe' enough to describe their difficulties and encouragement to articulate their needs. Tutors and trainers will have to help combat the individual's negative self-concept and help him or her to overcome particular barriers to learning.

It is well to be aware that the bravado so often demonstrated by young offenders often disguises low self esteem, which must be addressed before successful learning can take place. The way forward is an immediate taste of success, through learning tasks that are carefully set at an achievable level. It is important to maintain motivation by building in elements of personal interest and choice. Most learners develop a sense of what they want to achieve but not always know how to get there. As we know, learning based on what is meaningful to the learner is more likely to be retained. Jenny Lee's guide *Making the Curriculum Work for Learners with Dyslexia* contains a helpful section on raising self-esteem.

However, given their negative experiences of schooling, offenders with dyslexia may well stay clear of anything reminiscent of mainstream education. Avoiding class-based activities, they are more likely to be found in workshops, in the gym or on the wings doing jobs such as cleaning. Some are lucky enough to be drawn into the Toe by Toe reading scheme, in which a fellow prisoner becomes a mentor in highly structured one-to-one sessions.

Prison tutors and trainers should be directed to the wealth of materials on dyslexia support, given the inevitability of working with dyslexia offenders at some stage. I would recommend the distance learning training package: *Supporting Dyslexic Learners in Different Contexts*, produced by the CfBT Education Trust; this has a set of modules contextualised for prisons and probation.

Whatever learning or training activity is being delivered, it is necessary to take account of visual stress. This term encompasses a range of symptoms, such as being dazzled by the glare from white paper; seeing words appear to blur or move around on the page; frequently losing the place; omitting and misreading words; fatigue and/or headaches when reading. The specialised treatment necessary to treat any unresolved eye problems is seldom available in prisons. However, some people notice a benefit from coloured overlays or simply tackling reading matter which is not black on white, so these options should be tried. Guidelines on producing 'dyslexia-friendly' written materials are now widely circulated. Unfortunately the standard prison notices are prime examples of a non dyslexia-friendly style.

ICT and E-learning in prisons

Options for flexible learning, via technology, are opening up in some institutions; this is attractive to those offenders who say they 'cannot handle a group' and also for vulnerable prisoners. One of the attractions of ICT is that it can be an enabling technology; it can remove barriers and allow learners, who might otherwise be excluded to access the *Skills for Life* programme.

Recent figures suggest that 90% of all jobs now require ICT skills (NIACE figure). It is assumed that people with SpLDs take naturally to ICT but this is not always the case. Dyslexic difficulties such as a weak short-term memory and problems tracking text across the page can still impinge. The necessary hardware, such as ergonomic keyboard, a roller ball, or anir mouse (an ergonomic, vertical joy-stick type of mouse design) is unlikely to be available for dyspraxic learners in prisons. However, with patience and understanding of SpLDs, it should be possible for staff to make adaptations, such as slowing down mouse speed and changing background colours on monitors. An excellent book on making best use of technology has been produced in the NIACE e-guidelines series: *Supporting adult learners with dyslexia: Harnessing the power of technology.*

Many of us will have heard about *Touch-type, Read and Spell (TTRS)*, a multisensory approach to learning spelling, reading, touch-typing and computing skills, which is particularly appropriate to learners with dyslexia. First tried in Pentonville Prison, it was found to raise skills levels and self-esteem so has expanded into a number of prisons. In HMYOI Rochester TTRS is offered as part of the provision for offenders identified 'at risk' of having dyslexia. Prisoners come to the session for an hour and a half, combining the ICT package with other literacy based activities including individual tuition with a specialist dyslexia tutor. The TTRS tutor described why this program works so well for her dyslexic students: "They enjoy it and really benefit. It not only teaches them touch-typing skills but also to read and spell in a structured way using as many of their senses as possible. The kinaesthetic approach is effective. The computer screen and headphones often help the learners to concentrate and focus on the task." Ross, a learner on the program commented: "It's interactive learning. It allows you to learn actively."

The Offender's Learning Journey describes why e-learning is important: *Many offenders are demotivated by traditional learning and are unwilling to participate in traditional classroom environments where learning materials are paper-based..E-learning has already been successful in engaging offenders who are not willing to take part in traditional learning.*

Feedback from pilot studies has recorded the motivating effect of e-learning on offenders with the most severe learning problems (this is likely to include those with dyslexia). Technical problems, such as a lack of power points on the wings, have been largely overcome by the use of laptops. Security concerns, especially relating to internet access, are being resolved by surf control software and the careful installation of only the required programs into each individual learning account.

This area has expanded significantly over the last year. The offender learning website, [www.offenderlearning.net] launched in 2006, is a key on-line resource to support the development of e-learning. At the same time, £2 million was allocated to 49 e-learning offender projects that demonstrate innovative approaches to upskilling staff and offenders. One of these projects, managed by the Adult Dyslexia Organisation [www.adult-dyslexia.org], highlighted the particular support needs of dyslexic adults and produced the following useful resources: a CD Rom database of assistive technology; the *Good Practice Guide on Offending, E-Learning and Dyslexia*, and an accredited training course for prison staff.

Further initiatives include development of offender National Learning Network materials and a London-wide pilot of POLARIS (Prison Offender Learning and Resettlement Information System). It is important that we work to ensure that dyslexia awareness is integral to the roll out of these programmes for there is no doubt that e-learning is on the agenda to stay.

Dyslexia and foreign nationals

We now move to the consideration of a growing group within the prison population: 'foreign nationals'. By the end of 2006 they represented one in eight of the prison population – a 152% increase compared with ten years previously and three times higher than the increase in numbers of British nationals. Home Office statistics also recorded that at least one in five women in prison was a foreign national. Unfortuately, this is a specialist area for which prisons are ill-equipped.

It is all too easy to attribute the language difficulties of this population to their incomplete grasp of English, plus various cultural, educational and emotional factors, rather than exploring whether there might be complications such as dyslexia. Even if dyslexia is flagged up as a possible factor, the screening and testing materials available to staff in prisons are often inappropriate and it is unlikely that foreign nationals can be tested in their home language. Instead, staff need to consider dyslexia indicators that are independent of literacy.

It is necessary to be aware of three further factors:

1) the level of literacy in the home language;

2) 'language interference', i.e. features of the individual's own language which can contribute to the difficulties mastering another language; and

3) the nature of the first language; for example there may be language skills required in English in the home language.

These factors can mask dyslexia, compound it or simulate it. A further issue is a possible stigma that surrounds learning difficulties and disabilities in some cultures. For that reason it is better to refer to 'the learner profile', 'learning style' or 'differences in learning'. Useful guidance on all these matters is provided in *Dyslexia and the Bilingual Learner.*

One group of foreign nationals that has been growing in Women's Prisons in recent years are Jamaican women, convicted of bringing in drugs. Although they would not seem to fit in a class for learners of English, their language clearly differs from Standard English in many respects. Difficulties in gaining English literacy skills could be mistakenly attributed to dyslexia rather than the difference between Jamaican and Standard English.

Resettlement

The Prison Reform Trust sums up the scale of the resettlement challenge: *Half of all prisoners do not have the skills required for 96% of jobs and only one in five is able to complete a job application form* (Prison Factfile, Nov 2006). Resettlement and employability are government priorities; as a result preparation work now comes earlier in the sentence and employer involvement is seen as crucial. Again, dyslexic difficulties will impact on work preparation and training, especially if speaking and listening skills are affected. The importance of communication skills has been flagged up by their inclusion in the *Skills for Life* curriculum and by research undertaken by the Dyscovery Centre. The research compared the population of a certain prison with a control group, in terms social and communication skills, co-ordination, literacy and attention and concentration difficulties. A key extract of this investigation is quoted below.

The HMP group showed a generally higher score profile across all domains than the control group. The area of social and communication difficulties is the one that stands out and may not have been considered routinely in profiling individuals coming into the prison, which may in fact pose the greatest problem when leaving prison... Social and communication difficulties, coupled with poor literacy skills, may have a cumulative effect on the outcome in a range of settings socially, educationally and in employment. In the context of this research these difficulties may have a considerable influence on recidivism rates. A lack of social and communication skills affects individuals in all areas of their lives. Individuals may present as angry, reluctant, aggressive or as loners, because a lack of understanding of the nuances of their social setting and what is then expected of them. This may be misconstrued by others and this consequently may lead them into further troubles. (Identification and Implication of Specific Learning Difficulties in a Prison Population, 2005)

This research highlights the necessity of developing social and communication skills, rather than focusing solely on literacy, when delivering dyslexia support. This is very important in the area of work preparation: interviews call for at least adequate communication skills, especially when one already has the double handicaps of a criminal record and dyslexic difficulties.

All aspects of workplace skills, from form filling to interviews and completing time sheets, need to be explicitly practised in preparation for resettlement. At this stage individual support is needed, to explore ways of compensating for particular problem areas. As the release date nears, some offenders start to doubt their ability to cope 'on the out'. Schemes that offer support beyond the prison gate are invaluable – especially if staff and volunteers have awareness of SpLDs.

Supporting the offender with dyslexia and related SpLDs is a complex and many-staged process, only touched on in this article. But without this support there is little chance of avoiding the revolving door.

References and resources

Adult Dyslexia: A Guide for Learndirect Tutors. Adult Dyslexia Organisation / Ufi Ltd (currently undergoing 3rd revision) see www.ufi.com/dyslexia

Dyslexia and the Bilingual Learner. H. Sunderland et al. Avanti Books, 1997.

The Dyscovery Profiler (2007) Dyscovery Centre. www.dyscovery. co.uk

Education and Training for Offenders. T. Uden. NIACE, 2003.

E-guidelines 9: Supporting adult learners with dyslexia: Harnessing the power of technology. S. McKeown. NIACE, 2006.

The Good Practice Guide on Offending, E-Learning & Dyslexia. M. Jameson et al. Adult Dyslexia Organisation, 2007. [dyslexia.mj@dsl.pipex.com]

The Incidence of Hidden Disabilities in the Prison Population: Yorkshire and Humberside Research. Dyslexia Institute, 2005) [http://www.dyslexia-inst.org.uk/pdffiles/Hidden Disabilities Prison.pdf]

Identification and Implication of Specific Learning Difficulties in a Prison Population, Forensic Update 84, Dyscovery Centre, 2005.

Jameson Offenders Checklist. M. Jameson (1998) [dyslexia.mj@dsl. pipex.com]

Just Learning? Case Studies in improving offender education and training. NIACE/LSDA, 2006.

Making the Curriculum Work for Dyslexic Learners. J. Lee. Basic Skills Agency, 2002.

Supporting Dyslexic Learners in Different Contexts www.cfbt.com

Toe by Toe. K. & H. Cowling (1986) www.toe-by-toe.co.uk

Touch-type, Read & Spell. P. Alexander. www.ttrs.co.uk

Melanie Jameson is an adult dyslexia specialist who has taught in prisons and trained prison staff. She has also worked as an expert witness and undertaken consultancy for the Law Society and the Colleges of Law. Her current priority is to promote an understanding of specific learning differences within the legal system.

Alternative formats: your country needs you!

Ian Litterick

We are now used to being treated equally under the Disability Discrimination Acts. We are familiar with seeing *This document is available in Braille or large print* on the back of leaflets from large organisations. But, in practice, people with reading difficulties do not often get or read those documents in the most ideal format: they are still too difficult to get hold of. At Iansyst we print those words on documents but hope that nobody will take us up on them because it would be expensive to convert a document into Braille. However, we try to make these documents or similar information available on our websites in a form that people can read electronically. The BDA is also trying to go down a similar route, but with more emphasis on audio files, thanks, largely, to the efforts of volunteer Jean Hutchins.

The proportion of published material that is available to those who can't read is tiny. The law is mostly there. The software is mostly there. The format standards are mostly there. The necessary hardware devices are mostly there. The systems to make alternative formats available are mostly there. What is missing is the knowledge, the demand, the expectation, the belief amongst reading-impaired people, their parents, their teachers, their supporters that, in 2007, we have the right to have reading materials, as a matter of course, in the form that we can read them.

So the next step is up to **you**. As dyslexic person, teacher, SENCo, parent or support worker, you need to be asking, now, for any text to be in a readable form. Only if there is a full demand will the systems be set up to provide alternative formats as a matter of course. Many people should be involved in providing the various bits of the alternative format jigsaw. Only if there is full demand will these people themselves demand the tools and systems to do the job not just 'mostly' but completely and easily.

In a magnificently thorough 220-page report *Books for All: accessible curriculum materials for pupils with additional support needs* the Edinburgh Call Centre has produced a comprehensive overview of the difficulties and inadequacies of current provision of alternative formats for the whole range of people with reading difficulties. This report is available electronically at www.books4all. org.uk and makes many suggestions regarding what needs to happen if children with reading difficulties are not to be further handicapped throughout their education. It's written for Scotland but the content is universal. And the basic message is this:

A lot more needs to happen

A lot more **will** happen if we know it is possible, if we expect it, if we demand it, if we accept nothing else. And **we** means **you**!

Books for All calculates that 4–5% of school-age pupils could benefit from materials in alternative formats, either in addition to, or instead of, standard text. I think that is a very conservative number. At the moment, practically all the transcription centres that are producing alternative format materials are doing so for visually impaired students – usually Braille or large print. For every visually impaired student there are 14 with specific learning difficulties (including dyslexia) and another 14 with moderate general learning difficulties. The small amount that is currently being provided is catering for a small minority of the overall need.

What we should expect

It's not just books that we should expect to be available in alternative formats: novels, textbooks, reference books, catalogues and guidebooks. It's also notices, descriptions, assessment and exam papers, pamphlets, timetables, worksheets, reports and communications from school to home. And they need to be available at the right time, which is usually **now,** not in two days', or a week's time, when someone has found the time to prepare them. Students need to have them at the same time as their peers who are working alongside them.

For dyslexic people the format is likely to be electronic text. But it might be large print, or an audio recording of homework instructions or a report, or an e-mail of communications with home. In some circumstances it might even be a video recording. For children with general learning difficulties it may be simplified text or text with symbols. It's not good enough to expect people to get by or to miss out on information because it is not in format that they can readily digest. Nor is it acceptable to imagine that providing Braille or large print is sufficient.

Mostly there

I said above that the law, the software and the standards are mostly in place already. They will only get fully there when enough people are involved in the process on a daily basis, whether as readers, supporters or alternative format providers. Enough people, that is, to ensure that the law, the software, the standards, the hardware and the systems are all perfected so that the process works simply, quickly and routinely. However, for alternative formats to be quick, simple and routine, various things first need to be improved.

1. Better software

Tools for accessibility and creating alternative formats are a key area for software developers today. Dolphin's *EasyConverter* helps organisations convert from printed and electronic documents to Braille, large print, DAISY and audio. (DAISY is the Digital Accessible Information SYstem, a form of digital talking book designed for people with visual impairment but also of potential interest to people with other reading difficulties.) Web information is often the best alternative format and readers such as *BrowseAloud*, *ReadSpeaker* and *Textic Talklets* make it easy for websites to make themselves accessible by being readable aloud.

But there is also a lot of room for improvement. Most people use Microsoft Word to write text, but it is much too difficult to produce text that is 'accessible', i.e. text that is properly structured and has descriptions of pictures so that people with visual impairments can find their way around the document easily. It needs to be made possible to set Word up in such a way that it always asks the right questions and discourages the wrong type of formatting, so that it provides *Incidental Obligatory Accessibility* – without trying and without needing to be skilful. Text-to-speech engines need to improve their accuracy when they read numbers, abbreviations, and homophones like 'lead' that can be pronounced in different ways. It can still be very difficult to understand what the computer is reading out to you from the screen.

2. Better hardware

We still haven't quite got the ideal machine for reading electronic text – one that compares favourably with a book. Laptop computers are too big and heavy. There is, as yet, no electronic book that is light enough, has a good enough screen for use in sunlight, has good enough battery life and that will read out loud as well as display text. Mobile phones and PDAs have screens that are too small, are not bright enough, and have inadequate software for supporting reading. But they are in everybody's pocket.

CapturaTalk is an intelligent phone that reads out loud from a picture of text that its camera takes. It shows the way that everyday small devices that anyone might buy can develop for people with reading impairments. E-paper may be an answer. Coming soon, at first in black-and-white only, you will be able to roll your display up so that it is about as light and readable as paper.

3. Better habits

Authors will need to learn better habits to produce *Incidental Obligatory Accessibility*. They will need to learn to use Word's more efficient *Styles* rather than using the typical hodgepodge of ad hoc formatting that many of us do. And authors and print designers will need to spend a little bit of extra time when producing complex documents.

4. Better services

Where someone has gone to the trouble of converting a work into an alternative format we need to be able to find it. It is a waste of time if someone else has to duplicate the same work on the same document to produce the same result. *RevealWeb* is a database of alternative format materials for visually impaired people. It will shortly become part of the *UnityUK* database used by libraries and it will give this service the resources it needs to survive and grow. However, it will need to widen its remit to other disabilities and improve the quantity and quality of the information that it provides before it will be a really comprehensive and adequate service.

5. Better laws or licences

Since 2002 people have been able to convert materials for visually impaired people into alternative formats without getting permission from the publisher. But people with other reading impairments are still supposed to get permission. The law needs to be extended to cover all reading disabilities that are covered by the Disability Discrimination Acts. Meanwhile, and more easily, most of the organisations who are converting to alternative formats are doing so under a licence from the Copyright Licensing Agency. Their licences can readily be changed to cover all disabilities as they already have done for the Higher Education licence. Indeed, I hope this will have been agreed by the time you read this.

6. Better publisher' work flow

In principle, practically all books now go to the printers as electronic text. With small changes to processes and procedures this electronic text could be in a format that all people with reading impairments such as dyslexia require in order to be able to read it properly. And then the electronic texts needs to be made available through some central repository or via a database like *RevealWeb* so that individual reading-impaired people, or other organisations acting on their behalf, can download them easily. This provision may require a Digital Rights Management system to ensure that publishers do not lose income.

Conclusions

The basics of the system are already there to provide all reading-impaired people with the reading materials that they need in the format in which they can be read and at the time they are required. However, before this system works properly it needs a lot of developments and tweaks. These improvements will come about much quicker if we all insist that the system start working now, creaks and all.

A version of this article with links and occasional updates will be available on the web at www.dyslexic.com/altformat-needed

Ian Litterick is a member of the BDA New Technologies Committee and Executive Chairman of Iansyst Ltd, which specialises in technology solutions for dyslexia and other disabilities and runs the website dyslexic.com

Reports from Dyslexia Organisations

The Moat School

A Secondary Day School in London for Children With Dyslexia

Founded in 1998 The Moat School is London's first co-educational secondary school for dyslexic children offering an intensive and structured learning programme teaching the national curriculum.

Children receive a totally inclusive education, they understand their difficulties, but thrive academically, emotionally and socially in spite of them. Pupils have individual timetables that address their needs, and creative talent is nurtured in small classes enabling success in public examinations. The Moat School is CReSTED registered and has been described as the 'Gold Standard' in SpLD education.

The Good Schools Guide says: "Something special. Not for children wanting to be cosseted and comforted, but a hard-working haven for bright, determined dyslexics and dyspraxics who know what they want from life and will achieve when given a chance".

Come and see for yourself.

Bishop's Avenue, Fulham, London SW6 6EG

T: 020 7610 9018   **F:** 020 7610 9098

office@moatschool.org.uk   **www.moatschool.org.uk**

British Dyslexia Association

Jennifer Owen Adams

The British Dyslexia Association (BDA) exists to campaign and lobby for a dyslexia-friendly society. Our mission is 'a dyslexia-friendly society that enables all dyslexic people to reach their potential'. As the only impartial and objective dyslexia-focussed membership-based organisation in the UK, the BDA delivers support and information to over 6 million people throughout the country. The BDA tells society what dyslexia is, why having an understanding of dyslexia is important, and advises on how to become dyslexia wise. In practice, this means that the BDA listens, advises, signposts and provides impartial support, guidance and direction to policy-makers at national and regional level, as well as to parents, children, young people, employees and employers.

The BDA continues to be a dynamic charity that has worked since its inception in 1984 to raise awareness and change the experience of an all-age dyslexic community in the UK. Today it is the leading authority on dyslexia and related issues and is internationally renowned for its work. It disseminates all the latest thinking on dyslexia through its wide and diverse networks and uses its knowledge and experience to influence policy and bring about lasting change.

Strategic objectives

- To achieve a broad and inclusive membership, increasing the number of members and fostering a sense of belonging and identity in our members.

- To be visible and raise the public awareness of dyslexia and the profile of the BDA.

- To remove barriers to people with dyslexia by improving the level of dyslexia specific expertise.

- To support those at risk of disengagement; specifically offenders, those who feel unable to undertake education and the unemployed.

- To enable people with dyslexia to reach their potential.

- To increase the effectiveness and efficiency of the organisation through developing staff and volunteers and improving systems and processes.

How the BDA works

The BDA works on a number of levels. The Trustees and Senior Management Team shape and influence policy at the very highest level to ensure that changes designed for the benefit of dyslexic people is well founded and sustainable. We also advise and support people with dyslexia and those they come into contact with at a local level. It does this through its National Helpline, its national network of local associations , its website and regional based projects. Through its grassroots network, the BDA provides local and regional support services to help:

- every dyslexic child to access support in school,

- every dyslexic adult to access and achieve in further and higher education and in the workplace

- offenders to climb out of the 'offending cycle' and keep those 'at risk ' of offending out of the criminal justice system

- employers to embrace the potential of dyslexia

- parents and carers to gain as much information and advice as possible.

The information from 'the ground' forms the basis of our work in that it helps shape new methods and ideas that need developing, policy that needs establishing or changing and new standards that need to be set. This learning and best practice is then disseminated internationally, nationally, regionally and locally via conferences as well as a wide range of publications, this Dyslexia Handbook being an example. Below are some examples of the BDA's work:

Policy

Influencing policy is a key objective of the BDA. It works strategically with national and local organisations and government bodies to influence policy decisions that impact directly on the well being of dyslexic children, their families and employers. These close working relationships ensure that the needs of dyslexic people remain at the forefront of educational and employment policy and practice. Examples of our policy work include:

- Disability Rights Commission investigation into the potential risk of discrimination against thousands of public sector workers as a result of new government legislation.

- Right to Read campaign: a campaign to press for the same book, at the same time and at the same price for all print-impaired children and adults and for publications to be in alternative formats.

- Improving the professional standards of practitioners who assess dyslexia for the purposes of awarding Disabled Students Allowances and for access arrangements to assessments and examinations.

- Initiating a national debate on *Early Identification of dyslexia in schools: the way ahead.*

- Working with **Xtraordinary People** to press for a specialist dyslexia teacher in every school

- Meeting the Teacher Development Agency to raise their awareness of the need to incorporate SpLD awareness and training in Initial Teacher Training courses

- Advising the government on the structure, content and implementation strategy of the Inclusion Development programme

Training

The BDA has a rapidly expanding training provision that delivers training nationwide for teachers, school governors, parents, employers and other interested parties. The training programmes are designed to deliver the BDA's core objectives, which are to build awareness about dyslexia and to enable all dyslexic individuals to fulfil their potential. Thus many of our courses concentrate on what the dyslexia spectrum is and on the most recent research in this area. This is complemented by disseminating information regarding the most practical solutions to the problems faced by people with dyslexia. There is synergy with other BDA activities, including the **BDA Helpline**, where referrals are made both ways, the **BDA Quality Mark**, which recognises the journey made by organisations in becoming dyslexia friendly, and **conferences**, which assist in generating new knowledge.

We have now designed modules of training covering most areas of interest, from dyslexia to dyscalculia, building self-esteem. There are one-day programmes on teaching reading, writing and spelling. For clients within employment settings, the range covers everything from awareness to reasonable adjustments, performance and talent management. A priority for 2008 is to build on recent successes in alerting teachers to the potential that assistive technology can offer to adults and children with dyslexia.

Three types of training are offered: open, bespoke and accredited courses. Our **open courses** are delivered in a wide range of locations across England and Wales, with specialist courses for both educators and employers. We have also been able to use our spread of locations to gather information about best practice and disseminate this nationwide. Our **bespoke courses** are tailored to the needs of the client school or employer and are run on their site. We also have two **accredited programmes**, one on dyslexia and screening and another on the entire range of hidden difficulties and how to teach children with these. There are plans to expand the number of accredited programmes we offer. During the year ended March 2008, 112 open courses, 65 bespoke events and approximately 14 accredited programmes were run. We have trained almost 4,000 people since May 2007 and this number is likely to double in the current year.

Most teachers and teaching assistants attending our training are doing so because of their desire to help children in their classes who have learning difficulties. Employers are motivated to attend either because they perceive a threat posed by recent employment case law, or because they have personal experience of dyslexia and want to learn more. Whatever the motivation, the common reaction is that dyslexia and its related difficulties constitute a much more widespread issue than they ever envisaged. Some excellent feedback has been received from participants, who have not only displayed keen interest in the subject but also their willingness to instigate changes to help their dyslexic pupils or colleagues.

The most interesting and important aspect of training is, of course, what happens as a result. Dissemination of best practices has already been mentioned but we are also able to gather and collate relevant information, such as the extent of study skills support offered to dyslexic pupils. Most importantly, we are finding that the BDA training programme is having a considerable effects on the perception of dyslexia and the understanding of how common it is, in schools, colleges and at work. It is particularly gratifying to see schools and employers participating in training and then drawing up action plans which we are able to see implemented. For example, Oldfield School undertook an Inset day in October 2007 and immediately drew up plans with the whole staff for implementing ideas on confidence building for children, organisational tips and assistive technology. Similarly, a member of the training team of the Charities Aid Foundation came on one of our employer's courses and since then they have bought a dyslexia screening program for those employees who want to avail themselves of this opportunity, and have run awareness training for all managers.

Quality Mark

To support the raising of standards in the community to meet the BDA's vision of a dyslexia-friendly society, the BDA continues to expand its Quality Mark. This is a 'kite mark', which provides external recognition of an organisation's commitment to being 'dyslexia-friendly'. An article reviewing current developments for the BDA Quality Mark appears elsewhere in this handbook.

Helpline

The accredited BDA Helpline is run by 25 volunteers and linked to Local Associations who provide a localised service. The Helpline receives over 1,670 calls a month and 300 emails. Support, sign posting and information are given for all areas of learning difficulties, not just dyslexia. The web site is an excellent source of information that is regularly updated by the Helpline. Website hits averaged approximately 20,000 unique hits per month.

Local Association Board

The Local Association Board (LAB) continues to be the regular link between the network of Local Dyslexia Associations across England, Wales and Northern Ireland and the Trustee body. LAB has thirteen representatives who meet regularly and represent Local Associations. They discuss ideas and concerns covering all ages and all aspects of dyslexia in education, employment and the community. Most of its members are dyslexic themselves which helps them to understand the issues and their impact. LAB nominates three Trustees.

Accreditation Board

In educational terms, the Accreditation Board underpins the highest level work of the BDA. Accreditation, through this Board, is recognised as the 'gold standard' in teacher training internationally and is held in high regard by UK government bodies. Currently, the BDA Accreditation Board fulfils a number of different roles and functions:

- awarding individual qualifications to those who successfully complete approved courses

- approving courses based on detailed assessment of course content and on inspection visits

- actively working with academic institutions in order to develop courses

- setting standards and criteria.

Advisory Groups

There are two Advisory Groups who provide the Trustees with expert information as well as assisting the Charity with its work. These are:

- **The New Technologies Committee** works to raise awareness of information and communication technologies (ICT) for dyslexia. Members of the committee attend three meetings a year. Part of their remit is to raise the profile of the use of ICT in education to support learners with dyslexia. Committee members give talks with demonstrations, write articles and take part in events and exhibitions. They promote the potential of ICT in helping to overcome the challenges faced by people with dyslexia.

- **The Music Committee** supports the BDA Helpline with advice on examination issues related to the Association Board of the Royal Schools of Music and advises music students and professionals on all aspects of music and dyslexia. Members of the committee write publications and produce the music and dyslexia information sheet on the BDA website. A representative of the BDA attends committee meetings.

Membership

During 2007 Support Groups were the fastest growing section of membership. This newly formed category of membership offers a flexible approach which appeals to people who are passionate about offering support to children and adults with dyslexia but who do not always have the time or inclination to commit to a more formal structure.

Projects

The *Northern Ireland, Equipped Project* funded by the Big Lottery Fund is a three-year community-based project which is developing a regional wide information network at a local level. In Wales *Prosiect Llwyddiant (Project Success)* is funded by the European Social Fund (ESF) and works with 2000 13–19 year olds whose undiagnosed specific learning difficulties and related problems make it hard for them to engage with school and education. The project provides these students with the skills to access the curriculum, to assist them in gaining success and to encourage them to stay on at school (or college) or move from a learning environment into work or further education. Forty-one schools/colleges have signed up to the project and 1600 beneficiaries are receiving support. Assistive technology solutions are an integral part of this project.

The *INCLUDE project* which finished in 2007 involved the BDA working collaboratively with partner organisations from Poland, Hungary, Greece, Bulgaria and the UK on a two-year project. The purpose of the project was to develop a pan-Europe web based screening tool for adults to identify dyslexia. A report on this project can be found elsewhere in this Handbook.

The BDA's *ECUBE Project,* also completed in 2007, improved the services and support available to the education departments of offender institutions, developing the skills and knowledge of those working with offenders with dyslexia.

The *Liverpool Dyslexia Project,* funded by the Liverpool Children's Fund continues to provide dyslexia awareness training to providers of children's services in Liverpool. This project is bringing together best practice in dyslexia support for children and has been successful in building strong partnerships with children service providers.

7th International Conference 'Dyslexia: Making Links'

The 7th BDA International Conference, sponsored by Olympus, was held at the Harrogate International Conference Centre, 27 – 29 March 2008. The BDA was privileged to have Professor Maggie Snowling of the University of York, as chair of the conference. Maggie, along with her Conference Committee, brought together a hugely stimulating and thought-provoking conference, attended by over 800 delegates from countries all over the world.

The conference drew on a broad range of research and practitioner-led expertise and had, as its aim, the consideration of the relationship between dyslexia and other developmental learning difficulties, including dyscalculia, language impairment, ADHD and developmental coordination disorder. The conference theme *Making Links* reflected the aspiration to understand the common co-occurrence of these disorders from genetic, neuroscientific and cognitive perspectives and discussed how they affect the lives of individuals of all ages learning in different languages.
It was Maggie's view that bringing these different perspectives together was and remains fundamental to improving interventions for children, young people and adults with dyslexia and related difficulties.

Maggie expanded on this theme in her opening keynote address *Making Links: the broader phenotype of dyslexia.* Maggie commented on the rapid growth over the last ten years of research on dyslexia across the life span, its neurobiological bases and its manifestations in different languages. She noted important changes in the ways in which neurodevelopmental disorders, including dyslexia, are conceptualised. Her presentation reviewed research on the relationship between reading and other learning disorders, and she argued that dyslexia should be viewed as a dimensional disorder without clear boundaries. While some individuals reach a threshold for 'diagnosis', she postulated, others may show partial or co-morbid forms of dyslexia. Maggie went on to discuss the implications of this new conceptualisation for assessment and intervention.

This excellent start to the conference was immediately followed by a keynote address by Sir Jim Rose, formerly Her Majesty's Inspector and Director of Inspections for the Office for Standards in Education (OFSTED). Sir Jim talked about his independent review of the teaching of early reading, commissioned by the Secretary of State in June 2005 and published in March 2006. He discussed expected models of best practice in the teaching of reading and synthetic phonics how this related to the development of the birth to five framework and to the development and renewal of the National Literacy Strategy Framework for Teaching. He also covered what range of provision best suits children with significant literacy difficulties and what best enables them to catch up with their peers, as well as the relationship of targeted intervention programmes with synthetic phonics teaching. Finally, Sir Jim talked about how his review considered how leadership and management in schools could support the teaching of reading.

This opening day and subsequent days witnessed keynote speakers from across the world addressing the delegates on the contemporary issues emerging from their research. Aryan Van der Leij presented a paper on *International perspectives;* Cathy Price talked about her latest research in *Neuroimaging of dyslexia and language;* Stanislas Dehaene presented *Education as brain recycling:reading and arithmetic.* Development coordination disorder was the theme of David Sugden's address. Kate Nation talked about reading comprehension impairments and Eric Taylor on attention disorders. Dorothy Bishop presented a paper on *Treating reading disability without reading: evaluating alternative intervention approaches* and Barbara Maughan talked about adult outcomes. Barbara Foorman delivered the Bevé Hornsby Memorial Lecture on *Reading and language intervention.* Usha Goswami presented her latest research on *Auditory Rhythmic Processing ,*

Phonology and dyslexia: a cross-language analysis. Bob Burden discussed dyslexia and self esteem. Rebecca Treiman was invited to deliver the Nata Goulandris Lecture on *Learning to spell in English* and finally Richard Olson closed the conference with his paper *Reconciling strong genetic and strong environmental influences on reading ability and disability.*

These keynote presentations were supported by a packed programme of papers, symposia and workshops as well as interactive papers and posters. The conference closed with the announcement that Steve Chinn was awarded the Marion Welchman Award for his outstanding contribution to dyslexia research and practice and that the 8th International Conference of the British Dyslexia Association would be in 2011 and chaired by Joel Talcott of Aston University.

Proceedings of the conference are being made available free of charge to conference delegates via the BDA International Conference website at www.bdainternationalconference.org. Proceedings will also be made available for non-delegates via the same website for which a charge will apply.

The 7th BDA International Conference was a considerable success in terms of the number of delegates attending and the very impressive programme designed and delivered by Maggie Snowling, the Conference Committee and the BDA team. The conference theme of *Making Links* is one likely to have a lasting legacy. Sir Jim Rose is about to start his second review; this time focussing on an evaluation of what works best for learners with dyslexia in schools. Within that remit, Sir Jim is considering the requirement to look not only at best practice for all those children with dyslexia but also at best practice for children with related learning difficulties. This it is likely that the outcomes of the 7th International Conference of the BDA will be helping to shape the future direction of educational policy in the UK for the next ten years or more.

The future

The forthcoming year promises to be an exciting one for the BDA. As well as new initiatives, we will endeavour to continue to deliver a first-class service to all people with dyslexia in the UK. In everything we do at the BDA, meeting the needs and improving the lives of people with dyslexia remains our purpose.

Contact:

The British Dyslexia Association,
Unit 8, Bracknell Beeches
Old Bracknell Lane
Bracknell, RG12 7BW.
Tel (Helpline): 0845 251 9002
Tel (Admin): 0845 251 9003
Fax: 0845 251 9005
Web: www.bdadyslexia.org.uk/

Jennifer Owen Adams is Education and Policy Director of the British Dyslexia Association.

Dyslexia Action

Kerry Bennett

About Dyslexia Action

Dyslexia Action, a national charity, is the UK's leading provider of services and support for people with dyslexia and literacy difficulties. It specialises in assessments, teaching and training as well as developing and distributing teaching materials and undertaking research. Dyslexia Action was established in 2006 from the merger of the Dyslexia Institute (founded in 1972) and the Hornsby International Dyslexia Centre (founded in 1984). Dyslexia Action is an Organisational Member of the BDA.

Dyslexia Action is committed to improving public policy and practice. It partners schools, local authorities, colleges, universities, employers, voluntary sector organisations and the government to improve the quality and quantity of help for people with dyslexia and specific learning difficulties. Our services are available through our 26 centres and 160 teaching locations, including many schools, around the UK. Over half-a-million people benefit from our work each year. Dyslexia Action is the only national dyslexia-teaching organisation in the world with its own bursary fund to help families who could not otherwise afford specialist provision.

The work of Dyslexia Action is dependent on fees from assessments, tuition and training courses, and income from the sale of our products, as well as the generosity of benefactors. We employ over 250 specialist teachers, as well as Chartered Psychologists and support staff. Some 90 psychologists work with Dyslexia Action on a consultancy basis.

What does Dyslexia Action do?

Our mission is to ensure that all individuals with dyslexia are identified and educated to allow them to be successful by:

- providing accurate assessment and the most appropriate teaching

- working to influence and improve the practice of mainstream educational services for children and adults with dyslexia, through specialist teacher training, the development of high quality teaching tools, the evaluation of teaching methods to achieve better practice, and by improving awareness and understanding of dyslexia.

We have three main roles: assessment, teaching and teacher training. We also produce our own publications and teaching materials and undertake a continuous programme of research.

Each year we provide psychological assessments for over 9,000 children and adults, teach over 4,000 children and adults, and train over 200 teachers on our postgraduate courses.

How does Dyslexia Action work?

Our Head Office is based at Egham, Surrey. Our 25 main assessment and teaching centres are spread across the UK and our research office is based at the University of York. In addition, we have over 160 teaching locations, including many units in schools. As well as providing specialist tuition for literacy, most of our centres offer tuition in numeracy and run study skills courses.

We provide a range of specialist training courses for teachers, parents and others who are interested in dyslexia and literacy. Our postgraduate attendance courses are held in a number of UK locations and are also available to teachers throughout the world by distance learning. Shorter specialist courses for teachers, teaching assistants, adult tutors and parents are offered at a range of UK centres and tailor-made courses can be provided on request.

Dyslexia Action has used the expertise acquired over the past thirty five years to develop a number of teaching materials which have proved highly successful. These, as well as a wide range of assessment materials, can be purchased through our trading arm.

Dyslexia Actions partnerships and current projects

We work in partnerships and contracts to improve the quality and quantity of help for people with dyslexia and specific learning difficulties.

1. Consultancy with employers

Dyslexia Action works with companies to advise on the best options for them and their employees to support work performance in line with the Disability Discrimination Act (DDA). This might include work-focused psychological assessment followed up by a workplace consultation for individuals or groups. These workplace assessments are tailored to the needs of the company and can ensure employers meet the demands of the DDA.

2. Consultancy with schools and other providers

There are many ways in which Dyslexia Action works with schools, colleges, universities and private trainers to help address needs of their pupils and students. Sometimes our teachers work directly with learners, or alongside SENCOs (Special Needs Coordinators) and/ or teaching assistants. We offer all kinds of tailored packages to providers including tuition for learners, training for staff, mentoring, awareness raising, group teaching and consultancy.

3. Contract services

This includes partnerships with organisations such as the *Learning and Skills Council* or *Job CentrePlus* to provide screening, awareness training, assessment and tuition targeted to specific groups of people such as those living in deprived areas, or those working in key industries. Dyslexia Action also works with other agencies and charities to jointly promote or develop services for, for example, parents or local communities.

4. Probation, prison and young offender services

We offer a range of services that have proved invaluable to probation, prison, and young offenders groups. The results of our work contribute to our ongoing research.

Contact details

Dyslexia Action
Park House, Wick Road, Egham, Surrey, TW20 0HH
T: 01784 222300 F: 01784 222333
Email: info@dyslexiaaction.org.uk
Web: www.dyslexiaaction.org.uk

Kerry Bennett is Public Relations Manager for Dyslexia Action.

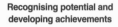

Patoss, The Professional Association of Teachers of Students with Specific Learning Difficulties is for all those concerned with the teaching and support of students with SpLD: dyslexia, dyspraxia, ADD and Asperger's syndrome.

Patoss aims to promote good practice amongst professionals and has published guidance for those moving into this field as well as for parents and established practitioners. Popular titles are:

How Dyslexics Learn: Grasping the Nettle by Saunders and White, helpful and accessible to parents, dyslexics and others interested in the field

Dyslexia: Assessing for Access Arrangements by Backhouse et al, published in conjunction with the Joint Council for Qualifications, essential for specialist teachers, heads of centres, governors, exam officers, SENCOs, ALS managers and all those involved in the process

Dyslexia? Assessing and Reporting edited by Backhouse and Morris, providing practical guidance for specialist teachers and educational professionals in training, as well as SENCOs and learning support staff working in schools and colleges.

For further information contact Patoss
tel: 013860 712650 email: patoss@evesham.ac.uk
or visit www.patoss-dyslexia.org

Patoss

Lynn Greenwold

As a **P**rofessional **A**ssociation of **T**eachers **o**f **S**tudents with **S**pecific Learning Difficulties, Patoss is for all those concerned with the teaching and support of pupils with SpLD, including dyslexia, dyspraxia, attention deficit disorders and Aspergers syndrome. We aim to promote good practice amongst professionals and have published guidelines for those moving into this field as well as for parents and established practitioners. Patoss is an Organisational Member of the BDA.

Publications

We work closely with the *Joint Council for Qualifications* (JCQ) in publishing guidelines in assessing for Access Arrangements in examinations. *Dyslexia: Assessing for Access Arrangements* supports all those involved in the examination process, which is published in its 3ʳᵈ edition this year. In addition *Dyslexia: Assessing and Reporting – The Patoss Guide* provides practical guidance needed by specialist teachers and education professionals in training, as well as by SENCOs and learning support staff working in schools and colleges. This publication focuses on the purposes, principles and practicalities of assessing for dyslexia across successive age groups. These two books join our popular *How Dyslexics Learn: Grasping the Nettle*, where jargon-free writing and full colour illustrations have made it accessible to parents, dyslexics and others interested in dyslexic learners. We also publish a *Tutor Index*, updated regularly.

Membership

Membership is open to professionals training or working in the field of SpLD. Many of our members teach in schools and colleges and some provide one to one tuition to students with specific learning difficulties.

Patoss aims are to:

- establish and maintain the professional status of those qualified to teach students with specific learning difficulties

- promote the continued provision and development of appropriate specialist qualifications in the teaching of students with SpLD

- enable members to update and extend their knowledge and skills and to exchange ideas through an annual conference, bulletins and local groups;

- promote fuller understanding and recognition of SpLD

- promote links with teachers working with SpLD students in all sectors of education

- promote links with other professionals involved in the field of SpLD

- give a professional corporate response to the Department for Education and Employment (DfEE) on matters affecting SpLD students

- maintain a register of the members of the association.

What Patoss offers:

- links with other professionals

- opportunities to keep in touch with recent research, and to exchange knowledge and experience

- a range of publications

- reduced fees for Patoss national conferences and local events

- a growing network of local groups
- different levels of insurance including professional indemnity.

SpLD Assessment Practising Certificate

Pressure for effective monitoring of standards in assessment has grown – from bodies such as Local Authorities, the DfES and Awarding Bodies who use assessment reports to make important decisions and from within the profession itself. This has led to the development of an *SpLD Assessment Practising Certificate*. These practising certificates recognise professional achievement in skills as an SpLD assessor. They also link the holder's practice to a commitment to continuing professional development. Holders of the Patoss SpLD Assessment Practising Certificates fulfil the criteria established by the DfES. These Practising Certificates, will, additionally assure Heads of Centres that the professional is suitably qualified to conduct assessments for examination access arrangements.

National Committee for Standards in SpLD Assessment, Training and Practice

We have several Patoss representatives on the *National Committee for Standards in SpLD Assessment, Training and Practice* [SASC] and the *SpLD Test Evaluation Committee* [STEC]. SASC is a standard-setting group concerned with the diagnostic assessment of specific learning difficulties in an educational setting. Its purpose and responsibilities are to:

- implement the training recommendations of the SpLD Working Group 2005/DfES Guidelines
- promote and monitor standards of SpLD assessor training relating to all age ranges
- promote continuing professional development in SpLD assessment
- advise on models of good practice in this continuing professional development
- monitor standards of this continuing professional development

- provide a forum for sharing good practice from a range of interested bodies

- draw on expertise across the sector

- provide guidance on training, and implementation of standards

- oversee and approve processes of awarding SpLD Assessment Practising Certificates

- maintain list of approved evaluators for APL/APE applications

- provide training for evaluators

- approve courses as meeting standards of SpLD assessor training.

Its associated committee, STEC, fulfils the role of evaluating and recommending new test materials to update guidance on tests acceptable for use in supporting DSA assessments.

To find out more

Visit the Patoss website: www.patoss-dyslexia.org

Lynn Greenwold is Chief Executive of Patoss.

Bangor Dyslexia Unit

Ann Rees and Ann Cooke

As always, the Bangor Dyslexia Unit continues to provide its regular services of teaching, assessment and student support. Research is also ongoing, particularly into links between dyslexia and bilingualism, with the emphasis on children in Welsh-medium education. This year has seen the launch at Bangor of the new ESRC (Education, Science and Research Council) Centre for Bilingualism. This exciting development will offer opportunities to the Unit to engage in research studies on dyslexia and the teaching and assessment of language skills. The Bangor Dyslexia Unit is an Organisational Member of the BDA.

'Dyslexia – A Matter of Words' Conference, June 2007

This year's T.R.Miles' lecture was delivered as part of the conference by Professor Usha Goswami. Her theme of 'Rhyme, Rhythm, Reading and Dyslexia' included a cross-language analysis. In an optional session in keeping with the bilingualism theme, papers were delivered on the teaching of dyslexic children in Malta and the assessment of Welsh dyslexic children. Other sessions were given over to practical teaching strategies.

It was pleasing to have good attendance including many teachers and parents from all over North Wales and beyond.

The Student Service

The original handbook for dyslexic students *Dyslexia at College* by Dorothy Gilroy and Tim Miles has been extensively revised by Liz Du Pré and previous authors. It is sad to record the death of Dorothy in September last year, after a long battle with cancer, just as the revision was in its final stages. Her contribution to students with dyslexia over many years was inestimable. She was a pioneer in this field and she is greatly missed both as a good friend and much-valued colleague.

This year, the Unit has supported around 450 students, undergraduates and post-graduates. Individual support continues to be available. A regular newsletter keeps students in touch and that and weekly group sessions allow students the chance to share and develop their strategies for learning and surviving at University. New staff have joined the team for screening students prior to a possible full assessment.

The Assessment Service

There is a constant demand for psychological assessments of children and adults. Assessments are becoming increasingly broad in their scope due to the demand for inclusion of other kinds of difficulties as well as dyslexia, including numeracy problems. Referrals for assessment are on the increase and this is likely to continue, particularly during the change in the professional training of educational psychologists, from a one-year course to a three-year doctoral training course, and the inevitable shortage of educational psychologists during the transition period. As the result of an assessment, adult individuals and students may be able to benefit from adjustments for exams or in the workplace, or to apply for Disabled Students Allowances (DSA).

The Teaching Service

Over 50 specialist teachers provide tuition (in English or in Welsh) for school children with Specific Learning Difficulties, including Maths, in the counties of Anglesey, Gwynedd and Conwy. Privately funded tuition is also available. A CPD programme is in place for all the teaching staff, most of whom have taken one or more of the modules on dyslexia in the Masters Degree Programme run by the School of Education at Bangor University. The Teaching Service offers workshops and training days for mainstream schools to raise awareness of specific learning difficulties and enable them more easily to identify and address the needs of those who are underachieving. A bilingual resource base for the teachers is constantly updated. It is good to note that the Welsh reading books written by the writing team have recently been published and that further work is planned, funded by an agency within the Welsh Assembly Government. Marie Jones (Director of Teaching) is a member of a Welsh Assembly Government Working Party looking into the provision of support for dyslexic learners across Wales.

In-service Training

We continue to run two in-service modular courses on dyslexia for qualified teachers in the School of Education Masters Programme: a one-year course on *Teaching of Dyslexic Learners*, and an extended two-year course. Both have a practical teaching requirement. A module on assessment is also available. This includes observed assessments, and can be extended for accreditation at Level A of the *British Psychological Society's Certificate of Competence in Educational Testing*. The courses are part-time and run on five weekends between October and May. BDA recognition on these courses can be achieved at either AMBDA or ATS level.

Publications

The Bangor Dyslexia Teaching System by Elaine Miles.
Tackling Dyslexia by Ann Cooke.
Dyslexia: the Pattern of Difficulties by Tim Miles *(may be out of print)*.
Dyslexia: a Hundred Years on by Tim and Elaine Miles.
English Words and their Spellings – a History of Phonological Conflicts by Elaine Miles.
Dyslexia at College by Liz Du Pré, Dorothy Gilroy and Tim Miles.
50 years of Dyslexia Research by Tim Miles.
Mathematics and Dyslexia by Elaine Miles and T.R.Miles.
Basic Topics in Mathematics for Dyslexics by Anne Henderson and Elaine Miles.
Music and Dyslexia edited by Tim Miles and John Westcombe (revised edition in press).

To find out more

Visit our website: www.dyslexia.bangor.ac.uk

Ann Rees is Head of the Assessment Service at Bangor Dyslexia Unit and Ann Cooke is the Co-director and Director of Teaching Modules.

Independent Dyslexia Consultants	2nd Floor, 1-7 Woburn Walk London WC1H 0JJ Telephone: 0207 388 8744 www.dyslexia-idc.org Email: info@dyslexia-idc.org

Directors: David McLoughlin and Carol Leather

Assessment, Coaching, Consultancy, Training

We have been working with dyslexic adults and children for 25 years

Our focus is on developing the individual's skills and abilities to enable them to become more successful

We provide a wide range of services for education and the workplace

Previously operating as The Adult Dyslexia & Skills Development Centre

Dyslexia Teaching Centre, London

Katherine Kindersley and Joanna Petty

The Dyslexia Teaching Centre is a busy teaching and assessment centre in the middle of London. It provides highly qualified, specialist support for children and adults of all ages, enabling individuals to acquire the skills needed for success in education, the workplace and everyday life. The Centre is situated in one of those 'hidden' places, overlooking the most delightful London garden at the back of Kensington Square on the premises of a large working convent. People speak of the oasis of calm and tranquillity that prevails on walking through the doors, which provides an ideal environment for assessment and learning.

The Teaching Centre had an interesting beginning. It was founded 30 years ago by Sister Mary John, who had retired from her position as head mistress of the Sisters' school in Sidmouth. As anyone who knew her would appreciate, Sister Mary John's retirement from education was unlikely. She trained at Barts in the then very new discipline of dyslexia therapy and set about establishing a school for children with dyslexia. Her energy and skill meant that the Centre grew rapidly and, by 1985, under the direction of Adrian Stokes, the Centre became a registered charity with a Board of Trustees and a Bursary Fund, supporting those who needed help but who were unable to fund assessment or tuition themselves.

Since those days, the Centre has continued to grow and flourish. In 2005, it moved to larger premises on the same site and it offers an ever-increasing range of support through its expanding teams of specialists. It works with people who have dyslexia as well as dyspraxia and other specific learning difficulties.

The multi-disciplinary team at the Centre includes:

- Specialist teachers
- Speech and language therapists
- Physiotherapists & Occupational therapists
- Educational psychologists
- Specialist teacher assessors
- Maths specialists
- Music and Art specialists

Who does the Centre support?

Children

Full and careful assessment leads to the development of a teaching programme, which is then specifically tailored to meet the needs of the individual child. The Centre's caseload is enormously varied. The majority of children are in mainstream school and receive specialist tuition once or twice a week, either at the Centre, or in the schools where the therapists work. Close liaison with classroom and subject teachers is maintained. The Centre is also well-known for managing children with a complex range of needs. Case conferences bring together all those working with the child, so there is a coherent and united approach, with everyone working together as a team. In addition, the Centre provides ongoing support for some children who, for a variety of reasons, do not attend school at all. For these children, the aim is to improve skills and confidence enabling them to return to specialist or mainstream school.

The Centre works in partnership with the Dyslexia Association of London to support parents who are having a difficult time gaining the support their child needs at school. It also supports parents through the appeal and tribunal processes.

As well as one-to-one tuition, the Centre provides paired and small-group tuition on literacy, maths and study skills. Touch-typing classes are increasingly popular. Tuition continues during school holidays and half-term breaks, ensuring that where needed, there is a continuity of support and newly gained skills are not lost through the long summer break, for example. Holiday support also means that children are able to boost their skills when there is less pressure from the school timetable.

Students

The Centre works with students at all stages of secondary schooling, providing study skills support through Key Stages 3 and 4, as well as for those approaching GCSE and 'A' level examinations. Work focuses on gaining more efficient strategies, e.g. in reading comprehension, the planning and structure of writing (whether it is at the level of the sentence, the paragraph or whole essay), revision techniques, organisation and memory strategies. Students become more confident and successful in their management of their studies.

Adults

All adults, whether they are in employment, or studying at undergraduate or post-graduate level, share the issues faced by people with Specific Learning Difficulties. These include dyslexia, dyspraxia, deficits in attention, memory and processing, and expressive language difficulties. Commonly the process of support begins with an assessment.

Individual diagnostic assessments are handled with sensitivity and insight and they explore the profile and the pattern of strengths and weaknesses. Where appropriate, a *Workplace Needs Assessment* can also be conducted. Recommendations are made for appropriate reasonable adjustments at work, as well as a training programme and items of equipment that will support the individual. The report can be used to apply for *Access to Work* funding.

Expert support for adults is also available. Assessment is used to inform the training programme, which is then planned with the individual in conjunction with their own priorities and needs. The experienced team of trainers draw on great depth of experience, a wide knowledge of the range of specific learning difficulties and a keen understanding of how to get effective change and forward progress with adults. Members of the team work with organisations, companies and government departments, as well as a wide range of educational institutions in and around London. Common areas needing support are:

- Writing reports, essays and dissertations
- Studying for exams, academic or professional
- Reading and researching
- Dealing with the complexities of high-level written and spoken language
- Developing confidence in conversational skills
- Developing confidence in addressing an audience or group & presentation skills
- Organisational and memory skills
- Timekeeping and 'multi-tasking'
- Work for maintaining focus and staying on track
- Managing incoming information at work
- Developing life skills and strategies
- Building self-esteem

Further Support at the Centre

- Educational counselling and advice.

- Work in conjunction with programmes of speech, motor or other therapies as required.

- The Centre employs a further range of therapies, such as Listening Sound Therapy, Neuro-Linguistic Programming, Brain Gym and perceptual awareness training.

- Touch-typing and computer skills training for all ages.

Many parents welcome guidance in choosing the right school for their child. The Centre has an excellent knowledge of specialist and mainstream schools and can advise on the 'best fit' for an individual child. Liaison with the schoolteachers and on-going monitoring of the child's progress can be provided.

Training activities

The Centre runs a variety of training programmes, including conferences for parents and professionals, parent workshops, and Inset days for schools and universities. The Inset training days are tailor-made to the specific requirements of the institution. Popular training days include dyslexia and dyspraxia awareness talks for staff, subject related workshops such as music and dyslexia/dyspraxia and ongoing consultation and training with teachers.

The following training days and workshops are held regularly through the year:

- *Dyslexia Awareness for Employers.* These training days are designed especially for managers, human resource and occupational health staff, and for all other groups interested in developing good practice in relation to employees with dyslexia or dyspraxia.

- *Dyslexia in the Workplace.* These training days are designed for professionals already working in the field of dyslexia who wish to gain further understanding about how to assess and support individuals with dyslexia at work.

- *Diagnostic Assessment in Higher Education.* These training days are designed for the specialist teacher or psychologist wishing to follow the current Government guidelines on assessment. They offer an opportunity to explore key aspects of adult assessment and to update knowledge of tests and assessment tools.

- *Workplace Training and Consultancy.* The Centre has experts who provide a range of training options for employers, on an individual basis, in a group setting for a team, or department, or whole day awareness training for managers. It also provides on-going consultancy for organisations and companies.

Conclusions

The Centre is committed to finding solutions to help all those with dyslexia and other specific learning difficulties move past the barriers which may hold them back, opening up the way forward for success. The Centre is an Organisational Member of the BDA. The Centre has an on-going programme of high-profile fund-raising events in order to support the Bursary Fund. Please contact us if you would be interested in being involved with this.

Contact details

The Dyslexia Teaching Centre
23 Kensington Square
London W8 5HN
Telephone: 020 7361 4790
Email: dyslexiateacher@tiscali.co.uk
Web: www.dyslexiateacher.co.uk

Katherine Kindersley and Joanna Petty are both directors of the Dyslexia Teaching Centre.

Adult Dyslexia Organisation

Donald Schloss

The Adult Dyslexia Organisation (ADO) is a national body for adult dyslexics. It is run by dyslexics for dyslexics and all those who are concerned with adult dyslexics, and provides a wide range of services to the public and to professionals. We exist to promote the cause of adults with dyslexia through lobbying, research, training and campaigning. A principal aim is to create awareness about dyslexia and to ensure that the needs of dyslexics are considered in the design and delivery of services.

ADULT
DYSLƎXIA
ORGANISATION

The Campaign

Launched at the House of Lord by Lords Addington and Laird on the 19th of May 2005, the *Dyslexia Friendly – User Friendly* campaign has achieved one milestone after another, benefiting not just dyslexics but everybody, both disabled and non-disabled. In addition to increasing awareness about dyslexia, we are campaigning to make communications more accessible for people with dyslexia, and to bring about adaptations and reasonable adjustments to enable dyslexics to reach their full potential.

The campaign aims to show that services and support have been put in place across education, employment, ICT, and day-to-day living. In the area of education, the campaign aims to create the awareness among tutors and education policy makers that dyslexics have a different way of learning, so that they receive the necessary support they need.

In terms of recruitment and employment, it is important to create awareness about dyslexia among employers, employees, managers and trade unions so that they can make reasonable adjustments and adaptation that will maximize the productivity of dyslexics. The *Dyslexia Friendly – User Friendly* campaign aims to create this level of awareness and bring about the necessary changes within the workplace.

The campaign also aims to target ICT, to create greater awareness of assistive technology. To achieve this, it will focus on those responsible for the policy and content of websites, to inform them on the needs of dyslexics and urge them to make available all specialist IT equipment, adaptations to existing technology, and to make their websites and intranets more accessible.

A greater awareness of dyslexia among people responsible for providing public services is also essential if the day-to-day living of dyslexics is to improve and if they are to be part of an inclusive society. The key outcome of the campaign has been for organisations, institutions, or individuals to sign up to one or more of the key campaign commitments, which include:

- Developing a dyslexia inclusive policy

- Putting in place specialist dyslexia support

- Making reasonable adjustments to accommodate dyslexics

- Setting up support groups

- Initiating awareness activities

- Producing guides on dyslexia or for dyslexic people

- Making specialist IT equipment available

- Adapting existing equipment
- Making websites and intranets more accessible
- Providing Readback facility on websites
- Signing up to our guidelines which can be downloaded from www.adult-dyslexia.org
- Setting up mentoring schemes
- Sponsoring an event
- Making a donation

What has been achieved so far

Thus far the campaign has contributed to:

- greater retention of people with dyslexia on education courses
- increased productivity within the workplace
- the setting of new benchmarks in the design of websites
- the setting up of a series of support groups within the community, and in education and employment.

These initiatives enable dyslexics and other people with disability to fulfil their potential and make a greater contribution to society. Other achievements of the campaign include:

Education

Adult Basic Literacy: ADO was a founder member of the then DfES *Skills for Life* Dyslexia Advisory Group, inputting into the roll-out of this major initiative. Through the project *Dyslexia in Different Contexts,* we are providing distance-learning training for skills-for-life teachers and trainers. The aim was to train about 1500 teachers and trainers. ADO sat on the reference group that directed this work.

Further/Higher education: ADO sat on the *National Working Party on Dyslexia in Higher Education,* a group of experts who surveyed current provision for students with dyslexia and outlined good practice in the areas of policy, identification, assessment, counselling and access to examinations. ADO contributed to the subsequent definitive report: *Dyslexia in Higher Education: Policy, Provision and Practice* (HEFCE, 1999) and also produced a digest entitled: *The Changing Face of Dyslexia in Higher Education* (HEFCE, 1999).

Prison education. ADO promoted the dyslexia-friendly approach in the government *Dyslexia Focus Group for Prisons.* Following a meeting with the Prisons Minister, the Home Office agreed to add dyslexia to the *Offenders' Learning Journey* so that contractors now have to demonstrate that they have the ability to identify and support dyslexics. This was written into their contracts.

National Union of Students (NUS). We have continuously provided *Guides to Further and Higher Education* for the NUS to support their disability and welfare advisers.

Ufi/learndirect. We produced and distributed *The Adult Dyslexia Guide: A Guide for learndirect tutors and support staff* to the 2000 learndirect centres and the 6,000 UK online centres [www.ufi.com/dyslexia]. Other work included forming a committee to address dyslexia and its overlapping conditions; providing guidance for the design of their dyslexia websites and the contents of the site; development of an accredited e-learning and dyslexia course in conjunction with BFAWU (Bakers Food and Allied Workers Union); producing a series of awareness conferences in conjunction with the then Department for Education and Skills' (now the Department for Children, Schools and Families) E-learning Strategy Unit and Ufi/learndirect.

We co-operated within the Ufi Single Equality Scheme Action Plan to deliver training to learn/direct centres. We developed an accredited e-learning course: *Adult Dyslexia Organisation – supporting learners with dyslexia in e-learning and a CD-rom on assistive technology.* We are also in the process of developing three centres of excellence. A series of awareness seminars has also been organised.

Exam bodies. We liaised with City and Guilds and Open College Network on accreditation of our courses.

Making courses dyslexia-friendly. ADO provided consultancy to Habia, the Hairdressing and Beauty Industry Authority Sector Skills Body as far back as 1999 and updated in 2006 in order to make their NVQ courses dyslexia-friendly and student-friendly.

Supporting Dyslexic Learners in Different Contexts project funded by the Skills for Life Strategy Unit, which is managed by CfBT Education Trust in partnership with CTAD and Dyslexia Action.

Learning and Skills Council (LSC): ADO provided a consultation report to address the LSC's Disability Equality Scheme.

Employment

Department for Work and Pensions (DWP): As a result of the *Dyslexia Friendly – User Friendly* campaign, the ability of occupational psychologists to identify and support dyslexics was upgraded by the DWP's Psychology Division. DWP provided compulsory dyslexia training for two years. We also produced the CD *Dyslexia and Employment, Enabling Full Potential*, working in partnership with the DWP and with support from JJ Charitable Trust. Additional assistance was given by five government departments, and a range of specialists in the fields of dyslexia and employment law. ADO also ran a conference to support the CD.

The Disability Rights Commission undertook a formal investigation into *Fitness, Standards in Social Work, Nursing and Teaching Professionals,* with *ADO* acting as professional witnesses and providing evidence of good and bad practice. This allowed us to introduce the *Dyslexia Friendly – User Friendly* approach.

The National Disabled Teachers Task Force, facilitated by the National Teaching Council for England, addressed the issue of fitness to teach in relation to the Disability Discrimination Act, working in conjunction with the LLU+ (formerly London Literacy Unit). Again, we were brought in as professional witnesses and asked to provide evidence of good and bad practice, which allowed us to introduce the *Dyslexia Friendly – User Friendly* approach.

Trade Unions. ADO has worked with a number of unions to develop and provide training for employers, employees, managers and union learning representatives, organizing short dyslexia and employment awareness courses.

Other areas

ICT: We have lobbied MPs throughout the UK to encourage central and local governments to make facilities for reading website contents available to the public.
We participated in the *MyGuide* project as stakeholders, carried out the website testing and are still in the process of developing new website accessibility guidelines. This project aimed to encourage ethnic minorities, disabled people, the 40+ age group, and economically disadvantaged groups to use the internet.

Day-to-day living: The ADO has worked with the Department of Transport over the last three years, assisting in their research on *Transport and Dyslexia*. Another initiative has been the *Brixton Challenge*. This was developed and run by the ADO, targeting dyslexics from black and ethnic minority communities. The campaign has been so successful that industry and government departments have invested in implementing some of our recommendations. We are now working in partnership with the National Health Service, reviewing the whole service and how it works. In addition, we are working with the Disability Rights Commission on internet accessibility, the Civil Service, on their *Guide, Fitness for Work for Nurses, Teachers and Social Workers;* the Fire Service, reviewing their disability policy in relation to dyslexia; the Ministry of Defence, developing dyslexia awareness training; and the Ministry of Justice, supporting their Civil Service Dyslexia Contact Group.

International activities: We are an active participant in many European dyslexia campaigns. Among these are:

- The *Provision and Use of ICT by Dyslexic Students at Universities in Europe* project

- Partners of the EU-funded project *"ADystrain – a project focusing on awareness training for employers, managers and trainers."*

- Production of, and support for, several publications in the areas of education, employment, ICT and day-to-day Living.

What is dyslexia?

We wish to propose that the definition of dyslexia be reframed. Up until now it has largely been thought of as a *disability*, as though there were something 'wrong' with being dyslexic. We wish to challenge this negative view. We believe that dyslexia is an experience that arises out of natural human diversity, together with an emphasis on the early learning of literacy, personal organisation and a good working memory. The problem here is seeing difference as 'deficit' and incorrectly linking it to intelligence.

Put in practical terms, it is disabling to expect that everyone:

- thinks in the same way

- learns to read in the same way

- makes sense of information in the same way

- can take in multiple instructions

- is able to take notes while trying to listen.

Without such disabling expectations, there is no difficulty and no disability. Let's turn this round: if we expected everyone to be able to think as fluently in 3D – as most dyslexics can – the majority of the population might be considered as having a 'disability'. We prefer to promote attitudes and strategies that are more inclusive and less likely to disable anyone. This is summed up in the Adult Dyslexia Organisation campaign slogan: *Dyslexia-Friendly, User-Friendly.*

Many dyslexics are extremely talented and many show exceptional powers of creativity. The suggestion that we are 'disabled' has arisen only because society has assumed that to be properly educated one has to be good at spelling and punctuation and that one has to be able to scan documents quickly and to write down notes at speed. In particular, to pass examinations that are gateways to success, involves for many the impossible task, for dyslexics, of reading at speed and having to remember facts which can perfectly well be looked up in a dictionary or encyclopaedia when needed.

In such an environment dyslexics are, indeed, disabled, and are entitled to the compensations that go with disability. In the case of students this may mean Disabled Students Allowances and, in the case of all employees, the protection arising from the Disability Discrimination Act, since employers are legally bound to make 'reasonable adjustments' for any employee who is disabled.

What we urge is that society should change its expectations and definitions of dyslexia. We urge the provision in education and in the workplace of dyslexia-friendly environments where dyslexics, like everybody else, are given the opportunity to demonstrate their skills and are not impeded by some of the traditional assumptions, which, in our view, over-value certain types of literacy and memory and undervalue many other skills, such as creativity and originality, at which dyslexics are sometimes very strong. Indeed, many dyslexics can be extremely gifted in many disciplines. Examples of famous and gifted dyslexics include Sir Richard Branson, Sir Jackie Stewart, Lord Rogers and Benjamin Zephaniah.

Why it is important to sign up to the Campaign

Signing up to the commitments of the *Dyslexia-Friendly – User-Friendly* campaign will cost you little or nothing, but will provide immense benefits. By signing up, your organisation can actually begin to fulfill its disability duties in relation to the Disability Discrimination Act and Disability Equality Duty, reaping benefits in the following ways:

- **Workplace**. Some of the outcomes of the campaign can actually improve your organisation's productivity.

- **Education**. By signing up you can increase retention and the number of students passing your courses

- **ICT**. Organisations signing up can benefit from guidance on building more accessible websites and making their literature more accessible.

- **Day-to-Day Living**. The campaign can also enable individuals to reach their full potential and contribute to the community and wider society.

You can get involved as an individual or an organisation by setting up a social, community or support group at the workplace, in college or at university. As a group you have a more effective voice. Your group's activities can range from putting on social events so that people can get to know each other, or becoming an effective lobbying and campaigning group.

Working through a group allows you greater input in your consultation and the ability to address dyslexia in its wider complexities. Your group can provide opportunities for sharing coping strategies that help build self esteem and confidence and which enable people to reach their full potential. It is important that the group is user-led to encourage ownership. You can also get involved in awareness-raising by taking part in training, poster campaigns, contributing to newsletters, taking part in media events or signing up to one or more of the campaign commitments.

Sign up to the campaign and make Britain a more inclusive society!

Contact details

The Adult Dyslexia Organisation
Ground Floor, Secker House, Minet Road
Loughborough Estate, London, SW9 7TP.
Tel: 020 7207 3911
Email: ado.dns@dial.pipex.com
Website: www.adult-dyslexia.org

Donald Schloss is Chief Executive of the Adult Dyslexia Organisation.

Xtraordinary People

Kate Griggs

My father had it. My brother's got it. And so do I. It's not some chronic life-threatening ailment, it's dyslexia. That awkward, often hidden, condition where words and numbers get muddled up – that awkward condition which means you sometimes can't concentrate or find it hard to take onboard too much information. That awkward condition that makes it harder to learn and to read, write and do maths. A condition that affects a staggering 10% of the population.

But my brother and I were lucky enough to benefit from supportive parents and an education that enabled us to do well at school. My father helped us to focus on our strengths and persevere with the things we found difficult. Last year, when fellow dyslexic Sir Richard Branson sold Virgin Mobile to NTL, my brother resigned from his role as CEO, a role he had held since the company's creation. His entrepreneurial flair earned him a very, very large handshake!

So having this hidden disability needn't hold you back; many of today's major employers have 'suffered' from this difficulty. But here's the rub: without the support from specially trained teachers a dyslexic child will probably have little or no hope of reaching this potential. There are around one million dyslexic children in our schools today. They are likely to go undiagnosed, without help, and needlessly struggle to cope with learning difficulties that could so easily be remedied by a change to the way teachers teach.

It's hard to believe that the teaching methods that have been used successfully to help dyslexics for decades aren't a compulsory part of teacher training. It's even harder to understand why this support isn't a statutory requirement for every school, particularly as this is a disability that affects so many children.

My personal battle to get my own sons' dyslexia recognised and supported gave me the motivation and determination to face this issue head on and to expose the desperate and unnecessary plight that so many children and parents are facing. So I set up *Xtraordinary People*, which operates as a restricted fund of the British Dyslexia Association, and I approached the leading dyslexia charities to join forces with XP and support my campaign for change.

To highlight the talents that so often accompany dyslexia I needed to rally celebrity support to the campaign in order to attract media attention. Richard Branson, Jamie Oliver, Robbie Williams and Orlando Bloom, to name but a few celebrities, were quick to pledge support. Like me, they all felt passionately that dyslexia-friendly education is something that should be available to all children who need it – regardless of their ability to pay.

Then, to bring this social injustice to the attention of both government and the media, I decided to stand against Ruth Kelly in the last general election and as a result had several meetings with Ruth over that period. Since the election I have been in talks with the government, given evidence to the Education Select Committee, the Rose Review of Reading and the 2020 Personalised Learning Review. Finally, the government were listening.

And so too were the media. Over the past two years I've written articles for the *Commons/Lords House Magazine*, Conservatives *Crossbow* magazine and been featured in a host of national newspapers and TV appearances including GMTV, BBC Breakfast, Newsnight, Channel 4, Sky, and Five News.

In 2006, BBC1 Real Story filmed a documentary about Xtraordinary People's work in a South London 'sink' school, working with 11-year-olds who had failed their SATs and gone 'off the rails'. After support from the charity, all children made dramatic progress.

In April 2007 I was immensely flattered to be awarded the 'Campaigner of the Year' Award presented in Downing Street by Gordon Brown, patron of the Sheila McKechnie Foundation, the awards charity. As a prize I receive invaluable advice on how to lobby Government and bring about change!

In May 2007 the Department for Children, Schools and Families (DCSF) awarded four dyslexia charities and Xtraordinary People £900,000 for the *No to Failure* project which will demonstrate and communicate effective support for children with dyslexia in our schools.

Clearly there is money in the education system, much of which is being spent in the wrong place. £990 million is being devolved to schools for personalised learning. You can only personalise learning for dyslexics if you are adequately trained. Around £4 billion is devolved to schools each year to support children with SEN. This money is often used to provide time with an untrained learning support assistant when many fewer hours with a trained teacher would get these children up to speed. A tiny percentage of either of these budgets would train our entire teaching workforce and it is this training that Xtraordinary People will continue to campaign for.

Can we, as a nation, continue to let these children remain hidden and unsupported or should we embrace their differences, and recognise and support their difficulties?

Contact:

Xtraordinary People
@ The British Dyslexia Association
Unit 8, Bracknell Beeches
Old Bracknell Lane
Bracknell, RG12 7BW
Tel: 0844 561 7977
Email: info@xtraordinarypeople.com
Web: www.xtraordinarypeople.com

Kate Griggs is founder of Xtraordinary People.

Index of Advertisers

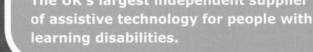